STATISTICAL
METHODS
FOR
CATEGORICAL
DATA ANALYSIS

STATISTICAL METHODS FOR CATEGORICAL DATA ANALYSIS

Daniel A. Powers
Department of Sociology
University of Texas at Austin

Yu Xie
Department of Sociology
Universtiy of Michigan

ACADEMIC PRESS

San Diego   London   Boston   New York   Sydney   Tokyo   Toronto

Academic Press
A Harcourt Science and Technology Company
525 B Street, Suite 1900, San Diego, California 92101-4495, USA
http://www.apnet.com

Academic Press
24-28 Oval Road, London NW1 7DX, UK
http://www.hbuk.co.uk/ap/

Library of Congress Catalog Card Number: 99-63219

International Standard Book Number: 0-12-563736-5

PRINTED IN THE UNITED STATES OF AMERICA
99   00   01   02   03   04   MM   9   8   7   6   5   4   3   2   1

To Our Wives
Jiwon and Yijun

and Children
Nathan, Hannah, Raissa, and Kevin

Contents

2 Review of Linear Regression Models

3 Logit and Probit Models for Binary Data

4 Loglinear Models for Contingency Tables

5 Statistical Models for Rates

6 Models for Ordinal Dependent Variables

7 Models for Unordered Dependent Variables

A The Matrix Approach to Regression

B Maximum Likelihood Estimation

Preface

In this book, we give a comprehensive introduction to methods and models for the analysis of categorical data and their applications in social science research. The primary audiences are graduate students and practicing researchers in social science. The book also serves as a reference.

One feature that distinguishes our book from other books on the topic is our explicit aim to integrate the transformational approach and the latent variable approach, two diverse but complementary traditions dealing with the analysis of categorical data. The statistical, or transformational, approach to categorical data analysis is most familiar to researchers in demography and biostatistics, whereas the latent variable approach is often taken by economists. A discussion of the two approaches is given in Chapter 1.

We assume that the reader has prior knowledge such as that covered in a typical applied regression course but not necessarily in advanced mathematical statistics. Although some technical details are unavoidable in a book like this, we make the book accessible by resorting to substantive examples. Some readers may wish to skip portions of the book that are technical without losing much appreciation of the book.

To utilize the internet technology fully, we have set up a website for the book at

http://www.la.utexas.edu/research/faculty/dpowers/book.[1]

The website contains the data sets and the programming codes in several popular statistical packages (e.g., GLIM [Numerical Algorithms Group 1986], LIMDEP [Greene 1995], SAS [SAS Institute 1990], STATA [Stata Corporation 1995], and TDA [Rowher 1995]) for the examples discussed in the book. The website provides some GLIM macros and GAUSS (Aptech Systems 1997) subroutines to illustrate details of estimation as well as several applications of specialized programs for models that cannot be estimated in a standard software package. We will continue to update the website (1) to provide exercises, (2) to add new examples, (3) to expand to other software packages, and (4) to provide other related materials.

USE OF THIS TEXT IN A COURSE ON CATEGORICAL DATA MODELS

This book is appropriate for a single-term course in categorical data modeling. Chapters 1 and 2 provide an introduction and basic foundation for the course. Our view is that, regardless of the type of data, a regression-type modeling approach can be an appropriate analytic method. Chapter 3 provides an introduction and detailed treatment of regression models for binary data. Chapter 4 goes into greater detail on the methods for analyzing contingency tables. Chapter 5 discusses models for transition rates. The core sections include Sections 5.1–5.3. Sections 5.4–5.6 can be omitted without loss of continuity. Chapters 6 and 7 provide an overview of methods for ordered and nonordered categorical responses. This material is linked to the contingency table approach of Chapter 4 and the latent variable framework outlined in Chapter 3.

ACKNOWLEDGMENTS

At various stages of the book project, we benefited from the encouragement of and association with the following scholars: Paul Allison, Mark Becker, John Fox, Richard Gonzalez, Leo Goodman, David Grusky, Robert Hauser, Michael Hout, Kenneth Land, Scott Long, Charles Manski, Robert Mare, Bill Mason, Susan Murphy, Trond Peterson, Adrian Raftery, Steve Raudenbush, Arthur Sakamoto, Herbert Smith, Michael Sobel, Chris Winship, Larry Wu, and Kazuo Yamaguchi. In addition, we extend our gratitude to many graduate students who have taken statistics courses from us and inspired us to write the book.

[1]Information is also available at www.academicpress.com/sbe/authors.

A Dean's Fellowship at the University of Texas at Austin to Dan Powers, a National Science Foundation's Young Investigator Award to Yu Xie, and University of Michigan's internal funds to Yu Xie provided partial support for this project.

We also thank the external reviewers for providing valuable critiques on early versions of the manuscript, and Pam Bennett, John Fox, Kimberly Goyette, and James Raymo for carefully proofreading the final version of the manuscript and providing programming examples. We alone are responsible for errors that remain. Last, but not least, we thank J. Scott Bentley, our editor at Academic Press, for initiating the project and then making efforts to bring it to completion.

Daniel A. Powers
Yu Xie

Chapter 1

Introduction

1.1 Why Categorical Data Analysis?

What is common about birth, marriage, schooling, employment, occupation, migration, divorce, and death? The answer: they are all categorical variables commonly studied in social science research. In fact, most observed outcomes in social science research are measured categorically. If you are a practicing social scientist, chances are good that you have studied a phenomenon involving a categorical variable. (This is true even if you have not used any special statistical method for handling categorical data.) If you are in a graduate program to become a social scientist, you will soon, if not already, encounter a categorical variable. Notice that even our statement of whether or not you have encountered a categorical variable in your career is itself a categorical measurement!

Statistical methods and techniques for categorical data analysis have undergone rapid development in the past 25 years or so. Their applications in applied research have become commonplace in recent years, due in large part to the availability of commercial software and inexpensive computing. Since some of the material is rather new and dispersed in several disciplines, we believe that there is a need for a systematic treatment of the subject in a single book. This book is aimed at helping applied social scientists use special tools that are well suited for analyzing categorical data. In this chapter, we will first define categorical variables and then introduce our approach to the subject.

1.1.1 Defining Categorical Variables

We define categorical variables as those variables that can be measured using only a limited number of values or categories. This definition distinguishes categorical variables from continuous variables, which, in principle, can assume an infinite number of values.

Although this definition of categorical variables is clear, its application to applied work is far more ambiguous. Many variables of long-lasting interest to social scientists are clearly categorical. Such variables include: race, gender, immigration status, marital status, employment, birth, and death. However, conceptually continuous variables are sometimes treated as continuous and other times as categorical. When a continuous variable is treated as a categorical variable, it is called categorization or discretization of the continuous variable. Categorization is often necessary in practice because either the substantive meaning or the actual measurement of a continuous variable is categorical. Age is a good example. Although conceptually continuous, age is often treated as categorical in actual research for substantive and practical reasons. Substantively, age serves as a proxy for qualitative states for some research purposes, qualitatively transforming an individual's status at certain key points. Changes in legal and social status occur first during the transition into adulthood and later during the transition out of the labor force. For practical reasons, age is usually reported in single-year or five-year intervals.[1]

Indeed, our usual instruments in social science research are crude in the sense that they typically constrain possible responses to a limited number of possible values. It is for this reason that we earlier stated that most, if not all, observed outcomes in social science are categorical.

---

[1]Education is another example. The substantive distinctions among "less than 12 years of schooling," "high-school diploma," "college degree," or "graduate degree" cannot be captured without categorization. A few categories offer a concise representation of the important points in the distribution of education.

What variables should then be considered categorical as opposed to continuous in empirical research? The answer depends on many factors, two of which are their substantive meaning in the theoretical model and their measurement precision. One requirement for treating a variable as categorical is that its values are repeated for at least a significant portion of the sample.[2] As will be shown later, the distinction between continuous and categorical variables is far more consequential for response variables than for explanatory variables.

1.1.2   Dependent and Independent Variables

A *dependent* (also called response, outcome, or endogenous) variable represents a population characteristic of interest being explained in a study. *Independent* (also called explanatory, predetermined, or exogenous) variables are variables that are used to explain the variation in the dependent variable. Typically, the characteristic of interest is the population mean of the dependent variable (or its transformation) *conditional* on values of an independent variable or set of independent variables. It is in this sense that we mean that the dependent variable depends on, is explained by, or is a function of independent variables in regression-type statistical models.

By "regression-type statistical models," we mean models that predict either the expected value of the dependent variable or some other characteristic of the dependent variable, as a regression function of independent variables. Although in principle we could design our models to best predict any population parameter (e.g., the median) of the dependent variable or its transformation, in practice we commonly use the term regression to denote the problem of predicting conditional means. When the regression function is a linear combination of independent variables, we have so-called linear regressions, which are widely used for continuous dependent variables.

---

[2]Note that a continuous variable can be truncated, meaning that it has zero probability of yielding a value beyond a particular threshold or cut-off point. When a continuous variable is truncated, the untruncated part is still continuous, whereas the part that is truncated resembles a categorical variable.

1.1.3   Categorical Dependent Variables

Although categorical and continuous variables share many properties in common, we wish to highlight some of the differences here. The distinction between categorical and continuous variables as dependent variables requires special attention. In contrast, the distinction is of relatively minor significance when they are used as independent variables in regression-type statistical models. Our definition of regression-type statistical models includes statistical methods for the analysis of variance and covariance, which can be represented by regressing the dependent variable on a set of dummy variables and, in the case of the analysis of covariance, other continuous covariates. Hence, including categorical variables as independent variables in regression-type models does not present any particular difficulties, as it mainly involves constructing dummy variables corresponding to different categories of the independent variable; all known properties of regression models are directly generalizable to models for the analysis of variance and covariance. As we will show later in this book, the situation changes drastically when we treat categorical variables as dependent variables, as much of our knowledge derived from linear regressions is simply inapplicable. In brief, special statistical methods are required for categorical data analysis (i.e., analysis involving categorical *dependent* variables).

Although the methods for analyzing categorical variables as independent variables in regression-type models have been a part of the standard statistical knowledge base that is now required for most advanced degrees in social science, methods for the analysis of categorical dependent variables are much less widely known. Much of the fundamental research on the methodology of analyzing categorical data has been developed only recently. We aim to give a systematic treatment of several important topics on categorical data analysis in this book so as to facilitate the integration of the material into social science research.

Unlike methods for continuous variables, methods for categorical data require close attention to the type of measurement of the dependent variable. Methods for analyzing one type of categorical dependent variable may be inappropriate for analyzing another type of variable.

1.1.4   Types of Measurement

The type of measurement plays a key role in determining the appropriate method of analysis when a variable is used as a dependent variable. We present a typology for four types of measurement based on three distinctions.[3] First, let us distinguish between *quantitative* and *qualitative* measurements. The distinction between the two is that quantitative measurements closely index the substantive meanings of a variable with numerical values, whereas numerical values for qualitative measurements are substantively less meaningful, sometimes merely as classifications to denote mutually exclusive categories of characteristics (or attributes) uniquely. Qualitative variables are categorical variables.

Within the class of *quantitative* variables, it is often useful to distinguish further between *continuous* and *discrete* variables. Continuous variables, also called interval variables, may assume any real value. Variables such as income and socioeconomic status are typically treated as continuous over their plausible range of values. Discrete variables may assume only integer values and often represent event counts. Variables such as the number of children per family, the number of delinquent acts committed by a juvenile, and the number of accidents per year at a particular intersection are examples of discrete variables. According to our earlier definition, discrete (but quantitative) variables are also categorical variables.

Qualitative measurements can be further distinguished between ordinal and nominal. Ordinal measurements give rise to ordered qualitative variables, or *ordinal* variables. It is quite common to use numerical values to denote the ordering information in an ordered qualitative variable. However, numerical values corresponding to categories of ordinal variables reflect only the ranking order in a particular attribute; therefore, distances between two adjacent values are not the same. Attitudes toward gun control (strongly approve, approve, neutral, disapprove, and strongly disapprove), occupational skill level (highly skilled, medium-skilled, low-skilled, and unskilled), and the classification of

---

[3]For an historical background, see Duncan's (1984) important book *Notes on Social Measurement*.

levels of education as (grade school, high school, college, and graduate) are examples of ordinal variables.

Nominal measurements yield unordered qualitative variables, often referred to as *nominal* variables. Nominal variables possess no inherent ordering, nor numerical distance, between category levels. Classifications of race and ethnicity (White, Black, Hispanic, and other), gender (male and female), and marital status (never married, married, divorced, and widowed) are examples of unordered qualitative variables. It is worth noting at this point, however, that the distinction between ordinal and nominal variables is not always clear-cut. Much of the distinction depends on the research questions. The same variable may be ordinal for some researchers but nominal for others.

To further illustrate the last point, let us use occupation as an example. Distinct occupations are often measured by open-ended questions and then manually coded into a classification system with three-digit numerical codes that do not represent magnitudes in substantive dimensions. Since the number of potential occupations is large (usually at least a few hundred in a coding scheme for a modern society), it is desirable, and indeed necessary, to reduce the amount of detail in an occupational measure through data reduction. One method of data reduction is to collapse detailed occupational codes into major occupational categories and treat them either as constituting an ordinal or even a nominal measurement (Duncan 1979; Hauser 1978). Another method of data reduction is to scale occupations along the dimension of a socioeconomic index (SEI) (Duncan 1961)—thus into an interval variable. More recently, Hauser and Warren (1997) challenged Duncan's approach and suggested instead that, to measure occupational socioeconomic status, occupations are best scaled into two separate dimensions of occupational income and occupational education. Hauser and Warren's work illustrates the importance of considering multiple dimensions when nominal measures are scaled into interval measures.

Figure 1.1 summarizes our typology scheme for the four types of measurements. According to this typology, there are three types of categorical variables: discrete, ordinal, and nominal, all of which will be discussed in this book. This distinction among the three types of categorical variables is useful only when the number of possible values equals or exceeds three. When the number of possible values is two, we

Figure 1.1: Typology of the Four Types of Measurements

have a special case called a binary variable. A *binary* variable can be discrete, ordinal, or nominal, depending on the researcher's interpretation. For example, if a researcher is interested in studying compliance with the one-child policy in China, the dependent variable is whether a couple has given birth to more than one child. For simplicity, assume that in a particular sample a woman has at least one child and no more than two children. Let us code y so that $y = 0$ if a woman has one child, and $y = 1$ if she has two children. In this case, the dependent variable can be interpreted as discrete (number of children-1), ordinal (one child or more than one child), or nominal (compliance versus noncompliance). Fortunately, the researcher may apply the same statistical methods for all three cases. It is the substantive understanding of the results that varies from one interpretation to another.

1.2   Two Philosophies of Categorical Data

The development of methods for the analysis of categorical data has benefitted greatly from contributions by scholars in such diverse fields as statistics, biostatistics, economics, psychology, and sociology. This multidisciplinary origin has given categorical data analysis multiple approaches to similar problems and multiple interpretations for similar methodologies. As a result, categorical data analysis is an intellectually rich and expanding field. However, this interdisciplinary nature has also made synthesizing and consolidating available techniques difficult due to the diverse applications and differing terminology across disciplines.

Part of this difficulty stems from two fundamentally different "philosophies" concerning the nature of categorical data. One philosophy views categorical variables as being inherently categorical and relies on transformations of the data to derive regression-type models. The other philosophy presumes that categorical variables are conceptually continuous but are observed, or measured, as categorical. In the one-child policy example, a researcher may view "compliance" as a behavioral continuum. However, he/she can only *observe* two distinct values of this dependent variable. This approach relies on latent variables to derive regression-type models. These very different philosophies can be traced back to the acrimonious debate between Karl Pearson and G. Udny Yule between 1904 and 1913 (Agresti 1990, pp. 26-28). Although these two approaches can be found in any single discipline, the first is more closely identified with statistics and biostatistics, and the second with econometrics and psychometrics. For simplicity, we will refer to the first approach as statistical or transformational and to the second as econometric or latent variable. We intend the terms *statistical* and *econometric* here as short-hand labels rather than as descriptions of the two disciplines.

1.2.1 The Transformational Approach

In the *transformational*, or statistical, approach, categorical data are considered as inherently categorical and should be modeled as such. In this approach, there is a direct one-to-one correspondence between population parameters of interest and sample statistics. The focus is on estimating population parameters that correspond to their sample analogs. No latent, or unobserved, variable is invoked.

In the transformational approach, statistical modeling means that the expected value of the categorical dependent variable, after some transformation, is expressed as a linear function of the independent variables. Given the categorical nature of the dependent variable, the regression function cannot be linear. The problem of nonlinearity is handled through nonlinear functions that transform the expected value of the categorical variable into a linear function of the independent variables. Such transformation functions are now commonly referred to as *link* functions.[4]

For example, in the analysis of discrete (count) data, the expected frequencies (or cell counts) must be nonnegative. To ensure that the predicted values from regression models fit these constraints, the natural logarithm function (or *log* link) is used to transform the expected value of the dependent variable so that a model for the logged count can be expressed as a linear function of independent variables. This *loglinear* transformation serves two purposes: it ensures that the fitted values are appropriate for count data (i.e., non-negative), and it permits the unknown regression parameters to lie within the entire real space (parameter space).

In binomial response models, estimated probabilities must lie in the interval $[0, 1]$, a range that is violated by any linear function if independent variables are allowed to vary freely. Instead of directly modeling probabilities in this range, we can model a transformation of probability that lies in the interval $(-\infty, +\infty)$. There are a number of ways to transform probabilities. The *logit* transformation, $\log[p/(1 - p)]$, can be used to transform the probability scale so that it can be expressed as a linear function of independent variables.

A *probit* transformation, $\Phi^{-1}(p)$, can be used in a similar fashion to re-scale probabilities. The probit link utilizes the inverse of the cumulative standard normal distribution function to transform the expected probability to the range $(-\infty, +\infty)$ (i.e., by transforming probabilities to z-scores). As in the logit model, the probit link transforms the probability so that it can be expressed as a linear function of independent variables. Both the logit and probit transformations ensure that the predicted probabilities are in the proper range for all possible values of parameters and independent variables.

1.2.2   The Latent Variable Approach

The latent variable, or econometric, approach provides a somewhat different view of categorical data. The key to this approach is to assume

---

[4]Models that can be transformed to linear models via link functions are referred to as *generalized linear models*. McCullagh and Nelder (1989) provide an extensive treatment of these types of models.

the existence of a continuous unobserved or *latent* variable underlying an observed categorical variable. When the latent variable crosses a threshold, the observed categorical variable takes on a different value. According to the latent variable approach, what makes categorical variables different from usual continuously distributed variables is partial observability. That is, we can infer from observed categorical values only the intervals within which latent variables lie but not the actual values themselves. For this reason, econometricians commonly refer to categorical variables as limited-dependent variables (Maddala 1983).

In the latent variable approach, the researcher's theoretical interest lies more in how independent variables affect the latent continuous variables (called structural analysis) than in how independent variables affect the observed categorical variable. From the latent variable perspective, it is thus convenient to think of the sample data as actual *realizations* of population quantities that are *unobservable*. For instance, the observed response categories may reflect the actual choices made by individuals in a sample, but underlying each choice at the population level is a latent variable representing the difference between the cost and the benefit of a particular choice made by an individual decision maker. Similarly, a binary variable may be thought of as the sample realization of a continuous variable representing an unobserved *propensity*. For example, in studies of college admissions, we may assume the existence of a continuous latent variable—qualification—such that applicants whose qualifications exceed the required threshold are admitted, and those whose qualifications fall short of the threshold are rejected (Manski and Wise 1983).

In studies of women's labor force participation, economic reasoning holds that a woman will participate in the labor force if her market wage exceeds her reservation wage (Heckman 1979). In practice, it is not possible for the researcher to observe applicants' qualifications, nor the difference between the market and reservation wages. We can, however, observe admission decisions and labor force participation status, which can be taken as *observed* realizations of the underlying population-level latent variable representing likelihood of admission or labor force participation.

Experimental studies in the biological sciences have also made good use of latent variables. In studies of the effectiveness of pesticides, for example, whether an insect dies depends on its *tolerance* to a level of dosage of an insecticide. It is assumed that an insect will die if a dosage level exceeds the insect's tolerance. The binary variable (lives/dies) is the realization of a continuous unobservable variable, the difference between dosage and tolerance.

The latent variable concept has been extended to the construction of latent *categorical* variables. A prime example is the latent class model, which capitalizes on independence conditional on membership in latent classes. This is analogous to factor analysis for continuously distributed variables. Heckman and Singer's (1984) nonparametric method of handling unobserved heterogeneity in survival analysis is also rooted in this fundamental idea.

1.3   An Historical Note

The development of techniques for the analysis of categorical data has been motivated in part by particular substantive concerns in fields such as sociology, economics, epidemiology, and demography (for an historical account in social science, see Camic and Xie 1994). For example, several innovations in loglinear modeling had their origins in the study of social mobility (e.g., Duncan 1979; Goodman 1979; Hauser 1978); the literature on sample selection models emerged from economic analyses of women's earnings (Heckman 1979); and problems in the analysis of consumer choices led to the development of many of the techniques for multicategory response variables (McFadden 1974). Methodological advances in survival analysis arose as extensions of the life-tables technique in demography by statisticians and biostatisticians to incorporate covariates in modeling hazard rates (Cox 1972; Laird and Oliver 1981). McCullagh and Nelder's (1989) theory of generalized linear models provided a unified framework which can be applied to most of these models.

Today's latent variable approach grew out of the early psychophysics tradition, where observed frequency distributions of qualitative "judgments" were used to scale the intensity of continuously distributed stimuli (e.g., Thurstone 1927). In the experimental framework of psychophysics, the "latent" variables were unobservable only to the subjects under an experiment, since the stimuli were manipulated by and thus known to the researcher. For illustration, imagine that a group of subjects are asked to rank the relative weights of two similar objects given by the experimenter. It is reasonable to assume that the probability of giving the correct answer is positively associated with the actual difference in weight. Thurstone (1927) explicitly assumed a normal distribution for the psychological stimulus and related it to the distribution of "judgments," thus paving the way to today's probit analysis. With time, social scientists have expanded this approach to uncover properties of latent variables from observed data, through such techniques as latent trait models and latent class models. For a treatment of sociologists' contributions to the latent variable approach, see Clogg (1992).

1.4   Approach of This Book

Two features distinguish this book from other texts on the analysis of categorical data. First, this book presents both the transformational and latent variable approaches and, in doing so, synthesizes similar methods in statistical and econometric literatures. Whenever possible, we shall show how the two approaches are similar and in what ways they are different. Second, this book has an applied as opposed to theoretical orientation. We shall draw examples from applied social science research and use data sets constructed for pedagogical purposes. In keeping with the applied orientation of this book, we shall also present actual programming examples for the models discussed, while keeping theoretical discussions at a minimum. We shall provide our data sets, program code, and computer outputs through a website.[5]

Combining the Statistical and Latent Variable Approaches

In many instances, the transformational and latent variable approaches are simply two parallel ways of looking at the same phenomena. More

---

[5]Our website is continuously updated with new examples utilizing several computer packages. The URL is www.la.utexas.edu/research/faculty/dpowers/book.

often than not, the two approaches yield exactly the same statistical procedures except for minor differences due to the manner in which the model is specified or parameterized. When this is the case, one's viewpoint about the underlying nature of observed categorical variables does not affect specific statistical techniques that we will cover but simply alters the substantive interpretations of results.

1.4.1   Organization of the Book

This book begins by considering the simplest models for categorical data and proceeds to more complex models and methods. We begin with a review of the general concepts behind regression models for continuous dependent variables. This is a natural starting point since many of the familiar ideas and principles used in the analysis of covariance and regression for continuous variables will carry over to the analysis of categorical dependent variables. These concepts are described in Chapter 2, along with a general orientation to regression models. Chapter 3 discusses models for binary data and issues pertaining to estimation, model building, and the interpretation of results. Chapter 4 provides an overview of measures of association, models for contingency tables, and models for discrete (count) data. Chapter 5 builds on the results from Chapters 3 and 4 by discussing models for the analysis of longitudinal data. Chapters 6 and 7 outline various methods for the analysis of polytomous (or multinomial) variables.

Chapter 2

Review of Linear Regression Models

This chapter reviews the classic linear regression model for continuous dependent variables. We assume the reader's familiarity with the linear regression model and thus will not delve into its details. Instead, we will highlight some general concepts and principles underlying the linear regression model that will be useful in later chapters focused on categorical dependent variables.

2.1 Regression Models

Regression is one of the most widely used statistical techniques for analyzing observational data. As mentioned in Chapter 1, the analysis of observational data typically requires a structural and multivariate approach. Regression models are used in this context to uncover net relationships between an outcome, or response, variable and a few key explanatory variables while controlling for confounding factors. Regression models are used to meet different research goals. Sometimes, regression modeling is aimed at learning the causal effect of one variable, or a set of variables, on a dependent variable. Other times, regression models are used to predict the value of a response variable. Finally, regression models are often intended as short-hand summaries providing a description linking a dependent variable and independent variables.

2.1.1   Three Conceptualizations of Regression

A researcher faced with a large amount of raw data will want to summarize it in a way that presents essential information without too much distortion. Examples of data reduction include frequency tables or group-specific means and variances. Like most methods in statistics, regression is also a data-reduction technique. In regression analysis, the objective is to predict, as closely as possible, an array of observed values of the dependent variable based on a simple function of independent variables. Obviously, predicted values from regression models are not exactly the same as observed ones. Characteristically, regression partitions an observation into two parts:

$$\boxed{\text{observed}} = \boxed{\text{structural}} + \boxed{\text{stochastic}} \, .$$

The observed part represents the actual values of the dependent variable at hand. The structural part denotes the relationship between the dependent and independent variables. The stochastic part is the random component unexplained by the structural part. In general, the last term may be regarded as the sum of three components: omitted structural factors, measurement error, and "noise." Omitting structural factors is inevitable in social science research because we can never claim to understand and measure all causal structures affecting a dependent variable. Measurement error refers to inaccuracies in the way in which the data are recorded, reported, or measured. Random noise reflects the extent to which human behavior or occurrence of events is subject to uncertainty (i.e., stochastic influences).

How to interpret regression models is contingent on one's conceptualization about what regression does to data. We propose three different conceptualizations.

Causation: $\boxed{\text{observed}} = \boxed{\text{true mechanism}} + \boxed{\text{disturbance}}$

Prediction: $\boxed{\text{observed}} = \boxed{\text{predicted}} + \boxed{\text{error}}$

Description: $\boxed{\text{observed}} = \boxed{\text{summary}} + \boxed{\text{residual}}$

These conceptualizations provide three different views of quantitative analysis. The first approach corresponds most closely to what might be perceived as a view in classical econometrics in which the model accurately represents the "true" causal mechanism that generates the data. The researcher's goal is to specify a model to uncover the data-generating mechanism, or "true" causal model. This first approach can be viewed as an attempt to get as close as possible to a deterministic model. More modern approaches would argue that there is no "true" model but rather that some models are more useful, more interesting, or closer to the truth than others.

The second approach is more directly applicable to fields like engineering where, given a relationship between explanatory variables and a response variable, the goal is to make useful response predictions for new data. For example, suppose that the strength of a material is related to temperature and pressure during the manufacturing process. Suppose that we produce a sample of materials by varying temperature and pressure in a systematic way. One objective of modeling might be to find the values of temperature and pressure that give the material maximum strength. Social scientists also employ this modeling approach in forecasting and may use this approach to identify people at risk of a particular outcome based on certain characteristics.

The third approach reflects the current view in modern econometrics and statistics in which a model serves to summarize the basic features of data without distorting them. A principle called Occam's razor, or the *law of parsimony*, is often invoked when assessing competing explanations of the same phenomenon. When applied to statistical models, this principle means that if two models equally explain the observed facts, the simpler model is preferred until new evidence proves otherwise. This approach differs from the first view in the sense that the question asked is not whether the model is "true" but whether it corresponds to the facts. The facts usually require formalization based on past research or theory. The model is then specified in accordance with theory or previous research.

These conceptualizations are not mutually exclusive; the applicability of a particular interpretation hinges on concrete situations, particularly the nature of the research design and objectives. With most applications in social sciences utilizing observational data, our inclination is to favor the last interpretation. That is, the primary goal of statistical modeling is to summarize massive amounts of data with simple structures and few parameters. With this conceptualization of regression models, it is important to keep in mind the trade-off between accuracy and parsimony. On the one hand, we desire accuracy in a model in the sense that we want to preserve maximum information and minimize errors associated with residuals. On the other hand, we prefer parsimonious models. More often than not, the desire to preserve information can only be achieved by building complicated models, which comes at the expense of parsimony or simplicity. The tension between accuracy and parsimony is so fundamental to social science research that we will revisit the issue several times in the book.

2.1.2   Anatomy of Linear Regression

There are three types of variables in a regression model: a dependent variable, a set of independent variables, and random errors. Because the exact nature of the dependency of the dependent variable on the independent variables is unknown, researchers often summarize it as a linear relationship in an approximation involving a set of unknown parameters or coefficients.

The continuous dependent variable, also called the response variable, is usually denoted by y. For a given sample of size n, we denote the individual data values as $y_i = y_1, y_2, \ldots, y_n$. We can think of the many possible values of y as forming a *population*. Like all random variables, y has a mean, a variance, and additional parameters to describe its distribution. The mean or expected value of y is denoted by $E(y) = \mu$. We can also let the mean of y be expressed as a function of independent variables. For example, if an independent variable assumes a unique value for each element in the population, and $E(y)$ is modeled as a function of the independent variable, there would be a different mean, say μ_i, for each observation.

More generally, associated with each observation is a set of independent variables, also called explanatory variables. The set of independent variables constitutes a data matrix indexed by n rows—corresponding to n individual units of analysis—and $K + 1$ columns—

corresponding to K distinct independent variables plus a constant.[1]
We will denote the $n \times (K + 1)$ matrix of independent variables as
$\mathbf{X}$, where K is the total number of explanatory variables. The values of $\mathbf{X}$ for the ith observation are denoted by the vector $\mathbf{x}_i = (x_{i0}, x_{i1}, \ldots, x_{iK})'$. With no loss of generality, we include as the first
column of $\mathbf{X}$ a vector of 1's (e.g., $x_{i0} = 1$), whose coefficient is the
intercept. We may write the expression for the mean of y, conditional
on the independent variables as

$$\begin{aligned} \mathrm{E}(y_i \mid \mathbf{x}_i) &= \beta_0 + \beta_1 x_{i1} + \beta_2 x_{i2} + \cdots + \beta_K x_{iK} \\ &= \sum_{k=0}^{K} \beta_k x_{ik} \\ &= \mathbf{x}_i' \boldsymbol{\beta}. \end{aligned} \tag{2.1}$$

The β_k $(k = 0, \ldots, K)$ terms are unknown regression coefficients, or
parameters, to be estimated from the sampled data. The intercept, β_0,
can be interpreted as the mean of y when all x variables are zero. The
remaining β_k $(k = 1, \ldots, K)$ terms are regression slopes, reflecting the
amount that $\mathrm{E}(y)$ changes when x_{ik} changes by one unit, while holding
other independent variables constant. The symbol $\boldsymbol{\beta}$ is used to denote
the $(K + 1) \times 1$ vector of regression coefficients, $\boldsymbol{\beta} = (\beta_0, \beta_1, \ldots, \beta_K)'$.

In focusing on the expected value of y, other characteristics of the
distribution of y are usually ignored. Since a model based on a set
of independent variables cannot predict exactly the observed values of
y, it is necessary to introduce ε_i (i.e., error, disturbance, or residual,
depending on one's viewpoint). For the ith observation, we have

$$\begin{aligned} y_i &= \beta_0 + \beta_1 x_{i1} + \beta_2 x_{i2} + \ldots + \beta_K x_{iK} + \varepsilon_i \\ &= \sum_{k=0}^{K} \beta_k x_{ik} + \varepsilon_i \\ &= \mathbf{x}_i' \boldsymbol{\beta} + \varepsilon_i. \end{aligned} \tag{2.2}$$

---

[1]Throughout this book we will use **bold-faced** symbols to indicate that a quantity is a matrix or vector. When possible, we will use the more familiar "scalar" representations. Some basic principles of matrix algebra are reviewed in Appendix A.

This expression describes the way in which y is decomposed into a linear function of x's with unknown parameters (β) and a residual term (ε_i). Since ε_i is intrinsically unobservable, simplifying assumptions about the characteristics of ε_i are necessary. A key assumption that yields the identification of the unknown parameters in Eq. 2.2 is the independence between ε and the x variables. Other assumptions are often invoked to improve efficiency. For example, it is common to assume ε_i to be independent of one another and identically distributed (i.i.d.). The independence assumption implies that the correlation in ε between a pair of observations is zero, whereas the identical distribution assumption assures a common variance of σ_ε^2 (i.e., homoscedasticity). With the i.i.d. assumption, Eq. 2.2 can be estimated using ordinary least squares (OLS), which is described in Section 2.2.1.

Even without the i.i.d. assumption, however, the OLS estimator is still a consistent estimator if ε is uncorrelated with the x's, meaning that it converges to the parameter vector when the sample size is large.

2.1.3   Basics of Statistical Inference

To understand estimation and statistical inference, it is necessary to introduce the distinction between population quantities (*parameters*) and their sample counterparts (*statistics*). This distinction is the basis for statistical inference, the practice of inferring characteristics of a population from more limited information contained in a sample drawn from the population. We begin with a general discussion of inference, although in this book inference is more narrowly limited to the estimation of parameters and their standard errors in regression and regression-type models.[2]

Let us assume that we wish to make inferences based on a simple random sample drawn from a population. Since we do not observe the whole population, key characteristics like the population mean of y are unknown. We can easily compute the mean and other moments for the sample, and such values are called sample statistics. However, there

---

[2]Because of this, we do not provide a *notational* distinction between the theoretical response variable and the sampled, or observed, values of the response variable.

is no guarantee that the sample statistics are good approximations of the population parameters. Statistical inference is the branch of statistics that is concerned with the problem of gaining knowledge about the values of unknown population parameters using information from sample statistics.

Estimation

The term *estimator* refers to the particular method or formula used to obtain sample statistics that are parameter *estimates*. There can be different alternative estimators for a given population parameter. With a few exceptions, different estimators yield distinct estimates of the population parameter of interest.

It is important to note that an estimate itself is a realization of a random variable that follows a probability distribution (or *sampling distribution*). Depending on the particular elements being sampled, sample statistics take on different values. One can view any particular estimate as one of many possible estimates that could have been obtained from multiple, equal-sized random samples drawn from the same population. Thus, the value of the sample mean from a single random sample is only one of numerous sample mean values that could have been calculated from such repeated samples. Moreover, different estimators or estimation methods will often produce different estimates of population parameters, in which case a choice must be made among competing estimators. For example, when the distribution is normal, both the sample median and the sample mean could be used as estimators of the population mean. The sampling distributions of these estimators are different.

Estimators can be judged according to how well they satisfy a few desirable properties. One desirable property of an estimator is unbiasedness. When the expected value of an estimator equals the value of the true parameter being estimated, the estimator is said to be *unbiased*. When there is more than one unbiased estimator, the choice of a good estimator would depend on criteria other than unbiasedness. Among all estimators that are unbiased, we prefer the estimator with the smallest variance in its sampling distribution. This desirable property of minimum variance is called *efficiency*. Information about the spread of a statistic around its mean value is used to place upper and lower limits on the value of a population parameter. These bounds form an *interval estimate* (or confidence interval) for the population parameter of interest. The width of this interval will depend on the researcher's desired level of confidence and the variance of the estimator. A probability statement that describes the chances that the true parameter lies in the interval constructed solely on the basis of the sample information and assumptions regarding the way that the population random variable is distributed can be formulated.

2.1.4   Tension between Accuracy and Parsimony

Estimation of the population mean is equivalent to estimating the following simple regression:

$$y_i = \beta_0 + \varepsilon_i. \tag{2.3}$$

That is, the model states that values of y_i are scattered around its mean value, β_0, with the random error, ε_i, being the difference. The predicted value would be $E(y) = \mu = \beta_0$. In an actual research setting, multivariate analysis is typically required, and numerous parameters accordingly need to be estimated.

There is always a tension between accuracy and parsimony in a statistical model. By "parsimony" we commonly mean statistical models with few parameters. By "accuracy" we mean the ability to reproduce the data, measured by goodness-of-fit statistics.[3] Although both accuracy and parsimony are desirable properties in statistical models, one is achieved only at the expense of the other. At one extreme, the most accurate model would exactly reproduce the data such that any predicted value would equal the corresponding observed value (i.e., predicted value = observed value). Such a model is called the *saturated model*. The saturated model would require that *mathematically* a separate parameter be estimated for each data point. In other words, there would be as many parameters as data points. The saturated model does not reduce the amount of information in observed data. At the

---

[3] The "data" in this case could be from a sample or from the entire population.

other extreme, a very parsimonious model, such as Eq. 2.3, would consist of a single parameter indicating the level of the global mean. Such parsimonious models may fail to reveal systematic variation in the data and thus paint grossly inaccurate pictures of reality. In practice, researchers often take a middle-ground and search for parsimonious yet informative models, thus achieving a good balance between the need for parsimony and the need for accuracy. The objective in model searching is to find models that describe the essential characteristics of the data using as few parameters as possible.

Nested, or hierarchical, models provide a way to motivate model searching. Two models are nested if one model is a special case of the other. Consider the following models:

$$(A) \quad y_i = \beta_0 + \beta_1 x_{i1} + \varepsilon_i,$$
$$(B) \quad y_i = \beta_0 + \beta_1 x_{i1} + \beta_2 x_{i2} + \varepsilon_i,$$
$$(C) \quad y_i = \beta_0 + \beta_2 x_{i2} + \varepsilon_i,$$
$$(D) \quad y_i = \beta_0 + \beta_1 (x_{i1} + x_{i2}) + \varepsilon_i.$$

Model (A) is said to be nested within Model (B), as (A) is a special case of (B) with the constraint that $\beta_2 = 0$. Likewise, (C) is nested within Model (B). Models (A) and (C), however, are not nested in each other. Model (D) is nested in Model (B) with the constraint that $\beta_1 = \beta_2$ but is not nested in (A) or (C).

For a pair of nested or hierarchical models, the model without the constraint is called the unconstrained model, and the model with the constraint is called the constrained model. It is important to know that for most goodness-of-fit statistics, adding constraints only improves, or at least does not worsen, goodness-of-fit. The right question to ask is not whether the unconstrained model fits better than the constrained model. It almost always does. The key question is whether the unconstrained model fits *significantly* better than the constrained model, relative to the number of additional parameters implied by the constraints. Specifically, we need to assess whether the improvement in fit is a real improvement or simply random fluctuation attributable to sampling error. For linear regressions, such assessments are conducted using F-tests based on reductions in residual sums of squares, or other proportionate reduction in error (PRE) criteria. For the nonlinear models introduced in this book, most assessments are chi-squared tests based on different criteria, such as reductions in the log-likelihood-ratio statistics.

2.2   Linear Regression Models Revisited

Linear regression models are appropriate for continuously measured dependent variables. This section revisits such models for conditional means of continuous dependent variables. Although the term *regression* has become less restrictive in recent years, conditional mean estimation remains the dominant objective associated with regression analysis. As we will show, regression-type models may be used in a number of situations; we use the term *regression* in the broad sense to refer to any conditional prediction problem.

2.2.1   Least Squares Estimation

For a continuously measured random variable, y, one objective of regression is to estimate the population mean of y conditional on a set of K independent variables from a sample of n observations and to ascertain how the expected value of y varies with x_k, or to learn the effect of x_k on y. The relationship between y and the explanatory variables is formulated as a linear model, shown in Eq. 2.2. Least squares (LS) estimation is a straightforward way to find the optimal values of the β's. The optimal values will be those that lead to the smallest possible error variance, or values that minimize the sum of squared deviations around the conditional mean. Let us rewrite the conditional mean function of y as μ_i, where $\mu_i = \sum_{k=0}^{K} \beta_k x_{ik}$. The goal of least squares estimation is to find estimates of β's that make the sum of squared errors around the conditional mean as small as possible. More formally, letting $\varepsilon_i = y_i - \mu_i$, the objective is to minimize

$$S(\boldsymbol{\beta}) = \sum_{i=1}^{n} \left(y_i - \sum_{k=0}^{K} \beta_k x_{ik} \right)^2 = \sum_{i=1}^{n} (y_i - \mu_i)^2 = \sum_{i=1}^{n} \varepsilon_i^2. \qquad (2.4)$$

Minimization of $S(\boldsymbol{\beta})$ is accomplished by evaluating the partial derivatives of $S(\boldsymbol{\beta})$ with respect to β_k

$$\frac{\partial S(\boldsymbol{\beta})}{\partial \beta_k} = -2 \sum_{i=1}^{n} \left(y_i - \sum_{k=0}^{K} \beta_k x_{ik} \right) x_{ik} = 0, \qquad k = 0, \ldots, K. \quad (2.5)$$

The partial derivatives describe the slope, or rate of change, of the sum of squares function at any given configuration of $\boldsymbol{\beta}$ values. The rate of change in the sum of squares function is zero at its minimum. The least squares technique yields a set of $(K+1)$ normal equations, which, when solved simultaneously for $\boldsymbol{\beta}$, give the least squares estimates. The least squares solution can be expressed conveniently in matrix form as

$$\mathbf{b} = \left[\mathbf{X'X} \right]^{-1} \mathbf{X'y}, \qquad (2.6)$$

where $\mathbf{b}$ is the vector of estimated regression coefficients, $\mathbf{X}$ is the $n \times (K+1)$ matrix of independent variables, and $\mathbf{y}$ is the $n \times 1$ vector of values for the dependent variable. The Gauss-Markov theorem states that $\mathbf{b}$ of Eq. 2.6 is the best (meaning most efficient) among all linear unbiased estimators (BLUE), with its variance and covariance being

$$\text{var}(\mathbf{b}) = \sigma_{\varepsilon}^2 (\mathbf{X'X})^{-1}. \qquad (2.7)$$

Note that var($\mathbf{b}$) is a $(K+1) \times (K+1)$ matrix, with diagonal elements equal to the variances of the estimates, and off-diagonal elements equal to the covariances between estimates.

2.2.2   Maximum Likelihood Estimation

The linear regression model may also be estimated using the maximum likelihood technique. The principal aim of maximum likelihood (ML) estimation is to find parameter values that maximize the sample likelihood, L, which may be thought of as the formula for the joint probability distribution (or joint density) of the sample.[4] The likelihood

---

[4]Appendix B provides additional technical details about ML estimation.

function yields a value that is proportional to the joint probability (or likelihood) of obtaining the particular data that are actually observed. Assuming independent observations, the individual components of the likelihood function can be multiplied using the general rule for joint probabilities of independent events.

For example, let $y_1, y_2, \ldots, y_n$ denote a random sample of independent observations from a population with a density function, $f(y \mid \theta)$, where θ is an unknown parameter describing some aspect of the population distribution of y. The joint density function of the sample is the product of the individual density functions, given by the expression

$$L = \prod_{i=1}^{n} f(y_i \mid \theta).$$

The goal of maximum likelihood estimation is to find the set of values of the unknown parameters that make L as large as possible.[5] Instead of maximizing the likelihood function, it is often more convenient to maximize the log-likelihood function. Because the logarithm is a strictly monotone transformation, the values that maximize L will also maximize $\log L$, which can be written as

$$\log L = \sum_{i=1}^{n} \log f(y_i \mid \theta).$$

For this example, which involves only a single parameter, the maximum is attained when the rate of change of $\log L$ with respect to θ equals zero. This condition is referred to as a first-order condition. Mathematically, this condition is expressed by equating the first partial derivative of $\log L$ with respect to θ to zero and solving for θ:

$$\frac{\partial \log L}{\partial \theta} = 0.$$

The solution of this equation yields the maximum likelihood estimate (MLE), $\widehat{\theta}$.

---

[5]Note that in the preceding example, L is maximized for a single parameter (θ). In general, L will depend on a vector of parameter values ($\boldsymbol{\theta}$).

To ensure that log L is maximized when solving for θ, it must be the case that the slope of log L is decreasing near the MLE. This condition is called the second-order condition, given by the expression for the second partial derivative of log L with respect to θ:

$$\frac{\partial^2 \log L}{\partial \theta^2} < 0.$$

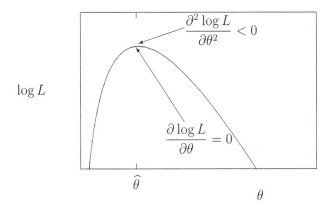

Figure 2.1: Maximization of $\log L$ with Respect to θ

Figure 2.1 depicts the principles of maximum likelihood estimation for a single parameter, θ. Note that in the context of multiple regression and other models considered in this book, the likelihood equations would need to be solved for $K + 1$ model parameters.

Unlike the least squares approach, the method of maximum likelihood requires that we make assumptions about the distribution of y, conditional on x's, or equivalently the distribution of the residual. The unobserved errors (ε_i) are assumed to be independent and identically distributed as normal with mean zero and variance σ_ε^2. We may write the probability distribution function or density function for ε as $f(\varepsilon)$

$$f(\varepsilon) = \frac{1}{\sqrt{2\pi}\sigma_\varepsilon} \exp\left[-\frac{1}{2}\left(\frac{\varepsilon}{\sigma_\varepsilon}\right)^2\right]. \tag{2.8}$$

Recall that $\varepsilon_i = y_i - \sum_{k=0}^{K} \beta_k x_{ik}$. For the ith observation, the density function may be written as:

$$f(\varepsilon_i) = \frac{1}{\sqrt{2\pi}\sigma_\varepsilon} \exp\left[\frac{-1}{2\sigma_\varepsilon^2}\left(y_i - \sum_{k=0}^{K} \beta_k x_{ik}\right)^2\right].$$

The likelihood for the sample is the product of the individual $f(\varepsilon_i)$'s over the entire sample. The resulting expression is a function of the data and the unknown parameters.

$$
\begin{aligned}
L &= \prod_{i=1}^{n} f(\varepsilon_i) \\
&= \frac{1}{\left(\sqrt{2\pi}\sigma_\varepsilon\right)^n} \exp\left[\frac{-1}{2\sigma_\varepsilon^2}\sum_{i=1}^{n}\left(y_i - \sum_{k=0}^{K} \beta_k x_{ik}\right)^2\right].
\end{aligned}
$$

The log likelihood can be expressed as

$$\log L = -\frac{n}{2}\log(2\pi\sigma_\varepsilon^2) - \frac{1}{2\sigma_\varepsilon^2}\sum_{i=1}^{n}\left(y_i - \sum_{k=0}^{K} \beta_k x_{ik}\right)^2.$$

The partial derivatives play a role in maximum likelihood estimation just as they do in least squares estimation since maxima and minima of functions are determined when the first partial derivatives are zero. Just as in the least squares case, one can find expressions for the partial derivatives of $\log L$ with respect to the unknown parameters. Maximum likelihood estimates are obtained by equating these expressions to zero and solving for the unknown parameters:

$$\frac{\partial \log L}{\partial \beta_k} = \frac{1}{\sigma_\varepsilon^2}\sum_{i=1}^{n}\left(y_i - \sum_{k=0}^{K} \beta_k x_{ik}\right) x_{ik} = 0, \quad k = 0, \ldots, K. \quad (2.9)$$

Since Eq. 2.9 differs from Eq. 2.5 only by a constant term that does not involve the β's, the value of $\mathbf{b}$ that maximizes Eq. 2.9 will also minimize Eq. 2.5. Thus, in this particular case, OLS estimates can be interpreted as MLEs. In general, this will not be the case except for a few kinds of models. The basic steps outlined earlier can be used to find any maximum likelihood estimate. For most models, however, simple closed-form solutions do not exist, and successive approximations to the MLEs must be carried out iteratively (see Appendix B).

2.2.3   Assumptions for Least Squares Regression

The key assumptions for least squares estimation of the regression model are linearity, independence between the x's and ε, and i.i.d. of ε. We will briefly review them.

Linearity: Linearity specifies that the conditional mean of y is a linear function of x variables: $\mu_i = \sum \beta_k x_{ik}$. *Specification errors* can result when there is a nonlinear relationship between the independent variables and dependent variable. In many instances, it is possible to transform nonlinear functions into linear functions. For example, a nonlinear regression with a multiplicative disturbance may be written as

$$y_i = \alpha x_i^\gamma \delta_i.$$

This equation can be transformed by taking natural logarithms of both sides resulting in a loglinear regression model

$$\ln y_i = \beta_0 + \beta_1 \ln x_i + \varepsilon_i,$$

where $\beta_0 = \ln \alpha$, $\beta_1 = \gamma$, and $\varepsilon_i = \ln \delta_i$. Ordinary least squares may be used on the transformed equation, yielding estimates that retain their desirable properties. Alternative estimation strategies, such as nonlinear least squares, are required when a transformation will not make the model linear in the parameters.

Independence of x's and ε: The assumption of independence between x's and ε is necessary in order to identify the $(K+1)$ unknown β parameters. This assumption can be satisfied in two ways. One is to hold the x's fixed by design. That is, under repeated sampling, the y's vary whereas the x's remain at fixed levels. Another way is to view both y and the x's as random variables but assume ε to be independent of the x's. The independence (or orthogonality) of the x's and ε is a condition that guarantees the unbiasedness of the least squares estimator. When this is true, the LS estimator is also asymptotically unbiased, or consistent.

i.i.d. of ε: Although the i.i.d. assumption says that ε is independent and identically distributed, it is not necessary to specify the actual distribution of ε. With large sample sizes, we can still draw statistical inferences about the β's using the usual t-tests due to the central limit theorem. However, in small samples the normality assumption about ε_i is needed to justify the use of t-tests.

Although the unbiasedness and consistency of the LS estimator do not require the i.i.d. assumption for ε, with the i.i.d. assumption, the LS estimator is made the best (meaning most efficient) among all linear unbiased estimators (BLUE). Note that i.i.d. means constant variance of ε (homoscedasticity) and no autocorrelation in ε.[6]

When ε is normally distributed, which is an extra assumption, the LS estimator coincides with MLE because both methods solve the same set of normal equations. The MLE is the *best unbiased estimator* (BUE) within the class of unbiased estimators. However, because the MLE can be nonlinear, efficiency is broader for the ML interpretation than for the LS interpretation. Broadly speaking, statistical inferences for MLEs are often evaluated on their large sample, or asymptotic, properties. It can be shown that, as the sample size goes to infinity, MLEs are consistent (asymptotically unbiased) and attain the smallest variance that a consistent estimator can have.

2.2.4   Comparisons of Conditional Means

Regression models for continuous dependent variables may contain continuous or categorical independent variables. Categorical indepen-

---

[6]Autocorrelation, or serial correlation, is defined as the correlation (nonindependence) of observation errors. Autocorrelation is most common in time-series data, where a high value of ε at time t is associated with a high value of ε at time $t + 1$.

dent variables can be easily handled in a regression model. Suppose, for example, we are interested in comparing earnings across three racial/ethnic categories: White, Black, and Hispanic. We can create dummy variables to represent the different groups. These dummy variables can then be used just like any other explanatory variables in a regression model.[7] A dummy variable takes a value of one when an attribute is present and zero otherwise. Suppose that individual earnings are related to race and ethnicity in a model as

$$y_i = \alpha_W W_i + \alpha_B B_i + \alpha_H H_i + \varepsilon_i,$$

where W is a dummy variable taking the value one whenever the respondent in question is White, and zero otherwise; B and H are defined similarly for Blacks and Hispanics. As written, this model provides the group means α_W for Whites and α_B and α_H for Blacks and Hispanics, respectively. In general, however, regression models include a constant term. Including a constant requires dropping one dummy variable term to avoid perfect linear dependence or underidentification. The resulting model with a constant and $J - 1$ dummy variable effects can be estimated. Dropping W results in

$$y_i = \alpha + \beta_B B_i + \beta_H H_i + \varepsilon_i.$$

The intercept in this model now represents the average earnings for Whites. The expected earnings for Blacks are given by this model as $\alpha + \beta_B$. Similarly, $\alpha + \beta_H$ gives the mean for Hispanics. Therefore, the parameters β_B and β_H represent the difference in average earnings between Blacks and Whites and between Hispanics and Whites, respectively.

The process by which one sets the arbitrary constraints in order to achieve unique identification of model parameters is called normalization. The normalization described earlier is termed regression coding or dummy-variable coding, and it is only one of a number of possible methods for handling nominal variables. In some situations, an alternative interpretation of the effects of categorical variables may be

---

[7]There are a number of ways to define dummy variables. Here we contrast the *regression* coding approach with the *effect* (or ANOVA) coding approach.

desired. Analysis of variance (ANOVA) is statistically equivalent to regression analysis with dummy variables. However, in ANOVA, categorical variables are, by convention, so coded that resulting parameters reflect differences from an average, rather than deviations from a reference category. This is also called ANOVA coding or centered coding. ANOVA coding constrains the sum of the dummy-variable effects to equal zero. That is, for a qualitative variable having J categories, $\sum_{j=1}^{J} \alpha_j = 0$ $(j = 1, \ldots, J)$. The intercept term represents the overall mean, or grand mean, with equal group sizes (i.e., when $n_1 = n_2 = \cdots = n_J$). With unequal group sizes, it is an arbitrarily standardized mean. The remaining J dummy-variable effects are interpreted as deviations from this average. Identical models result from either the regression-coded or ANOVA-coded design. However, the interpretation of the parameter estimates differs. In the chapters that follow, we will mostly use dummy variables.

2.2.5   Linear Models with Weaker Assumptions

In a research setting, the i.i.d. assumption is often unrealistic. The violation can take a number of forms, the principal two of which are heteroscedasticity and autocorrelation. For continuous dependent variables, the OLS estimator is inefficient when the i.i.d. assumption is violated but remains unbiased and consistent.

When the i.i.d. assumption is violated, the structure of the violation is sometimes known. Utilizing this additional information affords the researcher the ability to improve efficiency through the generalized least squares (GLS) approach, which is widely used to correct for heteroscedasticity as well as autocorrelation. The GLS estimator is a generalization of the familiar OLS estimator of Eq. 2.6. Let the variance-covariance matrix of the residuals be represented by the matrix $\mathbf{\Psi}_{n \times n} = V(\varepsilon)$. The GLS regression estimator is

$$\mathbf{b}_{GLS} = \left[\mathbf{X}'\mathbf{\Psi}^{-1}\mathbf{X}\right]^{-1}\mathbf{X}'\mathbf{\Psi}^{-1}\mathbf{y}, \qquad (2.10)$$

with variance-covariance matrix

$$\mathrm{var}(\mathbf{b}_{GLS}) = \left[\mathbf{X}'\mathbf{\Psi}^{-1}\mathbf{X}\right]^{-1}. \qquad (2.11)$$

The matrix Ψ^{-1} is referred to as the weight matrix. It can be shown that GLS basically transforms the original y and x variables so that the resulting regression equation meets the i.i.d. assumption. Thus, the GLS estimator has all the desirable properties of OLS when the i.i.d. assumption is satisfied: unbiasedness, consistency, efficiency, and asymptotic normality. When Ψ is unknown, it is replaced by its estimate. The resulting estimator is called the EGLS (estimated GLS) or FGLS (feasible GLS) estimator. The researcher may still choose to use OLS if the structure of the violation is unknown or difficult to specify, but the usual formula for the variances/covariances of the estimates (i.e., Eq. 2.7) is incorrect. The asymptotically "robust" formula should be used instead (also known as the Huber-White estimator) (Greene 1991).

Later in this section we provide an example of the FGLS estimator applied to grouped data. In this case, FGLS results in an estimator that has the same large sample properties as the maximum likelihood estimator. The FGLS estimator can also be used iteratively by updating the weighting matrix at each iteration. This technique results in the iteratively reweighted least squares (IRLS) estimator, which can be applied to many of the models in this book. Iteratively reweighted least squares estimation is equivalent to maximum likelihood for the models considered in Chapters 3 and 4, and most of the models in Chapter 5. Appendix B provides more detail about this estimator in the context of maximum likelihood estimation and generalized linear models.

Example of FGLS Estimation

We now illustrate how the FGLS technique can be applied to estimate a log-rate model using information on event counts and time spent at risk of an event. We will consider these models in more detail in Chapter 5. For now, we will briefly show how to estimate a nonlinear model using well-known regression techniques. In the example that follows, we would like to know the effects of age and period on the infant mortality rate. Table 2.1 provides the data for constructing the age- and period-specific empirical rates. Summary tables such as Table 2.1 are often provided in research papers, making it easy to carry

Table 2.1: Mortality in the First 6 Months of Life: Ümea, Sweden

	Period			
	1805–1807		1811	
Age	y	n	y	n
Week 1	19	1073	10	339
Weeks 2-4	70	3084	23	967
2-6 months	134	18520	69	4611

out secondary analyses (see e.g., Lithell 1981).[8]

Let us denote the empirical rates as

$$\widetilde{p}_i = y_i/n_i,$$

where y_i denotes the number of infants dying in an age interval in a given period (events), and n_i indicates the total number of person-weeks of life experienced by the individuals who were exposed to the risk of dying during a particular age interval in a given period. The n_i term in the denominator represents the exposure to the risk of mortality for that age and period.[9]

Since a rate must be positive, one way to guarantee this is to make the model linear in the logarithm of $\widetilde{p}$. A linear model in $\log \widetilde{p}$ is called a log-probability model. When the empirical rates can be constructed as the ratio of event counts to exposure, and $n_i \geq 20$ and $p_i < 0.05$, it is acceptable to call this model a log-rate model. We can estimate the log-rate model using FGLS. The regression model can be written as

$$\log p_i = \beta_0 + \beta_1 A2_i + \beta_2 A3_i + \beta_3 P2_i + \varepsilon_i,$$

---

[8]We thank Jan Hoem for sharing these data.

[9]What we are calling a "rate" is technically a proportion. However, when n_i is large (often taken as $n_i \geq 20$) and p_i is small (often taken as $p_i < 0.05$), the proportion is close to the rate. In this case, we are regarding each week of life as a Bernoulli trial. In a single trial (week), the infant either dies (with probability p) or survives (with probability $1 - p$). Then the age/period population mortality rate is actually a probability, which we estimate from a binomial experiment using the number of deaths (y_i) and trials (n_i) corresponding to a particular age/period classification.

where $A2$ is a $(0,1)$ dummy variable representing the second age interval (2–4 weeks), $A3$ is a dummy variable representing the third age interval (2–6 months), $P2$ is a dummy variable denoting the second period (1811), and $\varepsilon_i = \log \widetilde{p}_i - \log p_i$. The dummy-variable coding—which uses the first category of each variable as a reference category—would result in the *column-oriented* data matrix given in Table 2.2, which is suitable for input into standard regression programs.

Table 2.2: Column-Oriented Layout of Data File

y	n	$A2$	$A3$	$P2$
19	1073	0	0	0
70	3084	1	0	0
134	18520	0	1	0
10	339	0	0	1
23	967	1	0	1
69	4611	0	1	1

The log-rate model is an example of a heteroscedastic regression model where the error variance is not constant over age and period. In fact, it can be shown that the error variance is a function of the rates [i.e., $\text{var}(\varepsilon_i) = (1 - p_i)/n_i p_i$], so it is intuitively clear that the error variance is larger for smaller n's (see e.g., Maddala 1983).[10]

Generalized least squares estimation would use a weighting matrix given by the inverse of the variances. When the empirical rates are substituted, the FGLS weights are

$$w_i = \frac{n_i \widetilde{p}_i}{1 - \widetilde{p}_i}.$$

Instead of minimizing Eq. 2.4, we minimize the weighted sum of squares. Substituting $\mathbf{x}_i$ for the vector of independent variables (including the constant) and y_i for the dependent variable, $\log \widetilde{p}_i$,

---

[10] A more statistically correct approach would be to assume that the number of deaths y_i in a time interval of length n_i follows a Poisson distribution with rate p_i. In this case, it can be shown that the variance of $\log \widetilde{p}_i$ is simply $1/y_i$. A weighted least squares regression with weights y_i will give essentially the same results as those reported in Table 2.3.

$$S(\beta) = \sum_i w_i(y_i - \mathbf{x}_i'\beta)^2$$

$$= (y_i - \mathbf{x}_i'\beta)'\mathbf{W}(y_i - \mathbf{x}_i'\beta),$$

(2.12)

the solution of which is,

$$\mathbf{b}_{GLS} = [\mathbf{X}'\mathbf{W}\mathbf{X}]^{-1}\mathbf{X}'\mathbf{W}\mathbf{y},$$

where $\mathbf{W}$ is the diagonal matrix with w_i along the main diagonal and zeros elsewhere and is equal to $\mathbf{\Psi}^{-1}$.

The variance of the FGLS estimator is given by

$$\mathrm{var}(\mathbf{b}_{GLS}) = [\mathbf{X}'\mathbf{W}\mathbf{X}]^{-1}.$$

The FGLS solution can also be obtained using OLS on transformed variables. In this case (using Eq. 2.12), we would multiply $\log \widetilde{p}_i$ by $\sqrt{w_i}$ and multiply each independent variable (including the constant vector of ones) by $\sqrt{w_i}$. The standard errors of the estimates should then be divided by the square root of the reported MSE from the model.

Table 2.3 provides estimates and standard errors for alternative models fit to the data in Table 2.1. The results show that the FGLS estimates are close to the maximum likelihood estimates obtained by assuming a Poisson distribution for the number of infant deaths. Since the model is linear in the logged rate, we use an exponential transformation to retrieve the estimated mortality rates. Letting b_k ($k = 0, \ldots, K$) denote the FGLS estimates, the estimated (or predicted) rates, $\widehat{p}_i$, are given by

$$\widehat{p}_i = \exp(b_0 + b_1 A2_i + b_2 A3_i + b_3 P2_i).$$

We can estimate the risk of mortality at any age and period relative to any other age and period by forming the ratios of the estimated rates for different age intervals and periods. More on the concept of relative risk will be presented in Chapters 3, 4, and 5. In this example, the estimated risk of an infant dying in 1811 relative to the period from

Table 2.3: OLS, FGLS, and ML Estimates of the Log-Rate Model

Variable	OLS Estimate (Std. Error)	FGLS Estimate (Std. Error)	ML Estimate (Std. Error)
Constant	−3.993	−4.042	−4.037
	(0.206)	(0.188)	(0.190)
A2	0.017	0.136	0.112
	(0.246)	(0.211)	(0.213)
A3	−0.787	−0.821	−0.826
	(0.246)	(0.196)	(0.199)
P2	0.428	0.535	0.519
	(0.201)	(0.119)	(0.120)

1805 to 1807 (net of age) can be obtained simply by exponentiating the regression coefficient for $P2$, or $\exp(b_3) = \exp(0.535) = 1.71$. Thus, the estimated risk of dying in period 2 is 1.71 times that of period 1 based on this model. We can perform similar calculations using the estimates associated with $A2$ and $A3$ to get the estimated age-specific risks (net of period).

2.3   Differences between Categorical and Continuous Dependent Variables

Categorical variables assume a limited number of possible values. Their effects can be accounted for by dummy variables when used as independent variables in a regression. When used as dependent variables, however, categorical variables require special consideration. Both estimation and substantive problems arise if they are used as dependent variables in classical regression models designed for continuous dependent variables. Prediction poses a particularly significant problem in this case. Fitting a linear regression model to a categorical dependent variable can result in predictions being out of the plausible range for the dependent variable. To see this, consider a binary dependent variable y that takes on the values 0 and 1.

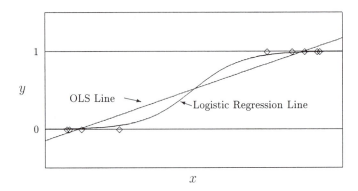

Figure 2.2: Logistic Versus Linear Regressions for Binary Data

As shown in Fig. 2.2, a linear regression of y on x means that the predicted line will inevitably fall outside the range of $[0, 1]$ if x is varied substantially. Clearly, this is not sensible. It often seems reasonable to assume that the relationship between y and x becomes less sharp as y approaches either 0 or 1. Such a nonlinear relationship can be represented by a logistic regression model to be explained in Chapter 3. However, there are many other transformations which will ensure that predicted responses lie in the $[0,1]$ range.

2.3.1   A Working Typology

Models for categorical dependent variables include those for binary, ordered, and unordered polytomous variables, frequency counts, and censored continuous variables. This book deals with regression-type models that can be written in the form of a single equation. The typology in Table 2.4 provides a schematic guide to regression models involving continuous and categorical data.

Cases 1–2 represent the classical regression approach for conditional mean estimation discussed in this chapter. Cases 3–4 involve binary response variables and will be discussed in Chapter 3 and, to a lesser extent, in Chapter 5. Cases 5–8 deal with ordered and unordered

Table 2.4: A Typology of Regression Models

Dependent Variable	Independent Variable	Method of Analysis	Case
Continuous	Continuous	Regression, correlation	1
Continuous	Categorical	Regression, ANOVA	2
Binary	Categorical	Logit/probit, loglinear	3
Binary	Continuous	Logit/probit	4
Unordered polytomous	Categorical	Loglinear, multinomial logit	5
Unordered polytomous	Continuous	Multinomial logit	6
Ordered polytomous	Categorical	Ordered logit/probit, loglinear	7
Ordered polytomous	Continuous	Ordered logit/probit	8
Cross-classified data	Categorical	Loglinear	9
Censored duration data	Categorical, continuous	Loglinear, logit/comp. log-log	10

responses and are covered in Chapters 6 and 7, and to some extent in Chapter 4. Case 9 represents the approach for cross-classified data, which is discussed in Chapter 4. Case 10 deals with the analysis of rates and will be discussed in Chapter 5. Under "Method of Analysis," we give only brief labels in reference to a rather broad—and sometimes heterogeneous—set of related methods and models.

Chapter 3

Logit and Probit Models for Binary Data

3.1 Introduction to Binary Data

In many areas of social science research, one encounters dependent variables that assume one of two possible values. For example, a youngster may graduate or fail to graduate from high school; a worker may be employed or unemployed; a patient in a clinical trial may respond or not respond to treatment during a period of observation. Data of this kind—having two possible outcomes—are said to be binary. By convention, the outcomes are commonly described as *success* and *failure*. In general, the substantive outcome of interest is considered to be a success ($y = 1$), whereas its complement is considered a failure ($y = 0$). With this in mind, researchers in the social and biological sciences often consider as a success a qualitatively *unsuccessful* outcome, such as failing to graduate from high school, being unemployed, or dying during a clinical study. Binary variables are also referred to as (0,1) variables. With binary dependent variables, the researcher's goal is to estimate or predict the probability of success or failure, conditional on a set of independent variables.

At the most basic level, the units of analysis for a binary (0,1) variable are individuals. In this case, there is only one trial for each individual, and the outcome is either 1 (success) or 0 (failure). This type of trial is called a Bernoulli trial. A Bernoulli trial has one parameter (p), the probability of success. The Bernoulli probability distribution function is given by

$$\Pr(y \mid p) = p^y(1-p)^{1-y}, \qquad (3.1)$$

which gives the probability of success, $\Pr(y = 1) = p$, and its complement, the probability of failure, $\Pr(y = 0) = 1-p$. In principle, success probabilities can assume different values for each sampled individual, when modeled as functions of explanatory variables. For example, the likelihood of high school dropout for the ith individual may depend on a number of individual characteristics and would be denoted as p_i. In practice, it is common that researchers group observations of binary (0,1) responses when explanatory variables are categorical. Such data are often represented in the form of contingency (or frequency) tables. For example, we may record the number of high school dropouts by sex in each racial or ethnic group. The data could be represented in the form of a $2 \times 2 \times R$ contingency table, with frequency counts cross-tabulated by the 2 possible outcomes, 2 sex categories, and R racial or ethnic categories. As we shall show later, the key information contained in such a table is the number of successes out of total trials, for each cell of sex $\times$ race/ethnicity. If all individuals within each cell are independent and identically distributed as Bernoulli trials, the sum of the total number of successes (or failures) follows a binomial distribution with two parameters, p and n, where n is the number of total trials for each cell. The binomial probability function is given by

$$\Pr(y \mid n, p) = \binom{n}{y} p^y (1-p)^{1-y}. \qquad (3.2)$$

This chapter considers models for grouped and individual-level binary data. We begin with binomial models for grouped (or replicated) binary data. These models are intuitively appealing and may be estimated using convenient least squares methods. Many of the concepts carry over to the discussion of individual-level binary data.

3.2   The Transformational Approach

The transformational, or statistical, approach to modeling binary data is based on the idea that there is a one-to-one correspondence between the sample data and the population quantities being modeled. This idea is the most intuitive when data are grouped according to an array of categorical independent variables. With grouped data, frequency counts are transformed to proportions, which are estimates of the population-level conditional probabilities. In the case of linear probability models, the dependent variable is the sample proportion or empirical probability (i.e., an estimate of the population proportion) and is modeled using the classical regression model and estimated by OLS or FGLS. As we shall see, this technique does not guarantee that predicted conditional probabilities lie in the range from zero to one. This shortcoming is avoided in logit and probit models in which transformations are used to ensure that the estimated conditional probabilities are constrained to be in the [0,1] range.

3.2.1   The Linear Probability Model

The linear probability model provides a good starting point for the discussion of binary dependent variables. With individual-level data, the linear probability model uses a binary (0,1) dependent variable. We do not recommend using a linear probability model with ungrouped data because this violates several of the assumptions of OLS estimation. With grouped data, this is less of a problem partly because there is more variation in the dependent variable, which is a proportion rather than a binary variable. With grouped data, a contingency table can be constructed containing all the sufficient information. Table 3.1 reports the number of high school graduates (y out of n) by race and ethnicity (White, Black, and Hispanic), sex (male and female), and family structure (intact and nonintact) from a subsample of young adults aged 25–30 from the National Longitudinal Survey of Youth (NLSY) (Center for Human Resource Research 1979).[1]

---

[1]Nonintact family structure is defined as not living with both biological parents at age 14.

Table 3.1: High School Graduates by Race, Sex, and Family Structure

	Intact				Nonintact			
	Male		Female		Male		Female	
Race	y	n	y	n	y	n	y	n
White	843	982	864	931	168	243	161	208
	(86%)		(93%)		(69%)		(77%)	
Black	346	441	360	410	231	337	225	283
	(78%)		(88%)		(69%)		(80%)	
Hispanic	237	305	208	259	82	128	78	98
	(78%)		(80%)		(64%)		(80%)	

The dimensions of the table are determined by the number of independent variables (or factors) and the number of categories (or factor levels) per variable. With three categories of race, two categories of sex, and two categories of family structure, we obtain $3 \times 2 \times 2 = 12$ cells. Within each cell (i), two quantities—the number of trials (n_i) and the number graduating (y_i)—are needed to estimate the population proportion of high school graduates in each category.

Adopting a dummy-variable coding for the factor levels corresponding to race, sex, and family structure, an *additive effects* model for this table can be written as

$$p_i = \beta_0 + \beta_1 \text{Black} + \beta_2 \text{Hispanic} + \beta_3 \text{Female} + \beta_4 \text{Nonintact},$$

where p_i is the probability of graduation controlling for race, sex, and family structure. The parameter β_0 is the intercept term, and the remaining coefficients $(\beta_1, \ldots, \beta_4)$ represent the "effects" of race (Black or Hispanic vs. White), sex (Female vs. Male), and family structure (Nonintact vs. Intact). A special version of the main effects model constrains graduation probabilities to be the same regardless of race, sex, and family structure (i.e., $\beta_1 = \beta_2 = \beta_3 = \beta_4 = 0$). This model is often referred to as the null model.

The additive effects model assumes that the effect of an independent variable does not depend on the values of another independent variable. A more general model can include interaction terms, allowing the effects of independent variables to vary depending on the levels of other variables with which they interact. When a model includes all possible interactions, the model would, in effect, fit a unique parameter to each cell in the table, thus exactly reproducing the observed data with the model parameters. This is called a saturated model. In practice, substantively meaningful models lie between the two extremes of the null model and the saturated model. However, the saturated model could be the best model for the data. For example, it could be the case that the preferred model for these data is one in which the effects of family structure on graduation vary by sex within ethnic groups.

As in any regression with categorical independent variables, normalization is necessary to identify model parameters uniquely. In the preceding example, we adopt dummy-variable coding, using the first categories of race (White), sex (Male), and family structure (Intact) as reference categories. For estimation purposes, it is often more convenient to arrange tabled data in column format, with dummy-variable coding, as shown in Table 3.2.

Table 3.2: Column-Formatted Summary of Data in Table 3.1 Using Dummy Variables

Black	Hispanic	Female	Family Structure	y	n
0	0	0	0	843	982
0	0	1	0	864	931
1	0	0	0	346	441
1	0	1	0	360	410
0	1	0	0	237	305
0	1	1	0	208	259
0	0	0	1	168	243
0	0	1	1	161	208
1	0	0	1	231	337
1	0	1	1	225	283
0	1	0	1	82	128
0	1	1	1	78	98

In Table 3.2, each row of data represents a cell from Table 3.1, with y_i denoting the number graduating and n_i denoting the total number of observations falling into the ith cell. The cells are treated as separate units of analysis in a manner similar to individual-level observations, with one proportion per group. The dependent variable in the linear probability model is the estimated (or *empirical*) probability of graduating, conditional on race, sex, and family structure, which we will denote as $\tilde{p}_i = y_i/n_i$.

Letting x_{ik} denote the kth variable in a set of K independent variables corresponding to the classification in the ith cell—and including a vector of ones for the intercept term—the OLS regression model can be written as

$$\tilde{p}_i = \sum_{k=0}^{K} \beta_k x_{ik} + \varepsilon_i, \tag{3.3}$$

where $\varepsilon_i = p_i - \tilde{p}_i$ is distributed with mean $\mathrm{E}(\varepsilon) = 0$ and variance $\mathrm{var}(\varepsilon) = \sigma_\varepsilon^2$.

Ordinary least squares estimation of the main effect linear probability model yields the following estimates and standard errors (in parentheses):

$$
\begin{array}{cccc}
0.82 & - & 0.027\ \text{Black} & - & 0.059\ \text{Hispanic} \\
(0.023) & & (0.025) & & (0.025) \\
& + & 0.089\ \text{Female} & - & 0.108\ \text{Nonintact} \\
& & (0.027) & & (0.021)
\end{array}
$$

Interpretation of the main effects model is straightforward. As in the classical regression model, the coefficients from the linear probability model have the familiar interpretation as the *marginal effect* of the independent variable on the dependent variable. That is, the marginal effect of x on p is the change in p associated with a unit change in x. In the case of categorical explanatory variables, the effect represents the case when $x = 1$, as compared to $x = 0$. In our example, the constant term ($b_0 = 0.82$) gives an estimated baseline probability of graduating when all covariates take the value zero (i.e., White males from intact families). The remaining terms give the estimated increase or decrease in the probability of graduation when covariates take the value one. For example, being Black decreases the probability of graduating by 0.027; being Hispanic decreases it by 0.059. Similarly, being female increases the chances of graduating by 0.089, whereas being from a nonintact family decreases the probability of graduating by 0.108. The estimates represent the effects of the independent variables after controlling for, or net of, the effects of other covariates in the model.

The foregoing main effects model explains over 85% of the variation in the empirical probabilities. The model is plausible for this particular data set as it produces no estimated graduation probabilities outside the [0,1] range. The linear probability model works well in this case because graduation probabilities do not vary dramatically by group, and the cell sizes (n_i's) are large. The smallest observed proportion is 0.64 among Black males residing in nonintact families, whereas the largest observed probability is 0.93 among White females living with both biological parents. The remaining probabilities lie between 0.69 and 0.88. As a rule of thumb, when the empirical probabilities exhibit little variation by group, a linear probability model may be attractive from the standpoint of ease of estimation and interpretation. However, there are several weaknesses with the linear probability model approach, and given the current state of the art in statistical software, such models are seldom fit to binary data.

In the framework of generalized linear models, we can express the linear probability model as

$$p_i = I(\eta_i) = \sum_{k=0}^{K} \beta_k x_{ik}, \qquad (3.4)$$

where $I(\eta) = \eta$ denotes the *identity* link function, and $\eta_i = \sum_{k=0}^{K} \beta_k x_{ik}$. McCullagh and Nelder (1989) illustrate how different specifications of the link function give rise to different models (see Appendix B).

Although the linear probability model appears to fit the data of our example, this approach has a number of drawbacks. First, the underlying assumption of linearity implies that the probability of graduation is a linear function of race, sex, and family structure. With dummy-variable coding for categorical independent variables, linearity does not seem to be a strong assumption. The functional constraints are really about the interactions. In the absence of interactions, the predicted probabilities could lie outside the plausible range for probabilities. For example, in the event that *all* young women in the sample had graduated from high school, the predicted probability of graduation among young White women would be greater than 1 under the linear probability model.[2] Moreover, if we were interested in computing group differences in probabilities, these quantities are confined to the range $[-1, 1]$ by the axioms of probability. A linear probability model could yield differences outside this range.

Another weakness is the assumption of homoscedasticity or constant variance in the observations. The variable y_i is distributed as binomial, with variance $n_i p_i (1 - p_i)$, whereas the sample proportion $\widetilde{p}_i$ has variance $p_i(1 - p_i)/n_i$. Thus, we find that the variance in the dependent variable depends on the size of the group (or number of trials) and the probability of success. Since these quantities are not constant across cells, the errors are heteroscedastic. This implies that a GLS estimation strategy incorporating the cell-specific variance should be used in this situation. Since p_i is unknown, a FGLS (weighted least squares) solution would substitute $\widetilde{p}_i = y_i/n_i$, which is an unbiased estimate of p_i, into the expression for the variance. Alternatively, we could substitute predicted probabilities from a previous OLS fit (i.e., $\widehat{p}_i = \sum_k b_k x_{ik}$). Using the empirical probabilities, the resulting regression weights are given by[3]

$$w_i = n_i / \left[\widetilde{p}_i (1 - \widetilde{p}_i) \right],$$

and the weighted sum of squares to be minimized is

$$S(\boldsymbol{\beta}) = \sum_i w_i (\widetilde{p}_i - \sum_{k=0}^{K} \beta_k x_{ik})^2.$$

---

[2]This can be verified by modifying the data in the example programs on the book's website.

[3]This estimator could be improved upon by iterating this process using the estimated values of p_i until convergence, called the iteratively reweighted least squares estimator.

This procedure is also known as the *minimum* χ^2 method (see, e.g., Maddala 1983).

Although FGLS estimation solves the problem of heteroscedasticity, it does nothing to guarantee that the estimated probabilities lie in the zero to one range. Because the β's and their estimates are unbounded, so too are the predicted values. For this reason, the linear probability model is not as useful for modeling binary responses as several competing models. However, provided that p_i is not close to 0 or 1, and the n_i are sufficiently large, the linear probability model is sometimes attractive due to its ease of use and its straightforward interpretation. Next, we consider logit and probit models that transform data to ensure that the parameters are unbounded, but the predicted values are constrained to lie in the range $[0, 1]$.

3.2.2   The Logit Model

The logit model is widely used in the social and biological sciences. The model is especially useful in epidemiological and demographic research in the assessment of the effects of explanatory factors on the relative risk of outcomes such as fertility, mortality, and the onset of disease or illness. The logistic transformation can be interpreted as the logarithm of the odds of success vs. failure, which is described in more detail in this section. The logistic transformation of the success probability p is given by

$$\text{logit}(p_i) = \log\left(\frac{p_i}{1 - p_i}\right). \tag{3.5}$$

We now treat Eq. 3.5 as a link function in the generalized linear model framework and obtain the logit model (see Appendix B):

$$\log\left(\frac{p_i}{1 - p_i}\right) = \eta_i = \sum_{k=0}^{K} \beta_k x_{ik}. \tag{3.6}$$

We solve for probability p_i:

$$p_i = \frac{\exp(\sum_{k=0}^{K} \beta_k x_{ik})}{1 + \exp(\sum_{k=0}^{K} \beta_k x_{ik})} = \Lambda(\eta_i), \tag{3.7}$$

where $\Lambda(\eta_i)$ is a shorthand notation for the function $\exp(\eta_i)/[1 + \exp(\eta_i)]$.

For all possible values of x and β, the logistic transformation ensures that p remains in the $[0, 1]$ interval. As p approaches 0, $\text{logit}(p)$ tends toward $-\infty$; as p approaches 1, $\text{logit}(p)$ tends toward $+\infty$. Using terminology from the theory of generalized linear models, the logit link makes the model linear in the unknown parameters.[4]

Odds, Odds-Ratios, and Relative Risk

The logit model is especially appropriate when the issue of interest is to describe the *odds* of success or another substantive outcome, or the odds of success faced by one group relative to another. Odds are defined as the ratio of the probability of one outcome to another. For example, letting p denote the probability of success and $1 - p$ (its complement) denote the probability of failure, the odds of success is the ratio $\omega = p/(1 - p)$. For the logit transformation, this quantity will be recognized as the antilog of the logit, $\exp(\eta)$. Proof of this fact is left as an exercise.

The concept of odds can be extended to describe the odds of success associated with belonging to one group as opposed to another. The *odds-ratio* is such a measure. Suppose we have two groups of binary data with probabilities of success p_1 and p_2, such that $\text{logit}(p_1) = \beta_0 + \gamma$ and $\text{logit}(p_2) = \beta_0$, where β_0 and γ are parameters. In this example, γ may be thought of as the regression coefficient corresponding to a dummy variable representing membership in the first group. The odds-ratio is a measure of the odds of success in the first group relative to the second, or

$$\theta = \frac{\omega_1}{\omega_2} = \frac{p_1/(1 - p_1)}{p_2/(1 - p_2)} = \frac{\exp(\beta_0 + \gamma)}{\exp(\beta_0)} = \frac{\exp(\beta_0)\exp(\gamma)}{\exp(\beta_0)} = \exp(\gamma).$$

$$(3.8)$$

If the two groups face the same odds of success, the odds-ratio is 1. The quantity $\exp(\gamma)$ represents the odds of success for the first group relative to the second.

---

[4]Most programs can use the individual data (binomial responses and trials) or the empirical proportions (y_i/n_i) as input.

The odds-ratio is closely related to the concept of *relative risk*. Risk is defined as a probability over an interval of time (or exposure interval). In general, we use the term *event* to denote whether a success (or some other outcome of interest) occurs in a given time period. At the start of the time period, all subjects are assumed to be at *risk* of a particular event or outcome. The risk is the number of *new* event occurrences that happen in the population over some time period to the total number at risk (or *exposed* to the risk). For example, suppose that 50 subjects who are at risk of developing a rare disease are followed over a ten-year period. In that period, 5 develop the disease. The risk is 5/50, or 0.10.

Suppose that the original sample actually contains two experimental groups of equal size 25, one group receiving an experimental drug (the *treatment* group) and the other group receiving a placebo (the *control* group). Suppose that 2 subjects in the treatment group develop the disease, whereas 3 subjects in the control group develop the disease. The risk is now 2/25, or 0.08 in the treatment group, and 3/25, or 0.12 in the control group. Let us denote the risk in the treatment group as r_t, and the risk in the control group as r_c. With these risks, it is possible to assess the relative risk, that is, the risk in one group relative to the other. The risk of disease in the treatment group relative to the control group is

$$\frac{r_t}{r_c} = 0.667.$$

The risk of disease in the treatment group is two-thirds that of the control group. Stated differently, the risk of disease in the control group is one and one-half times higher ($1/0.667 = 1.5$) than in the treatment group.

Odds ratios are often used to approximate relative risks when the success (or event) probabilities are small. To see this, consider the odds-ratio formed using the preceding example:

$$\theta = \frac{r_t/(1 - r_t)}{r_c/(1 - r_c)} = 0.64.$$

When r_t and r_c are small, the odds-ratio will closely approximate the relative risk since the denominators in the expressions for the odds approach one. This is one reason why the odds-ratio is used extensively in biostatistics and epidemiology in the study of the incidence of disease. These and related concepts are described more fully in Section 3.4 and in Chapters 4 and 5.

3.2.3   The Probit Model

The probit model provides an alternative to the logit model. Again, a nonlinear model in p is transformed so that a monotonic function of p is linear with respect to explanatory variables. The probability in the ith cell or the ith observation, p_i, is given by the standard cumulative normal distribution function:

$$p_i = \int_{-\infty}^{\eta_i} \frac{1}{\sqrt{2\pi}} \exp(-\frac{1}{2}u^2)du. \tag{3.9}$$

Note that Eq. 3.9 should be comparable to Eq. 3.7 for the logit model. Equation 3.9 can be more conveniently written as $p_i = \Phi(\eta_i)$, where $\Phi(\cdot)$ denotes the cumulative distribution function of the standard normal distribution. The probit (or normit) transformation, or probit link, is given by the inverse of the standard cumulative normal distribution function. Solving Eq. 3.9 for η_i yields

$$\eta_i = \Phi^{-1}(p_i) = \text{probit}(p_i). \tag{3.10}$$

Equation 3.10 defines the probit link. Thus, the probit model can be written as

$$\Phi^{-1}(p_i) = \eta_i = \sum_{k=0}^{K} \beta_k x_{ik} \tag{3.11}$$

or

$$p_i = \Phi\left(\sum_{k=0}^{K} \beta_k x_{ik}\right). \tag{3.12}$$

Like the logistic function, the probit function is symmetric around $p = 0.5$, where $\text{logit}(p)$ and $\text{probit}(p)$ are both zero. As p approaches 1, $\text{probit}(p)$ tends toward $+\infty$; as p approaches 0, $\text{probit}(p)$ tends toward $-\infty$. Letting $F^{-1}(p)$ denote the inverse of the cumulative logistic or standard normal distribution functions (i.e., the link functions),

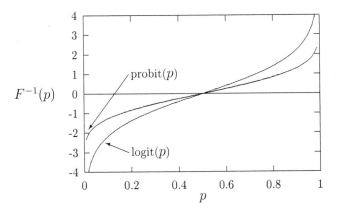

Figure 3.1: Logit and Probit Transformations of p

Fig. 3.1 shows the similarity between the probit and logistic transformations.

One finds that for ranges of p between 0.2 and 0.8 these transformations are essentially linear. For ranges of p outside this range, both functions are highly nonlinear. This implies that if p is modeled as a function of a continuous explanatory variable (x), the effect of x on p is not constant but varies with x. We would find, for example, that when $\text{probit}(p_i) = \text{logit}(p_i) = \beta_0 + \beta_1 x_i = 0$, the change in p associated with a change in x would be greater than when $\text{logit}(p_i)$ or $\text{probit}(p_i)$ are smaller or larger than 0. We provide a more detailed discussion of the implications of this on the interpretation of logit and probit coefficients in Section 3.4.

3.2.4   An Application Using Grouped Data

Table 3.3 shows estimates (with standard errors in parentheses) obtained from the linear probability, logit, and probit models applied to the data in Table 3.2. We apply the FGLS solution to estimate the linear probability (LP) model using the observed proportions in the weighting formula. We compare logit and probit models estimated using maximum likelihood (ML) and FGLS (see Appendix B).

Table 3.3: Estimates from Alternative Binary Response Models

Variable	LP FGLS	Logit ML	Logit FGLS	Probit ML	Probit FGLS
Constant	0.837	1.754	1.749	1.047	1.046
	(0.061)	(0.074)	(0.073)	(0.039)	0.040
Black	−0.034	−0.322	−0.312	−0.184	−0.183
	(0.071)	(0.091)	(0.090)	(0.051)	(0.051)
Hispanic	−0.073	−0.564	−0.567	−0.327	−0.328
	(0.081)	(0.105)	(0.104)	(0.060)	(0.055)
Female	0.082	0.575	0.558	0.323	0.319
	(0.065)	(0.081)	(0.081)	(0.045)	(0.047)
Nonintact	−0.120	−0.747	−0.750	−0.430	−0.430
	(0.062)	(0.083)	(0.082)	(0.048)	(−0.047)

The parameter estimates in Table 3.3 may be used to retrieve the predicted probabilities shown in Table 3.4. For example, the baseline probability of graduating from high school when all covariate values are zero (i.e., for White males residing in intact families) is 0.837, 0.852, and 0.852 for the linear probability, logit, and probit model.[5] The linear probability interpretation is straightforward. Each model term represents the effect on the probability so that the probabilities may be calculated directly. The logit and probit models require additional transformations. The baseline probability under the logit model is found by applying the transformation $\exp(\widehat{\beta}_0)/[1 + \exp(\widehat{\beta}_0)]$. For the probit model, we evaluate the cumulative normal distribution function $\Phi(\widehat{\beta}_0)$. This function is available in most computer packages and can be programmed on many pocket calculators or obtained from a normal probability table. The remaining cell probabilities are obtained by substituting the expression $\sum_k \widehat{\beta}_k x_{ik}$ for $\widehat{\beta}_0$ in the preceding expressions. Table 3.4 shows that the estimated probabilities are very similar, and close to the empirical probabilities.

---

[5]Maximum likelihood estimates of the logit and probit models are used to obtain the predicted probabilities.

Table 3.4: Estimated Graduation Probabilities by Race, Sex, and Family Structure

Race (x_1)	Sex (x_2)	Family Structure (x_3)	Empirical Probability	Linear Probability Model	Logit Model	Probit Model
White	Male	Intact	0.858	0.837	0.852	0.852
White	Female	Intact	0.928	0.919	0.911	0.915
Black	Male	Intact	0.785	0.803	0.807	0.806
Black	Female	Intact	0.878	0.885	0.882	0.882
Hispanic	Male	Intact	0.777	0.764	0.767	0.764
Hispanic	Female	Intact	0.803	0.846	0.854	0.851
White	Male	Nonintact	0.691	0.716	0.732	0.732
White	Female	Nonintact	0.774	0.799	0.829	0.826
Black	Male	Nonintact	0.685	0.683	0.665	0.668
Black	Female	Nonintact	0.795	0.765	0.779	0.775
Hispanic	Male	Nonintact	0.641	0.643	0.609	0.614
Hispanic	Female	Nonintact	0.796	0.726	0.735	0.730

3.3   Justification of Logit and Probit Models

The early origins of the logit and probit models can be traced to psycho-physics (Thurstone 1927). Modern developments of the logit and probit models, however, were developed in the field of bioassay or dose-response methodology (Cox 1970; Finney 1971). Binomial response models can be motivated by considering an experiment in which different amounts of a drug or other chemical compound are applied to batches of experimental subjects. For example, suppose that a particular insecticide is applied to batches of insects at a given dosage level u_i. At low dosages, none of the sampled insects may succumb; at high doses, all may die. The purpose of the experiment is to determine the lethal dosage levels (or response rates) or levels at which we would expect a certain proportion of the population to respond (by dying) to a given dosage level. Whether or not an insect dies is assumed to depend on its *tolerance* to the insecticide. Let c_i be a random variable denoting the tolerance of a particular insect. The ith insect dies $(y = 1)$ if $(u_i > c_i)$ and survives $(y = 0)$ if $(u_i < c_i)$. Thus, the probability of dying is

$$\Pr(y = 1) = \Pr(u > c). \tag{3.13}$$

3.3.1 The Latent Variable Approach

In social science applications, interpretations of u and c are straightforward. In studies of women's employment, for example, u is the market wage, and c is the reservation wage. In research on migration, u is the benefit of migration, whereas c is the associated cost. In general, u is often referred to as utility, whereas c is criterion. In economics, a behavioral interpretation links utilities to "revealed preferences." In actual research settings, we do not observe u and c directly. Instead, we only observe the outcome whether $y = 1$ or $y = 0$. The observed outcome is one that maximizes a rational individual's utility function. The researcher wishes to "reveal" the underlying u and c through Eq. 3.13, with the help of additional structural constraints. It is in this context that u and c are called latent variables.

One set of constraints implicit in the relationship between the latent variables (u, c) and the explanatory variables (x) is the linearity:

$$u = \sum_{k=0}^{K} \beta_k^u x_k + \varepsilon^u, \tag{3.14}$$

$$c = \sum_{k=0}^{K} \beta_k^c x_k + \varepsilon^c, \tag{3.15}$$

where β_k^u and β_k^c are, respectively, the coefficients of the kth independent variable for the u and c dependent variables, and ε^u and ε^c are disturbances for the two equations.

Combining Eqs. 3.13, 3.14, and 3.15, we obtain

$$
\Pr(y = 1) = \Pr(u > c)
$$

$$
= \Pr\left(\sum_{k=0}^{K} \beta_k^u x_k + \varepsilon^u > \sum_{k=0}^{K} \beta_k^c x_k + \varepsilon^c\right)
$$

$$
= \Pr\left(\varepsilon^c - \varepsilon^u < \sum_{k=0}^{K} \beta_k^u x_k - \sum_{k=0}^{K} \beta_k^c x_k\right) \tag{3.16}
$$

$$
= \Pr\left(\varepsilon^c - \varepsilon^u < \sum_{k=0}^{K} (\beta_k^u - \beta_k^c) x_k\right).
$$

The model implied by Eq. 3.16 is overparameterized. The main problem is that we can identify the differences in components between u and c but not both. To identify the model, it is necessary to add several constraints. One simple way to accomplish this is to normalize either u or c to be 0, by setting either

$$
\beta_k^u = 0 \quad (k = 0, \ldots, K); \quad \varepsilon^u = 0 \tag{3.17}
$$

or

$$
\beta_k^c = 0 \quad (k = 0, \ldots, K); \quad \varepsilon^c = 0. \tag{3.18}
$$

Equation 3.18 corresponds to a model with random utility but constant criterion. Similarly, Eq. 3.17 yields a model with constant utility but variant criterion. The two specifications may lead to different interpretations but cannot be separated statistically. In fact, they are also confounded with a third, general-form normalization, which encompasses the other two:

$$
\begin{aligned}
\varepsilon &= \varepsilon^c - \varepsilon^u \\
\beta_k &= \beta_k^u - \beta_k^c, \qquad k = 0, \ldots, K.
\end{aligned} \tag{3.19}
$$

The normalization of Eq. 3.19 simplifies Eq. 3.16 to

$$
\Pr(y = 1) = \Pr\left(\varepsilon < \sum_{k=0}^{K} \beta_k x_k\right) = F\left(\sum_{k=0}^{K} \beta_k x_k\right), \tag{3.20}
$$

where $F(\cdot)$ denotes the cumulative distribution function of ε. Still, it is necessary to standardize the mean and the variance of ε to identify the magnitudes of the β parameters. The reason for this is that, unlike continuously measured variables, binary dependent variables do not have inherent scales. The magnitude of the β parameters is meaningful only in reference to the mean (μ_ε) and the variance (σ_ε^2) of ε, which are unknown. It is thus useful to redefine ε to a common standard: $\varepsilon^* = (\varepsilon - a)/b$, where a and b are two chosen constants. The standardization changes Eq. 3.20 to

$$\Pr(y = 1) = F^* \left(\frac{\sum_{k=0}^{K} \beta_k x_k - a}{b} \right), \tag{3.21}$$

where $F^*(\cdot)$ stands for the cumulative distribution function of ε^*. Thus, it is necessary to define the location (a in Eq. 3.21) as well as the scale (b in Eq. 3.21) of ε^*. If we set $a = \mu_\varepsilon$, $b = \sigma_\varepsilon$, and $F^* = \Phi(\cdot)$, then Eq. 3.21 is the same expression as Eq. 3.12. Similarly, the logit model is obtained if ε is assumed to follow the standard logistic distribution (Eq. 3.7).

Both the standard logistic and the standard normal distributions have a mean of zero, but they have different variances: $\text{var}(\varepsilon^*) = 1$ for the standard normal and $\text{var}(\varepsilon^*) = \pi/\sqrt{3}$ for the standard logistic. This difference is translated to larger magnitudes for logit coefficients than comparable probit coefficients. In theory, multiplying a probit coefficient by approximately 1.81 (approximation of $\pi/\sqrt{3}$) should yield a value close to the logit coefficient. Similarly, multiplying logit estimates by approximately 0.55 should yield values that would correspond to probit estimates. As a rough rule of thumb, others have suggested that the multipliers 1.61 and 0.625 produce closer approximations (Amemiya 1981; Maddala 1983).

Because the normal and logistic distributions have similar shapes, probit and logit models are very similar. There is no compelling reason to prefer one model over another on substantive or theoretical grounds. Assuming that residual utility or criterion is due to a large number of small and accidental causes, some scholars have appealed to the central limit theorem and thus preferred the probit model. When this reasoning is invoked, the logit model may still be used as a good approximation. However, it is up to the researcher to defend this reasoning because the actual distribution of a latent variable is always up to anyone's conjecture. In practice, the logistic distribution may be preferred due to the simplicity of the probability distribution and density functions.[6] Because there is no simple closed-form expression for the odds-ratio in the probit model, the logit model may also be preferred because of its ease of interpretation in terms of log-odds-ratios. Furthermore, the binary logit, along with several other varieties of logit models, can be estimated as loglinear models, as we will show in Chapters 6 and 7.

3.3.2   Extending the Latent Variable Approach

The latent variable approach is commonly associated with the analysis of individual-level data. Suppose that we have a data set with data points x_{ik} and y_i $(i = 1, \ldots, n)$, where y is a dichotomous dependent variable $(y = 0, 1)$, and x_{ik} is the value of the kth covariate for the ith individual (including the constant term). For the ith individual, we define a continuous latent variable y_i^* representing the latent propensity that $y = 1$. Now express y_i^* as a linear function of x_{ik} and a residual ε_i:

$$y_i^* = \sum_{k=0}^{K} \beta_k x_{ik} + \varepsilon_i. \tag{3.22}$$

For simplicity, we will illustrate the individual-level model with the constant criterion normalization of Eq. 3.18, although other normalizations are statistically equivalent. We thus have the following "threshold-crossing" measurement model:

$$y_i = \begin{cases} 1 & \text{if } y_i^* > 0; \\ 0 & \text{otherwise.} \end{cases} \tag{3.23}$$

---

[6]The cumulative normal distribution function must be approximated numerically wheras the cumulative logistic distribution can be expressed in a closed form.

If ε_i is assumed to be i.i.d. as a standard normal, Eqs. 3.22 and 3.23 comprise the general formulation of the probit model. Likewise, if ε_i is assumed to be i.i.d. as a standard logistic, the logit model is obtained.

The observed values of y may be viewed as outcomes of a binomial experiment, where the number of trials is identically equal to one, and the response probabilities vary from trial to trial as functions of x_{ik}. This is only slightly different from the grouped data case, where the probabilities vary by groups, and the number of trials reflects the size of the group or the cell total in a contingency table. This distinction presents a slightly different estimation problem to be noted later. All the properties of the logit and the probit models for grouped data, however, are retained for the same models for individual data. Hence, we will not repeat the discussion here.

Index Functions

The latent variable approach has been used extensively in econometrics because of the close correspondence with the concept of utility. This section introduces a notational shorthand that is borrowed from this tradition.

Recall that the latent dependent variable is expressed as a linear function of unknown parameters, independent variables, and error. From Eq. 3.22, we have

$$y_i^* = \sum_{k=0}^{K} \beta_k x_{ik} + \varepsilon_i.$$

The systematic part involving the independent variables and the unknown regression parameters is referred to as an *index function*. It is often convenient to express this in matrix notation as

$$y_i^* = \mathbf{x}_i' \boldsymbol{\beta} + \varepsilon_i.$$

The expression $\mathbf{x}_i'\boldsymbol{\beta}$ denotes the index function for the ith individual, where $\boldsymbol{\beta} = (\beta_0, \dots, \beta_K)'$ is the $K+1$ column vector of regression coefficients, and $\mathbf{x}_i' = (x_{i0}, \dots, x_{iK})$ is the $K+1$ row vector of independent variables corresponding to the ith individual. This implies that the index function $\mathbf{x}_i'\boldsymbol{\beta}$ equals the conditional mean of the *latent* dependent variable y_i^*, $E(y_i^* \mid x_i)$. It is necessary to use a nonlinear transformation function to convert this conditional mean to a probability. For the logit model, the predicted probability is $\Lambda(x_i'\beta)$, which we express using the shorthand Λ_i; for the probit model, the predicted probability is $\Phi(x_i'\beta)$, or simply Φ_i.

Although both the logit and probit models are linear in the inverse transformations, they cannot be estimated using the usual least squares and weighted least squares techniques described earlier. Without grouping the data, we can not possibly form the empirical probabilities as the number of successes divided by the number of trials. Each observation represents a 0 or 1 outcome of a single (Bernoulli) trial. Nor can we construct the empirical logits and probits from the sample data.

3.3.3   Estimation of Binary Response Models

Unlike models for grouped data, models for individual-level data can include independent variables that, in principle, could have different values for all sampled individuals. In this sense, we have the potential to account for individual-specific sources of heterogeneity that might be "averaged out" when using grouped data. Model construction using individual-level data is exactly the same as in the grouped data model in other respects. In general, estimation is carried out using maximum likelihood or iteratively reweighted least squares for generalized linear models (see Appendix B).

Substituting $F(\cdot)$ for p in Eq. 3.1, the likelihood on data with n binary responses may be written as

$$L = \prod_i F(x_i'\beta)^{y_i} \left[1 - F(x_i'\beta)\right]^{(1-y_i)}. \tag{3.24}$$

The log-likelihood function is

$$\log L = \sum_i \left\{ y_i \log F(x_i'\beta) + (1 - y_i) \log[1 - F(x_i'\beta)] \right\}. \tag{3.25}$$

For models with more than one parameter, the first-order conditions require that we simultaneously solve the $K + 1$ equations to obtain an expression known as the score function[7]:

$$u_k = \frac{\partial \log L(\boldsymbol{\beta})}{\partial \beta_k} = 0, \qquad k = 0, \dots, K, \tag{3.26}$$

for which

$$h_{kl} = \frac{\partial^2 \log L(\boldsymbol{\beta})}{\partial \beta_k \beta_l} < 0 \qquad (k = 0, \dots, K) \quad (l = 0, \dots, K). \tag{3.27}$$

Solving the first-order conditions for the logit model, we obtain the following expression for the score function:

$$\frac{\partial \log L(\boldsymbol{\beta})}{\partial \boldsymbol{\beta}} = \mathbf{U}(\boldsymbol{\beta}) = \sum_i (y_i - \Lambda_i)\mathbf{x}_i, \tag{3.28}$$

where $\Lambda_i = \Lambda(\mathbf{x}_i'\boldsymbol{\beta}) = \exp(\mathbf{x}_i'\boldsymbol{\beta})/[1 + \exp(\mathbf{x}_i'\boldsymbol{\beta})]$.

For the probit model, the first-order conditions are given by

$$\frac{\partial \log L(\boldsymbol{\beta})}{\partial \boldsymbol{\beta}} = \mathbf{U}(\boldsymbol{\beta}) = \sum_{y_i=0} - \left[\phi_i/(1 - \Phi_i)\right]\mathbf{x}_i + \sum_{y_i=1} (\phi_i/\Phi_i)\,\mathbf{x}_i, \tag{3.29}$$

where ϕ_i denotes the standard normal density function, $\phi(\mathbf{x}_i'\boldsymbol{\beta})$, and Φ_i denotes the cumulative normal distribution function, $\Phi(\mathbf{x}_i'\boldsymbol{\beta})$. To ensure that these expressions yield maxima, the second derivative matrix (or *Hessian*) must be negative definite, meaning that the slope of the log-likelihood is decreasing near the MLEs (see Appendix B).

The matrix of second derivatives plays a key role in the estimation procedure and yields the estimated variance-covariance matrix of the estimates as a by-product. The asymptotic variance-covariance matrix of the logit and probit estimates is obtained by inverting the *negative* of the Hessian (or expected Hessian) matrix or *information matrix*. The information matrix for the logit model is given by the expression

---

[7]Different statistical packages rely on different methods to find maximum likelihood estimates of logit and probit models. Appendix B describes the iteratively reweighted least squares technique, which is used in the context of generalized linear models. Computer packages such as SAS (proc genmod) and GLIM use this approach. Other methods, such as the Newton-Raphson method and method of scoring, can be used to achieve the same results.

$$-\left[\frac{\partial^2 \log L(\beta)}{\partial\beta\beta'}\right] = \mathbf{I}(\beta) = \sum_i \Lambda_i(1 - \Lambda_i)\mathbf{x}_i\mathbf{x}_i'. \qquad (3.30)$$

For the probit model, the corresponding expression is

$$-\left[\frac{\partial^2 \log L(\beta)}{\partial\beta\beta'}\right] = \mathbf{I}(\beta) = \sum_i \frac{\phi_i^2}{\Phi_i(1 - \Phi_i)}\mathbf{x}_i\mathbf{x}_i'. \qquad (3.31)$$

In this case, iterative techniques must be used to obtain the MLEs because the functions Φ_i, ϕ_i, and Λ_i are nonlinear in the unknown parameters. After initial values from an OLS regression on the 0/1 binary variable are obtained, estimates are successively updated until the differences in estimates from one iteration to the next are negligible. At the tth iteration, estimates are obtained as

$$\widehat{\beta}^{(t)} = \widehat{\beta}^{(t-1)} + \left[\mathbf{I}(\widehat{\beta}^{(t-1)})\right]^{-1}\mathbf{U}(\widehat{\beta}^{(t-1)}).$$

The asymptotic variance-covariance matrix of the estimates is obtained from the final iteration as the inverse of the information matrix, $[\mathbf{I}(\widehat{\beta})]^{-1}$. The maximum likelihood estimates, $\widehat{\beta}$, are approximately normally distributed when the model is correct and the sample is large, with estimated variances equal to the diagonal elements of the inverse information matrix, $\text{Diag}[\mathbf{I}(\widehat{\beta})]^{-1}$. The quantity $\widehat{\beta}/\sqrt{\text{Diag}[\mathbf{I}(\widehat{\beta})]^{-1}}$ follows an asymptotic standard normal distribution (or z-distribution). This can be used to conduct significance tests on the individual parameters. Although this quantity is asymptotically a z-statistic, it is commonly called a t-ratio.

3.3.4 Goodness-of-Fit and Model Selection

Measures of Fit for Models Using Grouped Data

Consider a general regression model

$$y_i = \sum_k \beta_k x_{ik} + \varepsilon_i,$$

where ε is distributed with mean zero and variance σ_i^2. Let $\widehat{\mathbf{W}}$ denote the diagonal matrix of known weights used in the FGLS solution for the minimum χ^2 models given by

$$\mathbf{b}_{GLS} = (\mathbf{X}'\widehat{\mathbf{W}}\mathbf{X})^{-1}\mathbf{X}'\widehat{\mathbf{W}}\mathbf{y}.$$

We can define a weighted residual sum of squares from this regression model as

$$
\begin{aligned}
WSSR &= \sum_i \widehat{\sigma}_i^2 (y_i - \sum_k b_k x_{ik})^2 \\
&= (y_i - \sum_k b_k x_{ik})' \widehat{\mathbf{W}} (y_i - \sum_k b_k x_{ik}).
\end{aligned}
\tag{3.32}
$$

This statistic is asymptotically distributed as χ^2 with degrees of freedom (DF) equal to the number of observations minus the number of parameters in the model. We may compare any two nested models using this statistic. For example, let K_u denote the number of parameters in an unconstrained model ($k = 1, \ldots, K_u$), and let K_r denote the number of parameters in the constrained (or restricted) model ($k = 1, \ldots, K_r$), and $K_r < K_u$. The difference in $WSSR$ between the two models is distributed as χ^2, with DF of $K_r - K_u$.

R-Squared: Using the analogy to OLS regression, model fit in FGLS regression models may be judged using R^2. The R^2 measure, defined by Buse (1973) as a proportionate reduction in error (PRE) statistic, is

$$R^2 = \frac{WSSR_r - WSSR_u}{WSSR_r}.\tag{3.33}$$

For the logit model, where $\widehat{\mathbf{W}}$ is a matrix with diagonal elements $w_i = 1/[n_i \widetilde{p}_i (1 - \widetilde{p}_i)]$, the formula for weighted residual sum of squares may also be written as

$$WSSR = \sum_i n_i [\widetilde{p}_i (1 - \widetilde{p}_i)]^{-1} (\widetilde{p}_i - \widehat{p}_i)^2,\tag{3.34}$$

where $\widehat{p}_i = \exp(\sum_k b_k x_{ik})/[1 + \exp(\sum_k b_k x_{ik})]$.

Applying this to the FGLS grouped data logit model in Table 3.3, one obtains an R^2 value of $(1056.89 - 0.556)/1056.89 = 0.99$.[8]

Pearson X^2:   Other goodness-of-fit measures for grouped data may be constructed by considering how well the model predicts the observed data. The Pearson X^2 statistic can be constructed by considering the observed frequencies (y_i) and those expected under a given model $(n_i \widehat{p}_i)$:

$$X^2 = \sum_i \frac{(y_i - n_i \widehat{p}_i)^2}{n_i \widehat{p}_i (1 - \widehat{p}_i)}. \tag{3.35}$$

Small values of X^2 indicate agreement, or goodness-of-fit, between the observed and expected frequencies, whereas large values indicate disagreement, or lack of fit. The calculated statistic is compared to a χ^2 statistic with degrees of freedom equal to the number of cells minus the number of model parameters. For the logit model in Table 3.3, the Pearson X^2 is 20.66 with 7 DF.

The Log-Likelihood Function for Binomial Data

Other measures of fit stem from a consideration of the likelihood function, or the log of the likelihood function, $\log L$. Before discussing these goodness-of-fit measures, we will first develop the log-likelihood for binomial data. With i.i.d. observations, the likelihood on the data is the product of the individual probability density functions. Recall from Eq. 3.2 that the binomial probability function for exactly y successes—with success probability p—in n trials is written as

$$f(p) = \Pr(y \mid n, p) = \binom{n}{y} p^y (1 - p)^{n-y}. \tag{3.36}$$

Assuming independence of observations, the joint density, or likelihood, is the product of the individual densities:

$$L = \prod_i f(p_i) = \prod_i \binom{n_i}{y_i} p_i^{y_i} (1 - p_i)^{n_i - y_i}. \tag{3.37}$$

---

[8] High R^2 values are typically found with aggregated data.

Letting the individual probabilities depend on a smaller set of covariates ($\mathbf{x}_i$) and unknown parameters ($\boldsymbol{\beta}$), we can express the likelihood as

$$L = \prod_i \binom{n_i}{y_i} F(\mathbf{x}'_i\boldsymbol{\beta})^{y_i}[1 - F(\mathbf{x}'_i\boldsymbol{\beta})]^{n_i - y_i} \qquad (3.38)$$

and the log-likelihood as

$$\log L = \sum_i \left\{ \log \binom{n_i}{y_i} + y_i \log F(\mathbf{x}'_i\boldsymbol{\beta}) + (n_i - y_i) \log[1 - F(\mathbf{x}'_i\boldsymbol{\beta})] \right\},$$
$$(3.39)$$

where $F(\cdot)$ is a cumulative probability distribution function for the logistic, normal, or other suitable distribution.

The binomial coefficient $\binom{n_i}{y_i}$ appearing in Eqs. 3.38 and 3.39 is simply a constant multiplier, which does not involve unknown parameters. Therefore, in practice, we maximize the log-likelihood that is proportional to Eq. 3.39:

$$\log L = \sum_i \left\{ y_i \log F(\mathbf{x}'_i\boldsymbol{\beta}) + (n_i - y_i) \log[1 - F(\mathbf{x}'_i\boldsymbol{\beta})] \right\}.$$

This expression is maximized to yield optimal values of $\boldsymbol{\beta}$. Note that this expression is very similar to the log-likelihood function for individual data given in Section 3.3.3 (see Appendix B). Next we consider goodness-of-fit measures derived from a consideration of the log-likelihood function.

The Likelihood-Ratio Statistic

Log L cannot be used alone as an index of fit because it is not independent of the sample size. That is, smaller values of log L (i.e., bigger negative numbers) are associated with larger sample sizes. Competing models fit to the same data will result in different values of log L. When assessing model fit, we are generally concerned with how one model fits relative to another model. Three models are of particular importance in assessing fit—the null model, the saturated (or full) model, and the current model. Let L_0 denote the likelihood estimated from the null model. Recall that the null model constrains all parameters but the intercept (β_0) to zero. Let L_f denote the likelihood estimated from the full (or saturated) model. Recall that the full model contains a parameter for each cell (or observation) in the data and results in fitted values exactly equal to the observed data. L_f is the maximum attainable likelihood for the data. Let L_c denote the current model, which necessarily contains more parameters than the null model but fewer parameters than the saturated model and is therefore nested in the full model. When L_c is small relative to L_f, this is an indicator that the current model does not adequately fit the data (or poor model fit). Conversely, when the values of L_c and L_f are similar, then the current model fit is good. A commonly reported indicator of model fit is given by the likelihood-ratio statistic (or *deviance*), G^2, which measures the extent to which the current model deviates from the saturated model. The deviance is calculated as minus twice the logarithm of the ratio of likelihoods of the current to the full model, or

$$
\begin{aligned}
G^2 &= -2\log(L_c/L_f) \\
&= -2(\log L_c - \log L_f).
\end{aligned}
\tag{3.40}
$$

Letting $\widehat{y}_i = n_i\widehat{p}_i$ denote the fitted value of y_i, or expected number of successes under the model, the deviance for binomial models may be written as

$$
G^2 = 2\sum_i^n \left[y_i \log \frac{y_i}{\widehat{y}_i} + (n_i - y_i)\log\left(\frac{n_i - y_i}{n_i - \widehat{y}_i}\right) \right].
\tag{3.41}
$$

This expression shows how the deviance compares the fitted values of y_i to the observed values of y_i.

Interpreting the Deviance in Models for Grouped Data: In a linear model, the deviance is the residual sum of squares, which has a known distribution. In models for binomial data we must rely on asymptotic properties. As long as the group sizes (n_i) are reasonably large, the deviance follows an approximate χ^2 distribution. Unfortunately, there is no good rule of thumb for exactly how large the n_i

should be. A safe rule of thumb is that no more than 20% of the cells
in a given table should have frequencies less than 5. In cases where
the deviance can be used as a fit index, we can compare the deviance
to the appropriate χ^2 statistic with degrees of freedom equal to the
number of cells minus the number of parameters in the model. If the
G^2 statistic is higher than the χ^2 value associated with the upper 5%
($100 \times \alpha\%$, where $\alpha = 0.05$ by convention) of the χ^2 distribution given
the degrees of freedom, then the model does not fit the data. More
generally, fit can be judged as satisfactory if the current model's deviance is approximately equal to the degrees of freedom (i.e., $G^2 \approx DF$
or $G^2/DF \approx 1$). However, we stress that deviance as a goodness (or
badness) of fit statistic should be used only when there are an adequate
number of observations per cell.

Interpreting the Deviance for Individual-Level Data: Unlike
models for grouped data, the goodness-of-fit for models with individual-
level *binary* data (or very sparse binomial data) *cannot* be judged with
the deviance statistic. With binary data, the distribution of this statistic does not follow a χ^2 distribution, even asymptotically.[9] In the limit
(i.e., as the sample size goes to infinity), the number of parameters in
the saturated model becomes infinite as one parameter is required for
each observation. The problem is not as serious with grouped binary
data, or when individuals are exposed to more than one trial, provided
that the data are not too sparse. With grouped data, the proportions
being fit take the form $\widetilde{p}_i = y_i/n_i$. The number of parameters in the
saturated model remains the same as n_i tends to infinity. Increasing
the number of trials does not increase the number of parameters. This
condition is necessary to apply the distribution theory associated with
the G^2 statistic.

   With individual data, the likelihood for the saturated model is
equal to 1 ($L_f = 1$ and $\log L_f = 0$). Thus, the formula for the deviance
given by Eq. 3.40 is

$$G^2 = -2 \log L_c.$$

As we pointed out earlier, $\log L$ (or $-2 \log L$) should not be used as an

---

[9]See Simonoff (1998) for a more detailed discussion.

indicator of fit. However, as we shall see, the deviances from models for individual-level data can be used to select the best-fitting model from a set of competing nested models.

Differences in Deviance and Model χ^2: A better approach to assessing fit is to compare deviances from alternative models. We are generally interested in building the best model for the data. Comparing deviances from competing nested models provides a method for assessing improvements in fit due to the inclusion of new model terms. The difference in deviance follows an exact χ^2 distribution with degrees of freedom equal to the difference in the number of parameters in the competing models.

Table 3.5 presents two competing models. The first model is the original main effects model of Table 3.3; the second model adds the two-way interactions of race and family structure (i.e., Black $\times$ Nonintact and Hispanic $\times$ Nonintact) so that the less restricted model (Model 2) is

$$\begin{aligned} \text{logit}(p_i) = \beta_0 &+ \beta_1 \text{Black} + \beta_2 \text{Hispanic} + \beta_3 \text{Female} + \beta_4 \text{Nonintact} \\ &+ \beta_5 \text{Black} \times \text{Nonintact} + \beta_6 \text{Hispanic} \times \text{Nonintact}. \end{aligned}$$

Using the deviances themselves to judge goodness-of-fit, we find that both models provide an acceptable fit to the data. However, the ratio of the deviance to the DF in Model 1 is 2.87 compared to 2.18 for Model 2. Let G_1^2 denote the deviance for Model 1 and G_2^2 denote the deviance for Model 2. The difference

$$\Delta G^2 = G_1^2 - G_2^2 = 13.6$$

is distributed as χ^2 with degrees of freedom equal to the number of additional parameters in the less restricted model. In this case, the addition of the two interaction terms significantly improves the fit of the model ($p = 0.001$).

The deviance, or G^2 statistic, is a specific form of a more general measure known as the likelihood-ratio statistic. Many computer packages report the deviance (or a scaled deviance), along with the $\log L$ or $-2 \log L$ from the current model.

Table 3.5: Comparing Main Effects and Two-Way Interaction Models

	Model 1		Model 2	
Variable	Estimate	Std. Error	Estimate	Std. Error
Constant	1.754	(0.071)	1.867	(0.080)
Black	−0.322	(0.092)	−0.534	(0.118)
Hispanic	−0.564	(0.105)	−0.788	(0.128)
Female	0.575	(0.081)	0.568	(0.184)
Nonintact	−0.747	(0.083)	−1.121	(0.130)
Black × Nonintact			0.568	(0.184)
Hispanic × Nonintact			0.696	(0.222)
X^2	20.66		6.62	
G^2	20.12		6.56	
DF	7		3	
Log L	−2071.34		−2064.56	
Model χ^2	185.7		199.3	
DF χ^2	4		6	

Computer output may also include the value of $\log L_0$ or $-2\log L_0$, the corresponding values under the *null* model. In addition to these, a quantity known as the *model* χ^2 is often reported. The model χ^2 compares the fit of the current model relative to that of the null model:

$$\text{Model } \chi^2 = -2\log L_0 - (-2\log L_c). \tag{3.42}$$

The model χ^2 statistic assesses the improvement in fit over the null model provided by the additional parameters in the current model. The model χ^2 follows a χ^2 distribution with DF equal to the difference in the number of parameters in the current model and the null model (or K). Letting G_0^2 denote the deviance from the null model, the model χ^2 can be obtained as the difference $G_0^2 - G_c^2$. Fitting a null model to the data in Table 3.2, we obtain $\log L_0 = -2164.19$ and $G_0^2 = 205.82$. The model χ^2 values reported in Table 3.5 indicate that we can reject the null model over the alternative models for these data at conventional levels of significance.

Differences in model χ^2 can also be used to assess the fit of one model relative to another. In this case, we subtract the model χ^2 corresponding to the more restricted model from the model χ^2 of the less restricted model. Using the models in Table 3.5,

$$\text{model } \chi_2^2 - \text{model } \chi_1^2 = G_1^2 - G_2^2 = 13.6.$$

Pseudo-R^2 Measures: The log-likelihood can also be used to compute R^2-type measures. Given that $\log L_0 \leq \log L_c \leq \log L_f \leq 0$, the quantity

$$\frac{\log L_c - \log L_0}{\log L_f - \log L_0}$$

necessarily lies between 0 and 1. This quantity is 0 when the current model offers no improvement over the null model and equals 1 when the current model provides a perfect fit to the data.

Another R^2 measure proposed by McFadden (1974) is

$$D = \frac{\log L_0 - \log L_c}{\log L_0},$$

or, in the case of grouped binary (or binomial) data, this can be constructed using the deviance statistic, G^2:

$$D = \frac{G_0^2 - G_c^2}{G_0^2}.$$

Because there is no generally agreed upon R^2 measure for binomial data, the conventional wisdom is that these measures should be used cautiously, if at all.[10]

3.3.5   Hypothesis Testing and Statistical Inference

t-**Tests:**   For testing hypotheses about individual parameters, the *t*-test, or confidence interval approach, is probably the easiest. Maximum likelihood estimators possess a number of desirable properties

---

[10]Long (1997) provides a thorough overview of the properties of several R^2 measures for binomial data.

when certain general conditions apply. Independent and identically distributed observations, and independence of the x_i and the model errors (the ε_i) are all that is required. With these conditions satisfied, the maximum likelihood estimator is asymptotically unbiased (consistent), is normally distributed, and has the smallest variance among all consistent and asymptotically normal estimators. The inverse information matrix provides a lower bound on the attainable variance of the MLE and is a by-product of the estimation procedure. This matrix figures prominently in a number of statistical tests.

The t-ratios for the null hypothesis that $\beta_k = 0$ can be constructed in the usual way by dividing the estimate by the standard error obtained as the square root of the corresponding kth diagonal element of the inverse information matrix. This value can then be compared to entries in the standard normal table. Many computer programs output the t-ratio along with the probability of having obtained it under the assumption that the null hypothesis is true. Let t^* denote the calculated t-ratio. The p-value, $\Pr(\mid t \mid \geq \mid t^* \mid)$, gives the estimated significance level (α-level) or p-value of the test. Other statistical tests are constructed similarly.

The Wald Test: The Wald test is a more general test that may be used to test several constraints. Unlike the likelihood-ratio test, which requires estimating several nested models, the Wald test allows testing of one or more models, which are constrained versions of a single less-restricted model. Let $\widehat{\beta}_r$ denote a subvector of the estimated parameter vector $\widehat{\beta}$. Suppose that we wish to test whether the interaction effects are zero (i.e., that both β_5 and β_6 equal zero in Model 2 of Table 3.5). Then $\widehat{\beta}_r = (\widehat{\beta}_5, \widehat{\beta}_6)'$. Let $\mathbf{V}$ be the asymptotic variance-covariance matrix of $\widehat{\beta}$, and let $\mathbf{V}_r$ denote the corresponding submatrix of $\mathbf{V}$. The Wald chi-squared statistic for the hypothesis $\beta_r = \mathbf{0}$ is

$$W = \widehat{\beta}_r' \mathbf{V}_r^{-1} \widehat{\beta}_r. \tag{3.43}$$

The Wald statistic is distributed as χ^2 with degrees of freedom equal to the number of constrained parameters (r). With a single parameter, the Wald statistic is simply the square of the t-ratio. For more than a single parameter, the Wald statistic must be evaluated by extracting and manipulating the relevant matrix and vector quantities. For Model 2 in Table 3.5, the Wald statistic is 31.69 with 2 degrees of freedom. Thus, the constraint that $\beta_5 = \beta_6 = 0$ is not supported by the data.

We can generalize the Wald statistic to allow testing of other constraints. In the previous example, the null hypothesis can be written in the form

$$H_0 : \mathbf{R}\beta_r = \mathbf{q},$$

where $\mathbf{R}$ is a restriction matrix with each row corresponding to a single restriction of the coefficient vector, and $\mathbf{q}$ is a corresponding submatrix of zeros. In the previous example, we are testing two restrictions, $\beta_5 = 0$ and $\beta_6 = 0$.

Given these restrictions and our estimate vector $\widehat{\beta}_r$, we wish to test if the discrepancy vector $\mathbf{d} = \mathbf{R}\widehat{\beta}_r - \mathbf{q}$ is significantly different from zero, which, in this case, is a simultaneous test of both parameters. In the case of tests of one or more parameters equaling zero, the Wald statistic takes the form of Eq. 3.43. In general, however, we can test various *linear* constraints using a slightly modified statistic:

$$W = \mathbf{d}'\mathbf{V}_d^{-1}\mathbf{d}, \qquad (3.44)$$

where $\mathbf{V}_d = \mathbf{R}\mathbf{V}_r\mathbf{R}'$.

For example, the discrepancy vector for the test of these restrictions is

$$\mathbf{d} = \mathbf{R}\widehat{\beta}_r - \mathbf{q} = \begin{pmatrix} 1 & 0 \\ 0 & 1 \end{pmatrix} \begin{pmatrix} 0.568 \\ 0.696 \end{pmatrix} - \begin{pmatrix} 0 \\ 0 \end{pmatrix} = \begin{pmatrix} 0.568 \\ 0.696 \end{pmatrix},$$

with variance $\mathbf{R}'\mathbf{V}_r^{-1}\mathbf{R} = \mathbf{V}_d^{-1}$, as in Eq. 3.43.

Suppose we wish to test whether $\beta_5 = \beta_6$. This corresponds to a single interaction term, say, Nonwhite $\times$ Nonintact, and involves a single restriction, equivalent to the hypothesis that $\beta_5 - \beta_6 = 0$. This restriction can be expressed in terms of discrepancy vector

$$\mathbf{d} = \mathbf{R}\widehat{\beta}_r - \mathbf{q} = \begin{pmatrix} 1 & -1 \end{pmatrix} \begin{pmatrix} 0.568 \\ 0.696 \end{pmatrix} - (0) = (-0.1281).$$

This statistic can be viewed as analogous to a t-test on the difference $\beta_5 - \beta_6 = 0$, but taking the covariance of the estimates into account. In this case, using the usual formula for the variance of a difference, $\mathbf{V}_d = \text{var}(\widehat{\beta}_5) + \text{var}(\widehat{\beta}_6) - 2\text{cov}(\widehat{\beta}_5, \widehat{\beta}_6) = 0.0494$, so the Wald statistic is $W = -0.128^2/0.0494 = 0.332$, with 1 degree of freedom, which provides support for the hypothesis that $\beta_5 = \beta_6$.

Going one step farther, we test if the race effects can be collapsed into a single "Nonwhite" effect, implying that $\beta_2 = \beta_3$ in addition to $\beta_5 = \beta_6$. When these two constraints are tested, the Wald statistic is 3.898, with 2 degrees of freedom, providing support for the joint restrictions.

The Likelihood-Ratio Test: The most commonly used method for testing multiple constraints is the likelihood-ratio test described in Section 3.3.4. This test consists of a comparison of the log-likelihood of one model with that of a more constrained version. Using the results from Table 3.5, the more restricted model is Model 1 with a log-likelihood of -2071.34. The less restricted model (Model 2) has a log-likelihood of -2064.56. Let M_1 stand for the more restricted model and M_2 denote the less restricted model, where M_1 is nested in M_2. Letting L_1 represent the likelihood from M_1 and L_2 represent the likelihood for M_2, the likelihood-ratio chi-squared statistic is

$$-2(\log L_1 - \log L_2).$$

This statistic is distributed as χ^2 with degrees of freedom equal to $K_2 - K_1$ ($K_1 < K_2$), where K_1 and K_2 denote the number of parameters in M_1 and M_2, respectively. Using the results in Table 3.5, the likelihood-ratio statistic is 13.6 with 2 degrees of freedom. This provides further evidence against the hypothesis that $\beta_5 = \beta_6 = 0$. Note that the Wald and likelihood-ratio statistics are asymptotically equivalent but are not necessarily the same. This implies that substantive conclusions might differ depending on the test.

3.4   Interpreting Estimates

There are at least three alternatives for interpreting estimates from logit and probit models. The first interpretation comes from the latent variable framework of econometrics. Earlier, we noted that the index function, $\mathbf{x}_i'\boldsymbol{\beta}$, may be interpreted as the conditional mean of the latent variable y_i^*. Under this interpretation, the parameter estimates reflect the *marginal* effect of x_{ik} on y_i^*. This interpretation may be discomforting since a sample analog to the latent variable does not exist. However, if the focus is on describing the latent preferences or utilities, then this interpretation is adequate. If we wish to extend the discussion to probabilities, then it is preferable to interpret results using the odds-ratio or relative risk approaches when appropriate or to report the marginal effect of x_{ik} on the success probability $\Pr(y_i = 1)$.

3.4.1   The Odds-Ratio

In Section 3.2.2, we defined the odds-ratio for the grouped data logit model. This concept is easily extended to the case of the individual-level data logit model. Suppose we have a simple model for inclination (or propensity) to vote in a hypothetical community. Let y_i^* denote the latent continuous variable representing the propensity to vote and assume that this is a linear function of income and sex. At the sample level, we do not observe the propensity to vote per se, but we observe voting behavior. Let $y_i = 1$ if a respondent has voted and zero otherwise. Inclination to vote is assumed to be a function of a continuous independent variable x measuring income in thousands of dollars and a dummy variable d equal to 1 if the respondent is female and 0 if the respondent is male. The logit model can be written as

$$y_i^* = \beta_0 + \beta_1 x_i + \beta_2 d_i + \varepsilon_i.$$

Suppose that this model yields the following ML estimates (and standard errors):

$$\text{logit}[\Pr(y_i = 1)] \quad = \quad \begin{array}{ccc} -1.92 & + \quad 0.012x_i & + \quad 0.67d_i. \\ (0.26) & (0.005) & (0.21) \end{array}$$

For the dummy variable representing sex, the odds-ratio interpretation is straightforward. The odds-ratio is constructed as

$$\theta = \frac{\omega_1}{\omega_2} = \frac{\Pr(y_i = 1 \mid d_i = 1)/\Pr(y_i = 0 \mid d_i = 1)}{\Pr(y_i = 1 \mid d_i = 0)/\Pr(y_i = 0 \mid d_i = 0)}$$

$$= \exp(\widehat{\beta}_2) = \exp(0.67) = 1.95.$$

This result implies that, for this electorate, the odds of voting are nearly twice as high among females, holding income constant.

The odds-ratio has a less straightforward interpretation for continuous variables. In the case of continuous variables, we have no natural baseline group from which to construct the ratios. However, we can evaluate the odds at different values of the independent variable, or we can express the effect of the independent variable on the *odds*. In this sense, the interpretation involves the notion of a *multiplicative* effect rather than an odds-ratio per se. Suppose, for example, that we want to learn how the odds of voting varies by income level. We can construct an odds of voting for an individual with value $x + 1$, relative to an individual with value x as

$$\frac{\exp\{\widehat{\beta}_1(x + 1)\}}{\exp(\widehat{\beta}_1 x)} = \exp\{\widehat{\beta}_1(1)\} = 1.01.$$

In all of these examples, it is possible to state results in terms of the percentage change in the odds. In the preceding example, a unit change in income (a change of \$1,000 in this case) increases the odds of voting by 1%. Suppose we wanted to know how increasing income by c units would affect voting. Using the general format given earlier, we write

$$\frac{\exp\{\widehat{\beta}_1(x + c)\}}{\exp(\widehat{\beta}_1 x)} = \exp\{\widehat{\beta}_1(c)\}.$$

For example, if income increases by \$10,000, this increases the odds of voting by approximately 13%, or $\left\{\exp[\widehat{\beta}_1(10)] - 1\right\} \times 100\%$.

3.4.2   Marginal Effects

There is no natural analog for the odds-ratio in a probit model. For this reason, the marginal effects on the success probabilities are often reported.[11] A marginal effect expresses the rate change in one quantity relative to another. More specifically, the marginal effect is the change in the dependent variable per unit change in the independent variable. For the logit and probit models, a unit change in x_i produces a β change in y_i^*, since the models are linear in the parameters. Similarly, one could conceive of β as the marginal effect of x_i on the logit or probit. For example, in the model

$$y_i^* = \beta_0 + \beta_1 x_i + \beta_2 d_i + \varepsilon_i,$$

the change in y_i^* per unit change in x is given by the partial derivative

$$\frac{\partial y_i^*}{\partial x_i} = \beta_1.$$

This conceptualization will work as long as x_i is a continuous variable. With a discrete independent variable, such as the variable for sex in the previous example, the marginal effect is derived as the difference

$$E(y_i^* \mid d_i = 1) - E(y_i^* \mid d_i = 0) = \beta_2,$$

which is operationally identical to the foregoing expression, and where $E(y_i^*)$ is the expected value of y_i^*.

Marginal effects can also be constructed for the probabilities themselves. This is the most common usage in the literature. The marginal effect of the kth independent variable is given by

$$\frac{\partial \Pr(y_i = 1 \mid \mathbf{x}_i)}{\partial x_{ik}} = \frac{\partial F(\mathbf{x}_i'\boldsymbol{\beta})}{\partial x_{ik}} = f(\mathbf{x}_i'\boldsymbol{\beta})\beta_k,$$

where $F(\cdot)$ denotes the cumulative distribution function and $f(\cdot)$ denotes the density function. This quantity expresses the rate of change in the success probability in the neighborhood of a particular value of x. Figure 3.2 shows that the marginal effects are the slopes of tangent lines to the cumulative probability curve corresponding to each distinct value of x. Thus, we find that, unlike OLS regression, the "effect" of x on $\Pr(y = 1)$ varies with x. We can also see from Figure 3.2 that the maximum marginal effect for logit and probit models occurs when $\Pr(y = 1) = 0.5$.

---

[11]See Petersen (1985) for a review on the interpretation of marginal effects from binary logit and probit models.

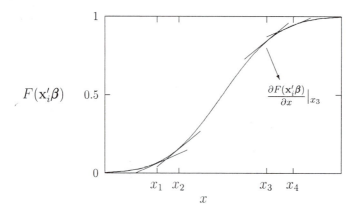

Figure 3.2: Marginal Effects as Slopes of Tangent Lines to the Cumulative Probability Curve

For the probit model, the marginal effect of x_{ik} is given by

$$\frac{\partial F(\mathbf{x}_i'\boldsymbol{\beta})}{\partial x_{ik}} = \phi_i\beta_k,$$

where $\phi_i = \phi(\mathbf{x}_i'\boldsymbol{\beta})$. For the logit model, the marginal effect is

$$\frac{\partial F(\mathbf{x}_i'\boldsymbol{\beta})}{\partial x_{ik}} = \Lambda_i(1 - \Lambda_i)\beta_k,$$

where $\Lambda_i = \Lambda(\mathbf{x}_i'\boldsymbol{\beta})$.

Because they vary with x, it is often instructive to compute the marginal effects associated with different values of x. In practice, the means of the independent variables and the parameter estimates are used in the expressions for ϕ_i and Λ_i to obtain "average" marginal effects, substituting $\bar{\mathbf{x}}'\widehat{\boldsymbol{\beta}}$ for $\mathbf{x}_i'\boldsymbol{\beta}$ in the preceding expression. In this way, there is an average marginal effect associated with each independent variable, as opposed to each possible value of x.

Table 3.6 presents the marginal effects for independent variables affecting inclination to vote. Both models yield very similar marginal effects. We find that when evaluated at the means of the independent

Table 3.6: Voting Inclination by Income and Sex

Variable	Logit Model		Probit Model	
	Estimate (Std. Error)	Marginal Effect	Estimate (Std. Error)	Marginal Effect
Constant	−1.918		−1.158	
	(0.262)		(0.150)	
Income (x)	0.012	0.0028	0.007	0.0027
	(0.005)		(0.003)	
Sex (d)	0.670	0.1219	0.394	0.1237
	(0.213)		(0.124)	

variables, the probability of voting is changed by 0.003 per $1,000 increase of income near the mean of income ($35,000). For the categorical variables like sex, marginal effects are calculated as differences in predicted probabilities. For the logit model, we estimate this marginal effect as

$$\Lambda(\widehat{\beta}_0 + \widehat{\beta}_1 \bar{x} + \widehat{\beta}_2) - \Lambda(\widehat{\beta}_0 + \widehat{\beta}_1 \bar{x}).$$

For the probit model, the marginal effect of sex is estimated as

$$\Phi(\widehat{\beta}_0 + \widehat{\beta}_1 \bar{x} + \widehat{\beta}_2) - \Phi(\widehat{\beta}_0 + \widehat{\beta}_1 \bar{x}).$$

Figure 3.3 shows how the marginal effect of a dummy variable can be interpreted as the difference in the cumulative probability functions at a given point on the x-axis. Again, we see that these effects are not constant for all values of x, and that the maximum difference occurs when $\Pr(y = 1) = 0.5$. In this example, being female increases the probability of voting by about 0.12 at the sample mean for family income.

It should be mentioned that odds-ratios and marginal effects are estimates of the "true" population quantities. As estimates, they possess sampling distributions, making it possible to construct confidence intervals around the true parameters. Statistical procedures grounded

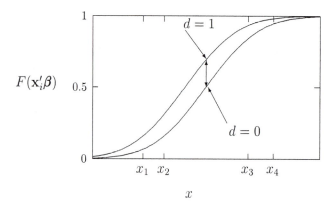

Figure 3.3: Marginal Effect of a Dummy Variable

in asymptotic theory can be used to determine the large-sample variances of the estimated quantities as *functions* of other estimates. Because these functions are nonlinear, the expressions are not in general straightforward. A technique known as the *delta method* is useful for calculating the variance of nonlinear functions. It states that given a function of a θ, $g(\theta)$, the asymptotic (or large-sample) variance of $g(\theta)$ is given by

$$\text{var}[g(\theta)] = \text{var}(\theta)\left(\frac{\partial g(\theta)}{\partial \theta}\right)^2.$$

This technique can be used to find confidence intervals for marginal effects. Greene (1991) offers a concise derivation of the asymptotic variance of the marginal effects for logit and probit models.

3.4.3   An Application Using Individual-Level Data

Table 3.7 provides maximum likelihood estimates from probit and logit models using individual-level data. The data are from a sample of 1,643 young men age 20−24 from the National Longitudinal Survey of Youth. The dependent variable is whether a youth had graduated from high school by 1985. We control for several independent variables, such as parents' education, race, family income, number of siblings, nonintact family structure, and measured ability. Both models yield essentially the same substantive conclusions. This is usually the case, except when many predicted values are very near 0 or 1.

Table 3.7: Logit and Probit Estimates from Individual-Level Data

Variable	Logit Model		Probit Model	
	Estimate	(Std. Error)	Estimate	(Std. Error)
CONSTANT	1.651	(0.274)	0.947	(0.151)
NONWHT	0.801	(0.171)	0.468	(0.097)
NONINT	−0.719	(0.160)	−0.400	(0.091)
MHS	0.349	(0.176)	0.193	(0.089)
FHS	0.309	(0.178)	0.186	(0.090)
INC/10000	0.531	(0.224)	0.293	(0.122)
ASVAB	1.488	(0.113)	0.836	(0.061)
NSIBS	−0.036	(0.029)	−0.023	(0.170)
$\log L_c$	−561.05		−558.84	
$\log L_0$	−765.73		−765.73	
Model χ^2	409.35		413.77	
DF	7		7	

Note: NONWHT = 1 if respondent is Black or Hispanic, and 0 otherwise; NONINT = 1 if respondent did not live with both biological parents at age 14, 0 otherwise; MHS = 1 if respondent's mother was a high school graduate, 0 otherwise; FHS = 1 if respondent's father was a high school graduate, 0 otherwise; INC/10000 is total family income in 1979 in ten-thousands of dollars (adjusted by family size); ASVAB is the standardized score on the Armed Services Vocational Aptitude Battery Test administered to each respondent in 1980; and NSIBS is the number of siblings.

The logits can be used to construct odds-ratios. For example, we find that, controlling for individual-level covariates, the estimated odds of graduating from high school for a young man from a nonintact family are $\exp(-0.719) = 0.487$ times that of a young man from an intact family. Stated somewhat differently, the odds of graduating for a youth residing in an intact family are $1/\exp(-0.719) = 2.05$ times that of a youth living in a nonintact family. Net of family-level and individual-level covariates, the estimated odds of graduation for nonwhites are over twice those of whites.

For continuous measures such as family income and ASVAB test scores, the odds-ratio is not entirely appropriate. Instead, we can use the term *multiplicative effect* to express the effect of changes in income or test score on the odds of graduating. For example, a $10,000 increase in family income raises the odds of graduating by $\exp(0.531) = 1.7$ or, in percentage terms, $100 \times \{\exp(0.531) - 1\}\% = 70\%$. Similarly, a 1 standard deviation increase in the standardized ASVAB test score increases the odds of graduation by 4.428, or over 340%. We obtain a similar substantive conclusion by examining the marginal effect of ASVAB score on the predicted probability. For the probit model, the change in the probability of graduation for a 1 standard deviation increase in ASVAB score is 0.146, when evaluated at the mean ASVAB score of -0.034.

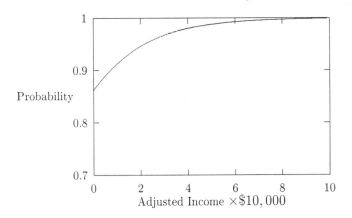

Figure 3.4: Graduation Probability by Family Income

Predicted Probabilities: As an alternative to computing marginal effects, another way to assess the effect of a continuous variable is to plot the predicted probability for a range of values of the continuous variable. For example, if we want to see how the probability of graduation changes by income level, we can fix all the covariates except income at their means (or some other specified values) and calculate predicted probabilities for different values of income. Using the probit estimates in Table 3.7, Fig. 3.4 depicts the relationship between the probability of graduation and family income.

3.5   Alternative Probability Models

There are a number of distributions other than the logistic and normal that could be used to model binary outcomes. One model that is commonplace in the literature is the complementary log-log model. Like the logit and probit model, the complementary log-log transformation ensures that predicted probabilities lie in the interval $[0,1]$. Unlike the normal and logistic, the distribution function is not symmetric around zero, but is skewed to the right. Figure 3.5 shows that the complementary log-log transformation [the inverse of the cumulative distribution function, $F^{-1}(p)$] is not symmetric around $p = 0.5$.

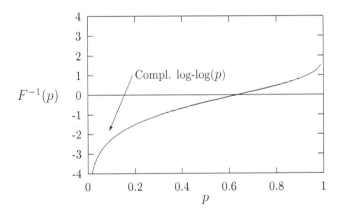

Figure 3.5: Complementary Log-Log Transformation of p

3.5.1   The Complementary Log-Log Model

The complementary log-log model is derived from the assumption that the error distribution (or distribution of the latent variable) follows a standard extreme value distribution. For the random variable U, the probability density function for the standardized extreme value distribution has the form

$$f(u) = \exp(u)\exp\{-\exp(u)\},$$

where $\mathrm{E}(U) = 0.5704$ and $\mathrm{var}(U) = \pi^2/6$. The cumulative distribution function has a convenient closed form

$$F(u) = 1 - \exp\{-\exp(u)\}.$$

The probability of success can be expressed as a function of unknown regression parameters

$$p_i = 1 - \exp\{-\exp(\sum_k \beta_k x_{ik})\}.$$

The model is linear in the inverse of the cumulative distribution function, which is the log of the negative log of the complement of p_i, or $\log\{-\log(1 - p_i)\}$, where

$$\log\{-\log(1 - p_i)\} = \sum_k \beta_k x_{ik}.$$

For small values of p_i, this function is approximately equal to $\log p_i$. This implies that $\log(1 - p_i) \approx \log p_i$, and $\log\{p_i/(1-p_i)\} \approx \log p_i + p_i$.

Aside from its use as an alternative probability model, this model has been used extensively to model grouped survival data, which is a topic that will be described in more detail in Chapter 5.

For individual-level data, we may again use the random utility function or latent variable framework

$$y_i^* = \mathbf{x}_i'\beta + \varepsilon_i,$$

where ε_i is assumed to have a standard extreme value distribution. The parameters have a similar interpretation to those from the logistic regression model. The term $\exp(\beta_k)$ represents a hazard ratio, relative risk, or multiplicative effect. Using the complementary log-log link, we find that the estimates based on the voting inclination data are very similar to those from the logit model presented in Table 3.6:

$$\log\{-\log(1 - p_i)\} \quad = \quad \underset{(0.230)}{-1.953} \quad + \quad \underset{(0.004)}{0.010 x_i} \quad + \quad \underset{(0.186)}{0.573 d_i}.$$

3.5.2   Programming Binomial Response Models

Binomial response models can be estimated using a number of widely available computer packages. The website for this book provides several programming examples using popular packages (GLIM, LIMDEP, SAS, and STATA), as well as a more in-depth look at the computational aspects of these models using the GAUSS matrix programming language and the programming features of LIMDEP.[12] The SAS package has procedures to estimate binomial models via generalized linear models (proc genmod) and more general versions via maximum likelihood (proc logistic). The LIMDEP program estimates a general multinomial response (multicategory) logit model for which the binary response model is a simple case. The probit model can also be estimated via maximum likelihood in LIMDEP. GLIM, LIMDEP, STATA, and SAS allow for grouped data models.

3.6   Summary

This chapter provides an overview of the most common techniques for modeling binary data. We first considered the transformational approach, and showed that when data are in the form of contingency tables (or fixed grids), FGLS estimation techniques can be used on the transformed empirical probabilities. With grouped or ungrouped data, the iteratively reweighted least squares (IRLS) technique can be used to obtain ML estimates from logit, probit, and complementary log-log models as generalized linear models. The IRLS technique thus provides a natural extension of the FGLS technique to individual-level data. Logit and probit models can be justified by invoking the concept of utility maximization. The latent variable formulation is a natural extension of this viewpoint.

---

[12]We are continuously updating our website to include examples of other software such as TDA.

Chapter 4

Loglinear Models for Contingency Tables

4.1 Contingency Tables

Contingency tables are joint frequency distributions of two or more categorical variables. More formally, a contingency table can be thought of as a cross-classification of possible values (or categories) of two or more variables, together with the number of observations in each cross-classified cell reported. When two variables are involved, the resulting contingency table is called a two-way table. When three variables are involved, it is called a three-way table. A three-way or higher-way table is also referred to simply as a multiway table.

Contingency tables, or "crosstabs," are among the oldest and the most widely used statistical tools available to social scientists. One major reason for their popularity is simplicity. Another reason is that contingency tables are nonparametric or require very weak parametric (or distributional) assumptions. More often than not, the researcher directly interprets the descriptive statistics revealed by a contingency table and reaches substantive conclusions without resort to explicit modeling. This eye-balling method, however, is very imprecise when the researcher explores complicated relationships or analyzes multiway tables. In this chapter, we will learn how to model contingency tables according to theoretically derived hypotheses and, in so doing, smooth out apparent irregularities due to sampling variability.

4.1.1 Types of Contingency Tables

Goodman (1981a) lists three ideal types of two-way contingency tables. They are:

1. The joint distribution of two explanatory variables (e.g., height and weight).

2. The causal relationship of an outcome variable depending on an explanatory variable (e.g., smoking and lung cancer).

3. The association between two outcome variables (e.g., attitude toward abortion and attitude toward premarital sex).

Note that the distinction among the three types of contingency tables is conceptual, for they appear in the same form. In fact, statistical models for contingency tables discussed in this chapter are estimated with frequencies rather than with the outcome variable as the expressed dependent variable in a generalized linear model. As in the case of correlations, cross-tabulations are inherently symmetric. For a simple regression involving only one independent variable, the slope coefficient can be recovered from the symmetric correlation coefficient between the dependent variable and the independent variable plus the scale parameters for the two variables. Likewise, statistical models for the analysis of contingency tables are also symmetric from the standpoint of estimation, although conceptual distinctions can be drawn between an outcome variable and an explanatory variable.

4.1.2 An Example and Notation

To go beyond the simplistic method of eye-balling, one needs to model contingency tables. Loglinear models are designed for this purpose. For the three types of contingency tables discussed earlier, the same statistical models are applicable. They are called loglinear models and are formally defined later in this chapter. For now, let us illustrate the setup and the notation with a concrete example.

Table 4.1 shows a cross-tabulation between level of education and attitude toward premarital sex.[1] The data are drawn from the 1987–1991 pooled General Social Surveys (GSS). For our illustration, let us assume the table to be of type II, with education being the explanatory variable and attitude toward premarital sex the outcome variable.

Table 4.1: Education and Attitude Toward Premarital Sex

	Attitude toward Premarital Sex		
Education	Disapproval	Approval	Total
High school or Less	873	1190	2063
College and above	533	1208	1741
Total	1406	2398	3804

In general, we denote a two-way contingency table as consisting of two variables: a row variable (R) and a column variable (C). Let R vary by a row index i, where $i = 1, \dots, I$, and let C vary by a column index j, where $j = 1, \dots, J$. When one of the two variables is an outcome variable and the other is an explanatory variable (i.e., type II), it is customary to let R denote the explanatory variable and C the outcome variable. We denote the cell frequency of the ith row and the jth column by f_{ij} and the expected frequency under a model by F_{ij}. The distinction between the observed frequency (f) and the expected frequency (F) disappears in the special case of a saturated model, in which $f = F$ for all the cells in the table. In this example, the observed frequencies and expected frequencies (in parentheses) are denoted by the notation in Table 4.2.

Note that we use the symbol $+$ to denote summation. Subscript $_{i+}$ stands for the row marginal total:

$$ f_{i+} = \sum_{j=1}^{J} f_{ij} \quad \text{and} \quad F_{i+} = \sum_{j=1}^{J} F_{ij}. $$

---

[1]The orginal GSS question was: "If a man and woman have sexual relations before marriage, do you think it is always wrong, almost always wrong, wrong only sometimes, or not wrong at all?" We collapsed the first two responses into "disapproval" and the last two responses into "approval."

Table 4.2: Observed (Expected) Frequencies

Education	Attitude Toward Premarital Sex		Total
	Disapproval	Approval	
High school or less	$f_{11}\ (F_{11})$	$f_{12}\ (F_{12})$	$f_{1+}\ (F_{1+})$
College and above	$f_{21}\ (F_{21})$	$f_{22}\ (F_{22})$	$f_{2+}\ (F_{2+})$
Total	$f_{+1}\ (F_{+1})$	$f_{+2}\ (F_{+2})$	$f_{++}\ (F_{++})$

Similarly, subscript $_{+j}$ stands for the column marginal total:

$$f_{+j} = \sum_{i=1}^{I} f_{ij} \quad \text{and} \quad F_{+j} = \sum_{i=1}^{I} F_{ij},$$

and subscript $_{++}$ represents the grand total:

$$f_{++} = \sum_{j=1}^{J} \sum_{i=1}^{I} f_{ij} \quad \text{and} \quad F_{++} = \sum_{j=1}^{J} \sum_{i=1}^{I} F_{ij}.$$

Obviously, $f_{++} = n$, the sample size. In practice, almost all models have the property $F_{++} = f_{++}$. As will be shown later in this chapter, most applications in social science actually maintain equality in marginal totals between the expected and observed frequencies.

4.1.3   Independence and the Pearson χ^2 Statistic

As with any observed data from a sample, we should treat frequencies in a contingency table as realizations of an underlying process. Because of sampling variation, observed frequencies may appear much less regular than an underlying pattern. One possible, and often interesting, pattern is the independence of the row and column variables. That is, we sometimes want to know whether or not observed frequencies fit the null hypothesis of independence (i.e., deviating from independence only within sampling error). For our GSS example, the independence hypothesis means that education is unrelated to attitude toward premarital sex.

To test the independence hypothesis, it is useful to think of it as a special statistical model. In general, let F_{ij} denote the expected value of f_{ij} under some model. Let the expected probability associated with the cell (i, j) be denoted by π_{ij}. By definition,

$$F_{ij} = n\pi_{ij}. \tag{4.1}$$

Likewise, we define π_{i+} and π_{+j} as the expected marginal probabilities of the row and column variables. For our example, the notation of expected probabilities is given in Table 4.3.

Table 4.3: Expected Probabilities

| Education | Attitude Toward Premarital Sex | | |
	Disapproval	Approval	Total
High school or less	π_{11}	π_{12}	π_{1+}
College and above	π_{21}	π_{22}	π_{2+}
Total	π_{+1}	π_{+2}	$\pi_{++} = 1$

The independence model means that the joint probability π_{ij} is the product of two associated marginal probabilities:

$$\pi_{ij} = \pi_{i+}\pi_{+j}. \tag{4.2}$$

Let the marginal probabilities be fitted as observed:

$$\pi_{i+} = f_{i+}/f_{++}, \tag{4.3}$$
$$\pi_{+j} = f_{+j}/f_{++}.$$

Combining Eqs. 4.1, 4.2, and 4.3, we have

$$F_{ij} = f_{i+}f_{+j}/f_{++}, \tag{4.4}$$

meaning that the expected frequency of any cell is determined by the sizes of its associated marginal totals. That is, the independence hypothesis allows for dissimilarity in the marginal distributions of the row and column variables. This makes intuitive sense. For our example in Table 4.1, we expect the cell (2,1) to be small in the absence of any relationship between education and attitude because, for our GSS sample, less than half (46%) of the respondents had attained college education, and less than half (37%) disapproved of premarital sex. Numerically, we can easily solve for the predicted frequencies under the independence model, as shown in Table 4.4.

Table 4.4: Expected Frequencies Under Independence

	Attitude Toward Premarital Sex		
Education	Disapproval	Approval	Total
High school or less	762.51	1300.49	2063
College and above	643.49	1097.51	1741
Total	1406	2398	3804

A widely used test statistic for testing the independence model is the Pearson χ^2 statistic. It is computed as

$$X^2 = \sum_{i=1}^{I} \sum_{j=1}^{J} (F_{ij} - f_{ij})^2 / F_{ij}, \qquad (4.5)$$

with degrees of freedom equal to $(I - 1)(J - 1)$. Since the difference between fitted and observed frequencies, $F_{ij} - f_{ij}$, is called the residual, χ^2 statistics such as Eq. 4.5 measuring the *lack* of fit are also said to be residual-based χ^2 statistics. More will be said about degrees of freedom later in this chapter. For our example, the Pearson χ^2 statistic is 55.50 for 1 degree of freedom, which is significant beyond the 0.001 α-level, meaning that the chance of observing the actual association between education and attitude toward premarital sex in Table 4.1 is very small if the two variables are independent of each other in the population. The contribution of specific cells to χ^2 (as in Eq. 4.5) is given in Table 4.5.

Note that Eq. 4.5 is a generic formula for calculating the residual-based Pearson χ^2 statistic, although it is commonly associated with the independence model with the expected frequencies defined by Eq. 4.4. Statistical programs that compute cross-tabulations routinely report this statistic under the independence hypothesis.

Table 4.5: Contribution to Pearson χ^2

| | Attitude Toward Premarital Sex | | |
Education	Disapproval	Approval	Total
High school or less	16.01	9.39	25.40
College and above	18.97	11.12	30.10
Total	34.98	20.51	55.50

4.2   Measures of Association

4.2.1   Homogeneous Proportions

An alternative way to express the independence model is to examine conditional proportions. This is particularly appropriate when one of the two categorical variables in a two-way cross-tabulation is an outcome variable, as in our attitude example. Table 4.6 presents the row-specific proportions for the expected frequencies under independence (i.e., Table 4.4).

Table 4.6: Row-Specific Proportions Under Independence

| | Attitude toward Premarital Sex | | |
Education	Disapproval	Approval	Total
High School or Less	0.370	0.630	1.000
College and Above	0.370	0.630	1.000
Total	0.370	0.630	1.000

We see that the proportion is the same in each row. This should not surprise us because the expected frequencies were derived under the independence model, which implies the homogeneity of proportions. Let the conditional proportion be denoted by $\pi_{j|i}$. It is easy to show that under independence

$$\pi_{j|i} = \frac{F_{ij}}{f_{i+}} = \frac{f_{i+}f_{+j}}{f_{i+}f_{++}} = \frac{f_{+j}}{f_{++}} = \pi_{+j}. \tag{4.6}$$

Clearly, the independence model constrains all row-specific proportions to be equal to the marginal proportion and thus to each other. By symmetry, the same property holds true for column-specific proportions. Conversely, if the proportions are not homogeneous across rows or columns, there is dependence between the row and column variables. From an earlier test with the Pearson χ^2 statistic, we infer that the proportions are not homogeneous for our data set. To show this, Table 4.7 presents the row-specific proportions in the observed data.

Table 4.7: Row-Specific Proportions for Observed Data

| | Attitude toward Premarital Sex | | |
Education	Disapproval	Approval	Total
High school or less	0.423	0.577	1.000
College and above	0.306	0.694	1.000
Total	0.370	0.630	1.000

This table reveals that respondents with higher education are more likely to approve of premarital sex than are those with a high school education or less. The Pearson χ^2 statistic reported earlier shows that this relationship is unlikely to be due to chance alone.

4.2.2 Relative Risks

For a dichotomous outcome variable, only one proportion is sufficient for summarizing the information. The other is its complement and thus redundant. In general, for an outcome variable with J categories, only $J - 1$ proportions are nonredundant. For our attitude example, we only need to know either the proportion of disapproval or the proportion of approval. After focusing on either of the outcome categories, it is often useful to have a summary measure of the difference by the explanatory variable. When there are only two categories for the explanatory variable, such as in our attitude example, only one summary measure is needed. One convenient measure is to take the ratio of conditional proportions, treating the first category for both row and column as the reference:

$$\frac{\pi_{2|2}}{\pi_{2|1}}. \tag{4.7}$$

Formula 4.7 is called the relative risk, as defined in Chapter 3. Note that the relative risk for the first outcome category is a different but constrained number: $\pi_{1|2}/\pi_{1|1} = (1 - \pi_{2|2})/(1 - \pi_{2|1})$. In general, there are $(I-1)$ nonredundant comparisons for an explanatory variable with I categories. For our attitude example, the relative risk of approval between the respondents with higher education and those without higher education is $0.694/0.577 = 1.203$.

4.2.3   Odds-Ratios

Odds-ratios are the basic building blocks of loglinear models, since many loglinear models can be characterized in terms of odds-ratios. Before we define odds-ratios, let us first review odds. As discussed earlier in connection with the logit model, the odds are the ratio of the probability of an event occurring to the probability of the event not occurring. For the first and second rows of a 2×2 table, with $j = 2$ as the positive outcome, the odds are

$$\omega_1 = \pi_{12}/\pi_{11},$$
$$\omega_2 = \pi_{22}/\pi_{21}.$$

A monotonic transformation of a probability, odds measure the likelihood that an event occurs. A higher value means that the likelihood of outcome 2 in reference to outcome 1 is higher. To measure the *relative* likelihood, we can take the ratio in odds between two categories of another (often explanatory) categorical variable, called the odds-ratio. Formally, the odds-ratio for a 2×2 table is

$$\theta = \frac{\omega_2}{\omega_1} = \frac{\pi_{22}/\pi_{21}}{\pi_{12}/\pi_{11}} = \frac{\pi_{22}\pi_{11}}{\pi_{12}\pi_{21}} = \frac{F_{11}F_{22}}{F_{12}F_{21}}. \tag{4.8}$$

Although formula 4.8 refers to expected frequencies (F's), observed frequencies (f's) are also often used in practice. When observed frequencies are used, the resulting odds-ratios are called observed odds-ratios. Note that odds-ratios are always positive, varying in the range

$(0, \infty)$. Like all relative measures, the interpretation of odds-ratios depends on the choice of reference categories. As defined by Eq. 4.8, an odds-ratio higher than 1 means that the second categories of the row and column variables, or conversely, the first categories of the row and column variables, are positively associated. An odds-ratio of 1 indicates a null relationship between the two variables, corresponding to statistical independence. It is often convenient to take the natural logarithm of an odds-ratio to convert it to a log-odds-ratio (LOR). Log-odds-ratios vary in the range $(-\infty, \infty)$, with 0 corresponding to independence. For our attitude example, the odds-ratio is 1.663, and the LOR $= 0.508$.

For a 2×2 table, there is only one meaningful odds-ratio. Rearranging reference categories yields either the same odds-ratio or its reciprocal. Due to formula 4.8, odds-ratios are also called cross-product ratios, with the product across the main diagonal as the numerator. For a general two-way table of dimension $I \times J$, there are $(I-1)(J-1)$ nonredundant odds-ratios, from which other odds-ratios can be derived. For convenience, we define as the basic nonredundant odds-ratios those from the $(I-1) \times (J-1)$ 2×2 subtables with adjacent rows and columns. Let θ_{ij} denote these "local odds-ratios," defined as

$$\theta_{ij} = \frac{F_{ij} F_{(i+1)(j+1)}}{F_{i(j+1)} F_{(i+1)j}}, \qquad i = 1, \ldots, I-1; \; j = 1, \ldots, J-1. \quad (4.9)$$

To see how these fundamental local odds-ratios constrain other odds-ratios, first recognize that for an $I \times J$ table, there are many possible odds-ratios, since each odds-ratio involves the combination of two categories of the row variable and two categories of the column variable. For illustration, we use a fuller table for our attitude example (Table 4.8), which is based on four categories of education and four Likert-scale categories of attitude toward premarital sex.

For this 4×4 table, we can easily calculate the nine local odds-ratios, each involving a 2×2 subtable with adjacent rows and columns. They are reported in Table 4.9.

Any other odds-ratio can be derived from the local odds-ratios. For example, say that we wish to know the odds-ratio involving rows 2 and 3 and columns 2 and 4. Using the notation of Eq. 4.9, we see that (by

Table 4.8: Full Table for the Attitude Example

	Premarital Sex is			
	Always Wrong (1)	Almost Always Wrong (2)	Sometimes Wrong (3)	Not Wrong At All (4)
Education				
Less than H.S. (1)	332	99	141	311
High school (2)	313	129	258	480
Some college (3)	199	87	218	423
College and above (4)	176	71	208	359

Table 4.9: Local Odds-Ratios Based on Adjacent Rows and Columns

	Attitude Toward Premarital Sex		
Education	C: 2 versus 1	C: 3 versus 2	C: 4 versus 3
R: 2 versus 1	1.382	1.404	0.843
R: 3 versus 2	1.061	1.253	1.043
R: 4 versus 3	0.923	1.169	0.890

multiplying $F_{23}F_{33}$ in both numerator and denominator)

$$
\begin{aligned}
\frac{F_{22}F_{34}}{F_{32}F_{24}} &= \frac{F_{22}F_{34}F_{23}F_{33}}{F_{32}F_{24}F_{23}F_{33}} \\
&= \left(\frac{F_{22}F_{33}}{F_{23}F_{32}}\right)\left(\frac{F_{23}F_{34}}{F_{33}F_{24}}\right) \\
&= \theta_{22}\theta_{23}.
\end{aligned}
\tag{4.10}
$$

As an exercise, verify that Eq. 4.10 is true numerically using the observed frequencies in Table 4.8.

4.2.4   The Invariance Property of Odds-Ratios

Odds-ratios are invariant to changes in (1) the total sample size, (2) the row marginal distribution, and (3) the column marginal distribution.

This can be easily demonstrated with the following example. Say that for the following 2×2 table, the observed frequencies are denoted by f's, and the odds-ratio by θ:

$$
\begin{array}{cc}
f_{11} & f_{12} \\
f_{21} & f_{22}
\end{array}
$$

$$
\theta = \frac{f_{11}f_{22}}{f_{12}f_{21}}.
$$

If we change the sample size by a factor of c, all the frequencies are changed by the same factor c, but the odds-ratio remains unchanged:

$$
\begin{array}{cc}
cf_{11} & cf_{12} \\
cf_{21} & cf_{22}
\end{array}
$$

$$
\theta = \frac{cf_{11}cf_{22}}{cf_{12}cf_{21}} = \frac{f_{11}f_{22}}{f_{12}f_{21}}.
$$

If we alter the distribution of the row marginals so that the first row total is changed by a factor of c, and the second row is changed by a factor of d, the odds-ratio still remains unchanged:

$$
\begin{array}{cc}
cf_{11} & cf_{12} \\
df_{21} & df_{22}
\end{array}
$$

$$
\theta = \frac{cf_{11}df_{22}}{cf_{12}df_{21}} = \frac{f_{11}f_{22}}{f_{12}f_{21}}.
$$

Likewise, if we alter the distribution of the column marginals so that the first column total is changed by a factor of c, and the second column by a factor of d, we have the same result:

$$
\begin{array}{cc}
cf_{11} & df_{12} \\
cf_{21} & df_{22}
\end{array}
$$

$$\theta = \frac{cf_{11}df_{22}}{df_{12}cf_{21}} = \frac{f_{11}f_{22}}{f_{12}f_{21}}.$$

In general, odds-ratios are invariant to changes in marginal distributions, since such changes in marginal distributions are translated to proportional increases or decreases across rows or columns. This invariance property makes odds-ratios the measure of choice in studies that wish to partial out differences in marginal distributions (e.g., Featherman, Jones, and Hauser 1975). It is due to this invariance property that maximum likelihood estimation for simple random samples can be directly applied to situations where samples are stratified on either the explanatory variable (i.e., stratified samples) or the outcome variable (i.e., case-control studies), as far as the estimation of odds-ratios is concerned (Xie and Manski 1989).

Odds-ratios are closely related to the independence model, which allows free marginal distributions. As we commented earlier, the independence model for an $I \times J$ table has $(I-1)(J-1)$ degrees of freedom, or $(I-1)(J-1)$ constraints. We now can be more explicit: the independence model specifies that the $(I-1)(J-1)$ nonredundant odds-ratios are equal to 1. Rejection of the independence model implies that some of these odds-ratios are not equal to 1. This explains why most models for contingency tables begin with independence as the baseline model (i.e., controlling for the marginal distributions), and when this is the case, more complicated models can often be expressed in terms of odds-ratios.

4.3   Estimation and Goodness-of-Fit

For any given data, there are always many potential models. Which model the researcher believes to be true depends to a large extent on the researcher's theoretical assumptions and beliefs. However, more often than not, several models are equally appealing on theoretical grounds. To aid in such situations, the researcher may wish to estimate the different models and use empirical tests to assess their relative plausibility. Thus, it is important that we discuss estimation and measures for evaluating a model's goodness-of-fit.

4.3.1 Simple Models and the Pearson χ^2 Statistic

Equation 4.5 provides the general formula for computing the Pearson χ^2 statistic. Although it is most commonly used for computing the Pearson χ^2 statistic under the independence model, it can be used in connection with any model. Let us use the earlier attitude example as an illustration, focusing on model constraints and degrees of freedom. From our earlier discussion, we already know that the independence model does not fit the data. In this subsection, we will discuss some more naive but simpler models. Let us first consider the model of "equal probability" (Model A). The equal probability model says that the distribution of frequencies is equal for all cells:

$$F_{ij} = F.$$

The constraints of the model are such that the expected cell frequencies do not vary either with i or with j. The estimation is simple:

$$\pi_{ij} = 1/4 \quad \text{or} \quad \widehat{F}_{ij} = n/4 = 951.$$

The model consumes 1 degree of freedom for estimating the mean frequency. Thus, $DF = 4 - 1 = 3$.

Applying formula 4.5 for computing the Pearson χ^2 statistic for this model, we obtain the results in Table 4.10.

Table 4.10: Pearson χ^2 Components Under Model A

	Attitude Toward Premarital Sex		
Education	Disapproval	Approval	Total
High school or less	6.40	60.06	66.46
College and above	183.73	69.45	253.18
Total	190.12	129.52	319.64

Obviously, the model provides a very poor fit to the data. The model is "naive" in the sense that it does not recognize the unequal distributions across categories, either for the explanatory variable (education) or the outcome variable (attitude).

We now consider the model of "equal probability conditional on column" (Model B). The model specifies that the distribution of frequencies is equal for both cells within each column:

$$\pi_{i|j} = 1/2.$$

From this, it is easy to derive the estimates of $\widehat{F}_{ij}$, which is invariant with i:

$$\pi_{ij} = \pi_{+j}\pi_{i|j} = \pi_{+j}/2; \qquad \widehat{F}_{ij} = \widehat{F}_{+j}/2 = f_{+j}/2.$$

The last equality holds because we fit the column marginals exactly. Thus, in this model, 2 degrees of freedom are used for two column marginal totals: $DF = 4 - 2 = 2$.

The calculated Pearson χ^2 statistic from the model is 82.35. Model B is an improvement over Model A in that it takes into account the lower proportion of respondents in the first category of the outcome variable than in the second category. The marginal distribution of the education variable is left unaccounted for.

Similarly, we may also fit a naive model of "equal probability conditional on row" (Model C). Model C would fit the row marginals but not the column marginals (with Pearson χ^2 statistic being 310.41 with $DF = 2$). If we fit both row and column marginal distributions, the model becomes the "independence" model (Model D). The Pearson χ^2 statistic under Model D is 55.50 with 1 degree of freedom, as shown before. Only 1 degree of freedom remains because 3 degrees of freedom are consumed for the independence model: total sample size, the column proportion (either π_{+1} or π_{+2}), and the row proportion (either π_{1+} or π_{2+}): $DF = 4 - 3 = 1$.

From the preceding examples, we see that the Pearson χ^2 statistic is very easy to compute. The major step is to obtain expected frequencies ($\widehat{F}$'s). Once $\widehat{F}$'s are known, it is straightforward to apply formula 4.5. Under the hypothesis that the model is true, the Pearson χ^2 statistic is asymptotically distributed as χ^2. The researcher can compare the calculated χ^2 with the corresponding critical value from a χ^2 table.

4.3.2   Sampling Models and Maximum Likelihood Estimation

The class of models that we wish to introduce in this chapter are called loglinear models, with $\log(F)$ as the dependent variable. As discussed in an earlier chapter, such nonlinear models are best estimated by using maximum likelihood or, equivalently, by using iterative reweighted least squares for generalized linear models. The key requirement for ML estimation, however, is the prior knowledge of (or assumptions about) the sampling distribution for the stochastic component of a model. For the problem of contingency tables, three sampling models are usually invoked.

A. Poisson: The Poisson model is the most natural sampling model for observed counts within a fixed space and time. It is one of the simplest distributions with a single parameter, λ. If variable f follows a Poisson distribution with $\lambda = F$, its probability mass function is

$$p(f \mid F) = \frac{\exp(-F)F^f}{f!} \text{ for } f = 0, 1, 2, \ldots . \qquad (4.11)$$

Equation 4.11 ensures that $\mathrm{E}(f) = \mathrm{var}(f) = F$. Note that we are omitting subscripts for f and F, respectively, denoting observed and expected frequencies, since they may contain two or more subscripts for multiple dimensions of a contingency table. What is important here is the assumption that the frequency count defined within each cross-classified cell follows an independent Poisson distribution. Examples are accidents, arrests, scientific discoveries, and births. In the context of contingency tables, we assume that these counts are cross-classified by certain characteristics defining either the outcome or the explanatory variables (such as age and education). The sum of independent Poisson-distributed variables, the total sample size (n), is a random variable that is also distributed as Poisson.

B. Multinomial: The multinomial distribution is a generalization of the binomial distribution. If the total sample size n is fixed, the distribution of n observations into multiple categories can be thought of as following a multinomial distribution. When we use notation for a two-way table, the probability mass function of a multinomial distribution is

$$p(f_{11}, \ldots, f_{IJ}) = \frac{n!}{\prod\limits_{i=1}^{I} \prod\limits_{j=1}^{J} f_{ij}!} \prod_{i=1}^{I} \prod_{j=1}^{J} \pi_{ij}^{f_{ij}}. \tag{4.12}$$

Equation 4.12 is an extension of the more familiar binomial distribution. The uncertainty here does not pertain to sample size, as in the case of the Poisson model, but to the assignment of elements in a sample of fixed size into a classification. For example, the researcher may create a grid for classifying marital status by gender, with marital status categorized as single, married, divorced/separated, and widowed. Every sampled individual in a survey has to fall into one of the eight mutually exclusive categories.

C. Product-Multinomial: Fixing the total sample size is very often insufficient. In many studies, particularly in experiments or in stratified samples, the marginal totals of the different categories of the explanatory variable are fixed by design. In other situations, marginal totals of the outcome categories are also fixed either by study design or by research needs. For example, situations like this occur when a sample is drawn using disproportionate stratification. Thus, it is sometimes more natural to condition a contingency table on the marginal totals of either the row or the column variable. When this is the case, the sampling distribution reduces to an independent multinomial distribution within a broader class, which is the same as the product-multinomial sampling for the entire dataset. When we condition on row totals, for example, the probability mass function is

$$p(f_{i1}, \ldots, f_{iJ}) = \frac{n_{i+}!}{\prod\limits_{j=1}^{J} f_{ij}!} \prod_{j=1}^{J} \pi_{j|i}^{f_{ij}}. \tag{4.13}$$

Fortunately, maximum likelihood estimation under the three sampling models is identical (see e.g., Fienberg 1979, pp. 167–170). Appendix B outlines the procedures involved under Poisson sampling.

The main difference among the three sampling models is the treatment of the grand total and marginal totals. In practice, this distinction is inconsequential, since researchers usually include parameters to fit the grand total and marginal totals exactly. Thus, it is not necessary to choose a particular sampling model, so long as the marginal totals are fitted.

4.3.3   The Likelihood-Ratio Chi-Squared Statistic

As reviewed in Appendix B, maximum likelihood estimation yields parameter estimates that maximize the joint probability of all observed events occurring. Since it is common that only a part of the likelihood function involves unknown parameters, we can focus on just this part, called the kernel, and ignore the rest. For example, under multinomial sampling (Eq. 4.12), the likelihood function is proportional to

$$\prod_{i=1}^{I}\prod_{j=1}^{J}\pi_{ij}^{f_{ij}}, \text{ where all } \pi_{ij} \geq 0, \text{ and } \sum_{i=1}^{I}\sum_{j=1}^{J}\pi_{ij} = 1. \qquad (4.14)$$

Formula 4.14 is the kernel. The part of the likelihood function containing a ratio in factorials does not involve unknown parameters and thus can be left out of the expression for the kernel. When the kernel is maximized, the likelihood is maximized as well. In practice, we maximize the logarithm of the likelihood function and thus the logarithm of the kernel for ease of computation. Let M_r denote a restricted model and M_u the saturated model. Under M_r, let us denote the ML estimate of π_{ij} by $\widehat{\pi}_{ij}^r$, and the ML estimate of F_{ij} by $\widehat{F}_{ij}^r$, or simply $\widehat{F}_{ij}$ when there is no confusion. $\widehat{F}_{ij}^r = \widehat{\pi}_{ij}^r n$. Under M_u, $\widehat{\pi}_{ij}^u = f_{ij}/n$, and $\widehat{F}_{ij}^u = f_{ij}$. The ratio in the kernel between M_r and M_u is

$$Q = \frac{\prod_{i=1}^{I}\prod_{j=1}^{J}(\widehat{\pi}_{ij}^r)^{f_{ij}}}{\prod_{i=1}^{I}\prod_{j=1}^{J}(\widehat{\pi}_{ij}^u)^{f_{ij}}} = \frac{\prod_{i=1}^{I}\prod_{j=1}^{J}(\widehat{F}_{ij}^r/n)^{f_{ij}}}{\prod_{i=1}^{I}\prod_{j=1}^{J}(\widehat{F}_{ij}^u/n)^{f_{ij}}} = \prod_{i=1}^{I}\prod_{j=1}^{J}(\widehat{F}_{ij}/f_{ij})^{f_{ij}}. \qquad (4.15)$$

$Q \leq 1$, as a restriction can only deteriorate the goodness-of-fit. Now let us define the test statistic G^2 (sometimes also denoted as L^2) as

$$G^2 = -2 \log Q = -2 \sum_{i=1}^{I} \sum_{j=1}^{J} f_{ij} \log(\widehat{F}_{ij}/f_{ij})$$

$$= 2 \sum_{i=1}^{I} \sum_{j=1}^{J} f_{ij} \log(f_{ij}/\widehat{F}_{ij}). \tag{4.16}$$

The statistic G^2 is called the likelihood-ratio chi-squared statistic. Always nonnegative, G^2 is asymptotically distributed as χ^2 under the assumption that the restricted model is true. The degrees of freedom can be calculated as the difference between the number of cells to begin with (i.e., IJ) and the number of parameters fitted.

In general, G^2 can been seen as the difference in $-2 \times$ log-likelihood:

$$G^2 = -2(L_r^2 - L_u^2), \tag{4.17}$$

where L_r and L_u respectively denote the log-likelihood for the restricted and unrestricted models. When G^2 is reported for a model without an explicit unrestricted model, the implicit reference is the saturated model. In this case, G^2 is also called the scaled deviance in the output of several computer packages. For the saturated model, $G^2 = 0$. When the researcher is interested in testing the statistical significance of the difference between two nested models, it does not matter whether he/she works directly from the general formula Eq. 4.17 or indirectly from the difference in G^2 between the two models, since the two formulas lead to the same chi-squared test.

For the independence hypothesis ($\pi_{ij} = \pi_{i+}\pi_{+j}$ for all i and j), for example, the likelihood is maximized when $\widehat{\pi}_{i+} = f_{i+}/n$ and $\widehat{\pi}_{+j} = f_{+j}/n$. We can then calculate G^2 according to Eq. 4.16. G^2 is distributed as chi-squared with $(I-1)(J-1)$ degrees of freedom if the null hypothesis is true. For our example of attitude toward premarital sex (2×2 version in Table 4.1), $G^2 = 55.89$ for 1 degree of freedom. The Pearson chi-squared statistic (X^2) and the likelihood-ratio chi-squared statistic (G^2) are asymptotically equivalent.

4.3.4　Bayesian Information Criterion

The use of the G^2 statistic as a goodness-of-fit measure has been criticized by Raftery (1986, 1995) as an unsatisfactory procedure for rejecting one model in favor of another in large samples. The essence of the argument is that, when the sample size is large, it is much easier to accept (or at least harder to reject) more complex models because the likelihood-ratio test (G^2) is designed to detect *any* departure between a model and observed data. Adding more terms to a model will always improve the fit, but with large samples it becomes harder to distinguish a "real" improvement in fit from a trivial one. In this sense, the likelihood-ratio test often rejects acceptable models. One solution to this problem is to use the BIC (Bayesian Information Criterion) statistic in searching for parsimonious models that provide an "adequate" fit to the data.

The BIC index provides an approximation to a $-2 \times$ log-transformed *Bayes factor*, which may be viewed as the ratio in likelihood between one model (M_0) and another model (M_1). The basic idea is to compare the relative plausibility of two models rather than to find the absolute deviation of observed data from a particular model. In practice, the researcher often chooses the saturated model to be M_1 as the reference in assessing the adequacy of M_0. The statistical methods for calculating the Bayes factor are complicated and beyond the scope of this book. Many applied researchers have found the BIC statistic popularized by Raftery (1986, 1995) to be useful. It is defined as

$$BIC = G^2 - DF \log n. \qquad (4.18)$$

This expression shows that BIC penalizes G^2 more, per degree of freedom, for a larger sample than for a smaller sample, at the rate of $\log n$. A negative BIC means that model M_0 is more likely than model M_1 so that the researcher should choose M_0 over M_1. When comparing multiple models, a lower value of BIC means a better-fitting model. However, the researcher should not blindly rely on BIC as the sole criterion for model selection, since it is based on an approximation. In practice, we recommend that the researcher consider a variety of goodness-of-fit criteria, including but not restricted to G^2 and BIC. Numerical examples will be given later.

4.4   Models for Two-Way Tables

4.4.1   The General Setup

There are two ways to express the loglinear model for a contingency table. Let R denote row, C denote column, and f_{ij} $(i = 1, \ldots, I; j = 1, \ldots, J)$ denote the observed frequency for the ith row and the jth column. We begin with the multiplicative version of the model, with the expected frequency (F_{ij}) specified as a function of multiplicative terms:

$$F_{ij} = \tau \tau_i^R \tau_j^C \tau_{ij}^{RC}, \tag{4.19}$$

where the τ parameters are subject to normalization constraints to be discussed in depth later. With the ANOVA-like normalization constraints (i.e., τ's multiply to one along all appropriate dimensions), τ represents the (unweighted) grand mean; τ^R and τ^C represent respectively the marginal effects of R and C; and τ^{RC} represents the two-way interaction between R and C. As will be shown later, the interaction τ^{RC} parameters essentially measure the odds-ratios between R and C. When $\tau_{ij}^{RC} = 1$ for all i and j, the model is the familiar independence model.

Given that frequency is always positive, we further restrict the τ parameters to be positive. A τ parameter greater than 1 raises the expected frequency, and a τ parameter less than 1 lowers it. A τ of 1 does not affect the expected frequency at all. Since multiplication is harder to work with than addition, we can transform the multiplicative version of the model in Eq. 4.19 into the log-additive form:

$$\begin{aligned} \log F_{ij} &= \log(\tau) + \log(\tau_i^R) + \log(\tau_j^C) + \log(\tau_{ij}^{RC}) \\ &= \mu + \mu_i^R + \mu_j^C + \mu_{ij}^{RC}. \end{aligned} \tag{4.20}$$

Note the one-to-one correspondence between the τ parameters in the multiplicative form (Eq. 4.19) and the μ parameters in the log-additive form of Eq. 4.20. Since loglinear is a more familiar and more general term than log-additive, we will refer to the second version as the loglinear form.

4.4.2 Normalization

Not all parameters in Eqs. 4.19 and 4.20 are uniquely identified. This is no different from situations in linear regressions where the researcher can use only up to $J - 1$ dummy variables for a nominal independent variable with J categories. For an $I \times J$ table, the upper limit of the number of parameters identifiable is given in Table 4.11.

Table 4.11: Identifiable Parameters

Type of Parameters	Notation in τ	Notation in μ	Number of Parameters
Grand Total	τ	μ	1
Row Marginals	τ_i^R	μ_i^R	$I - 1$
Column Marginals	τ_j^C	μ_j^C	$J - 1$
Interactions	τ_{ij}^{RC}	μ_{ij}^{RC}	$(I - 1)(J - 1)$
Sum			IJ

This upper limit is achieved when a saturated model is fitted. There are many different ways to normalize the parameters to achieve identification. Some of them are not widely used by researchers but can be useful in certain situations. For example, the parameter for the grand total sometimes can be conveniently deleted in order to identify uniquely I row marginal totals or J column marginal totals.

For most applications, two conventions are used. One is ANOVA-type coding (also referred to as effect coding) that preserves the meaning of the grand total:

$$\prod_i \tau_i^R = \prod_j \tau_j^C = \prod_i \tau_{ij}^{RC} = \prod_j \tau_{ij}^{RC} = 1 \quad \text{or}$$
$$\sum_i \mu_i^R = \sum_j \mu_j^C = \sum_i \mu_{ij}^{RC} = \sum_j \mu_{ij}^{RC} = 0. \tag{4.21}$$

The second convention is dummy-variable coding, which is equivalent to blocking out one category for R and C. Let us block out the first category for both:

$$\tau_1^R = \tau_1^C = \tau_{1j}^{RC} = \tau_{i1}^{RC} = 1 \quad \text{or}$$
$$\mu_1^R = \mu_1^C = \mu_{1j}^{RC} = \mu_{i1}^{RC} = 0. \tag{4.22}$$

Which normalization system to use often depends on the computer program. ECTA, for example, uses ANOVA coding. Most other computer programs, such as GLIM, STATA, S-Plus, and SAS (proc genmod) use dummy-variable coding. For empirical examples in this chapter, we will use the dummy-variable normalization with the first category as reference, unless otherwise stated. However, it is important to realize that the difference between the two normalization systems is an arbitrary one. The reader should be able to go back and forth between the two. Let us take a simple example to illustrate this point in the linear regression context. Say that we have a dichotomous variable sex (male vs. female). We can create two dummy variables with the following design matrix:

Sex	x_1	x_2
Male	1	0
Female	0	1

However, in general, we cannot use both x_1 and x_2 because they are redundant when an intercept is included in the model. For any data set coded in this manner, $x_1 + x_2 = x_0$, where x_0 is a vector of ones. Thus, using x_1 and x_2, together with an intercept term (β_0), introduces perfect multicollinearity in the model. There are a number of ways to remedy this problem. A common dummy-variable normalization sets $\beta_1 = 0$ so that $\beta_0 + \beta_1 x_1 + \beta_2 x_2 = \beta_0 + \beta_2 x_2$.

In contrast, the ANOVA-type normalization uses both x_1 and x_2 with the constraint that $\beta_1 + \beta_2 = 0$ so that $\beta_1 = -\beta_2$.

In general, a normalization takes the form

$$\sum_{k=1}^{K} w_k \beta_k = 0,$$

where $K =$ the number of categories, and w_k is the category-specific weight. For example, the dummy-variable normalization is achieved by setting $w_1 = 1$; $w_k = 0$ for $k \neq 1$. The usual (unweighted) ANOVA-type normalization is achieved by setting $w_k = 1$, for all k. Sometimes, w_k is set to the sample proportion in the kth category in the marginal distribution of the variable to enable the interpretation of the intercept as the weighted grand mean.

In short, both the dummy-variable and ANOVA-type normalizations identify parameters of a loglinear model. Depending on the particular normalization, resulting parameters will be different. However, there should not be any substantive difference due to the choice of normalization per se.

4.4.3 Interpretation of Parameters

Loglinear models are different from linear regressions in that the "dependent" variable in loglinear models is the frequency rather than the outcome variable. That is, the outcome variable and the explanatory variable appear in a loglinear model symmetrically. It is up to the researcher to infer causal association between them, if it is present, from model parameters. This fact has certain implications for appropriate interpretations of loglinear parameters. Loglinear models often contain many parameters. The researcher should mentally separate "nuisance" (or uninteresting) parameters from substantively meaningful parameters. In most applications, the substantively meaningful parameters are interaction parameters. This is true because the "main" effect parameters serve to saturate, or fit exactly, the marginal distributions of the row and column variables.

One way to interpret loglinear parameters is to consider conditional odds. For example, assume that the row variable is the explanatory variable and that the column variable is the outcome variable. Let j and j' denote two arbitrary categories for the column (outcome) variable. We have

$$
\begin{aligned}
\log(\pi_{j|i}/\pi_{j'|i}) &= \log(F_{ji}/F_{j'i}) = \log(F_{ji}) - \log(F_{j'i}) \\
&= \mu + \mu_i^R + \mu_j^C + \mu_{ij}^{RC} - (\mu + \mu_i^R + \mu_{j'}^C + \mu_{ij'}^{RC}) \quad (4.23) \\
&= \mu_j^C - \mu_{j'}^C + \mu_{ij}^{RC} - \mu_{ij'}^{RC}.
\end{aligned}
$$

If the researcher uses the dummy-variable normalization with j' as the reference category, Eq. 4.23 simplifies to $\mu_j^C + \mu_{ij}^{RC}$. Under the independence model, $\mu_{ij}^{RC} = 0$, and the marginal parameters for the column variable (μ_j^C's) define conditional odds or log-odds, as well as marginal odds or log-odds due to the homogeneity of proportions property.

If the independence model does not hold, then the conditional odds vary by row, with the amount of variation determined by the interaction parameters (μ_{ij}^{RC}'s). In general, marginal parameters absorb marginal distributions, and two-way interaction parameters measure two-way associations. In fact, two-way interaction parameters correspond directly to log-odds-ratio measures. For $\log \theta$ involving the four cells in the subtable of rows (i, i') and columns (j, j'):

$$
\begin{aligned}
\log \theta = \log \frac{F_{ij} F_{i'j'}}{F_{ij'} F_{i'j}} &= \log F_{ij} + \log F_{i'j'} - \log F_{ij'} - \log F_{i'j} \\
&= (\mu + \mu_i^R + \mu_j^C + \mu_{ij}^{RC}) + (\mu + \mu_{i'}^R + \mu_{j'}^C + \mu_{i'j'}^{RC}) \\
&\quad - (\mu + \mu_i^R + \mu_{j'}^C + \mu_{ij'}^{RC}) - (\mu + \mu_{i'}^R + \mu_j^C + \mu_{i'j}^{RC}) \\
&= \mu_{ij}^{RC} + \mu_{i'j'}^{RC} - \mu_{ij'}^{RC} - \mu_{i'j}^{RC}.
\end{aligned}
\tag{4.24}
$$

If dummy-variable coding is used for normalization, and i' and j' happen to be the reference categories for the row and column variables, Eq. 4.24 simplifies to μ_{ij}^{RC}. That is, with dummy-variable coding, two-way interaction parameters represent the log-odds-ratio between the current row and column categories and their reference categories. Log odds-ratios involving any other two pairs can be easily obtained according to Eq. 4.24.

4.4.4   Topological Model

With the marginal totals fitted exactly, the substantive interest of a researcher in a two-way table lies in the association between R and C. This interest is represented as two-way interaction parameters (τ_{ij}^{RC} in Eq. 4.19 and μ_{ij}^{RC} in Eq. 4.20). One of the easiest ways to understand this association is to estimate all nonredundant interaction parameters in a saturated model. For an $I \times J$ table, this means that we can

Table 4.12: Hauser's Mobility Table

	Son's Occupation				
Father's Occupation	(1)	(2)	(3)	(4)	(5)
Upper nonmanual (1)	1414	521	302	643	40
Lower nonmanual (2)	724	524	254	703	48
Upper manual (3)	798	648	856	1676	108
Lower manual (4)	756	914	771	3325	237
Farm (5)	409	357	441	1611	1832

Note: Son's occupation (column) is defined in the same way as father's occupation (row).

estimate the local odds-ratios for the $(I-1) \times (J-1)$ 2×2 subtables with adjacent rows and columns. Let us take a closer look at the following example of an intergenerational social mobility table (Table 4.12) cross-tabulating son's occupation by father's occupation (taken from Hauser 1979).

Let us now estimate the saturated model for this table using a dummy-variable normalization with the first row and the first column as reference categories. The estimated μ_{ij}^{RC} coefficients are given in Table 4.13 (with asymptotic standard errors in parentheses).

Table 4.13: Interaction Parameters of the Saturated Model: Intergenerational Mobility Example

	Son's Occupation				
Father's Occupation	(1)	(2)	(3)	(4)	(5)
Upper Nonmanual (1)	0	0	0	0	0
	—	—	—	—	—
Lower Nonmanual (2)	0	0.675	0.496	0.759	0.852
	—	(0.077)	(0.097)	(0.071)	(0.219)
Upper Manual (3)	0	0.790	1.614	1.530	1.565
	—	(0.074)	(0.080)	(0.064)	(0.190)
Lower Manual (4)	0	1.188	1.563	2.269	2.405
	—	(0.071)	(0.081)	(0.062)	(0.177)
Farm (5)	0	0.862	0.862	2.159	5.065
	—	(0.089)	(0.089)	(0.073)	(0.169)

Interpretation of the estimates in terms of odds-ratios (Eq. 4.24) should be straightforward. We observe, for example, the likelihood of son's occupation in farm highly depends on father's occupation in farm. For concreteness, contrasting the last and the first columns and the last and the second rows, we obtain the logged ratio in odds of being a farm worker rather than an upper nonmanual worker between the son of a farm worker and the son of a lower nonmanual worker:

$$\log \frac{F_{55}/F_{51}}{F_{25}/F_{21}} = 5.065 + 0 - 0.852 - 0 = 4.213.$$

The saturated model is not very interesting because it is not parsimonious. In searching for parsimonious models, the researcher may group cells with similar values of odds-ratios into a type, or level, and thus map out the interaction parameters into a topological pattern or levels. Hauser (1979), for example, designed the following matrix based on the observed odds-ratio pattern in Table 4.12:

$$
\begin{array}{ccccc}
2 & 4 & 5 & 5 & 5 \\
3 & 4 & 5 & 5 & 5 \\
5 & 5 & 5 & 5 & 5 \\
5 & 5 & 5 & 4 & 4 \\
5 & 5 & 5 & 4 & 1 \\
\end{array}
$$

The values in this matrix delineate unique interaction parameters. A model that fits such a levels matrix for two-way interactions with row and column marginals fitted is called a levels model, or a topological model. If we use dummy-variable coding with category 1 as the reference category, four levels parameters will be estimated. Let us denote them as μ_2^h, μ_3^h, μ_4^h, and μ_5^h. Our estimation yields $G^2 = 66.57$ for 12 degrees of freedom, a huge improvement over the independence model with $G^2 = 6170.1$ for 16 degrees of freedom. Given the large sample size (19,912), Hauser's topological model fits the data well ($BIC = -52.22$).[2] The estimated coefficients of the interaction parameters are given in Table 4.14.

---

[2] This is not surprising given that the levels were chosen to maximize goodness-of-fit.

Table 4.14: Estimated μ^h Parameters

Parameter	Estimate	(S.E.)
μ_2^h	-1.813	(0.076)
μ_3^h	-2.497	(0.080)
μ_4^h	-2.803	(0.058)
μ_5^h	-3.403	(0.060)

A log-odds-ratio involving any two rows and two columns can be obtained from these μ^h parameters. For example, consider rows 2 and 3, columns 2 and 3.

$$\log \theta_{22} = \log \frac{F_{22}F_{33}}{F_{23}F_{32}} = \mu_4^h + \mu_5^h - \mu_5^h - \mu_5^h$$
$$= \mu_4^h - \mu_5^h = -2.803 + 3.403 = .6.$$

Note that Hauser's design matrix covers the whole table, not just the 16 cells with nonzero values in Table 4.13. In general, a design matrix for a topological model assigns levels to all cells in a table. The saturated, or full-interaction, model is a special case of the topological model with the following design matrix:

$$\begin{array}{ccccc} 1 & 1 & 1 & 1 & 1 \\ 1 & 2 & 3 & 4 & 5 \\ 1 & 6 & 7 & 8 & 9 \\ 1 & 10 & 11 & 12 & 13 \\ 1 & 14 & 15 & 16 & 17 \end{array}$$

In fact, as will be shown later, many special models can be conveniently parameterized as topological models.

4.4.5 Quasi-Independence Model

In mobility tables and similar tables where there is a correspondence between row and column variables, diagonal cells tend to be large. That is, there is a tendency for tables to exhibit clustering along the main diagonal. Researchers in social stratification call such tendency to cluster along diagonal cells inheritance effects. These large diagonal cells often contribute significantly to the poor fit of the independence model. One substantively interesting hypothesis is whether the rest of the table satisfies the independence hypothesis net of the diagonal cells. This leads to the quasi-independence model.

A square table satisfies quasi-independence if R and C are independent of each other in off-diagonal cells. That is,

$$\pi_{ij} = \pi_{i+}\pi_{+j}, \qquad \text{for } i \neq j.$$

Compared to the independence model, the quasi-independence model consumes I additional degrees of freedom, thus with $(I-1)(I-1) - I$ degrees of freedom for residuals. The loss of the I degrees of freedom can be interpreted either in terms of the reduction of the number of data points by I, or in terms of the increase of I additional parameters. In fact, each interpretation corresponds to an estimation method. For the first interpretation, the researcher can block out the diagonal cells (e.g., by using a weight matrix) while estimating the independence model. For the second interpretation, the researcher can add unique parameters to the diagonal cells, effectively estimating a topological model. For a 5×5 table, the design matrix is

$$
\begin{array}{ccccc}
2 & 1 & 1 & 1 & 1 \\
1 & 3 & 1 & 1 & 1 \\
1 & 1 & 4 & 1 & 1 \\
1 & 1 & 1 & 5 & 1 \\
1 & 1 & 1 & 1 & 6
\end{array}
$$

The two estimation methods yield identical results. The main difference is that the second method yields estimates for diagonal cells, whereas the first does not. The second method can also be used to constrain some diagonal parameters to be equal. For this example, the quasi-independence model is a significant improvement in goodness-of-fit over that of the independence model, with $G^2 = 683.34$ for 11 degrees of freedom. As shown by Goodman (1972), this method can be used effectively to test for partial independence in limited regions or account for a few especially large cells.

4.4.6   Symmetry and Quasi-Symmetry

For square $I \times I$ tables, the researcher may be interested in whether or not the row and column variables are symmetric with respect to each other. The symmetry model is

$$\log F_{ij} = \mu + \mu_i + \mu_j + \mu_{ij}, \qquad (4.25)$$

where $\mu_{ij} = \mu_{ji}$. Here we purposely omit the superscripts R and C for the μ terms because they pertain to both R and C. The symmetry model means that all cells are symmetric to each other across the main diagonal: $F_{ij} = F_{ji}$. Obviously, it is highly constrained and thus of limited use. The residual degrees of freedom are one-half of the number of off-diagonal cells, or $I(I - 1)/2$.

We can decompose the symmetry of Eq. 4.25 into two components: marginal homogeneity and symmetric interactions. If we replace marginal homogeneity with marginal heterogeneity while retaining symmetric interactions, we have the model of quasi-symmetry:

$$\log F_{ij} = \mu + \mu_i^R + \mu_j^C + \mu_{ij}^{RC}, \qquad (4.26)$$

where $\mu_{ij}^{RC} = \mu_{ji}^{RC}$. That is, the quasi-symmetry model allows for marginal heterogeneity but restricts the interaction parameters to be symmetric across the main diagonal. Many researchers find the quasi-symmetry model to be more useful because it conditions on differences in marginal distribution that should be left unconstrained. Sobel, Hout, and Duncan (1985), for example, use the quasi-symmetric model to describe structural mobility with parameters measuring the difference in row and column marginal distributions. Because the quasi-symmetry model adds $I - 1$ additional parameters compared to the symmetry model, the residual degrees of freedom for the quasi-symmetry model are $I(I - 1)/2 - (I - 1) = (I - 1)(I - 2)/2$.

The quasi-symmetry model can be easily estimated using a topological coding. For the 5×5 case, for example, the design matrix for the interactions can be expressed as

$$
\begin{array}{ccccc}
2 & 1 & 1 & 1 & 1 \\
1 & 3 & 7 & 8 & 9 \\
1 & 7 & 4 & 10 & 11 \\
1 & 8 & 10 & 5 & 12 \\
1 & 9 & 11 & 12 & 6
\end{array}
$$

For our mobility example, $G^2 = 27.45$ with 6 degrees of freedom; $BIC = -31.95$. Quasi-symmetry is more general than quasi-independence.

4.4.7   Crossings Model

Not all models of potential interest can be expressed in terms of topological models with a single design matrix. One such example is the crossings model (Goodman 1972). The hypothesis implied by the crossings model is that different categories of a nominal variable present varying degrees of difficulty for crossing. The further apart two categories are for the row variable, the smaller the interaction parameter between two categories for the column variable. Formally, the crossings model simplifies Eq. 4.19 to

$$
F_{ij} = \tau \tau_i^R \tau_j^C \nu_{ij}^{RC}, \tag{4.27}
$$

with

$$
\nu_{ij}^{RC} = \begin{cases}
\displaystyle\prod_{u=j}^{i-1} \nu_u & \text{for } i > j, \\
\displaystyle\prod_{u=i}^{j-1} \nu_u & \text{for } i < j, \\
\xi_i & \text{for } i = j.
\end{cases}
$$

For a 5×5 table (such as the mobility example of Table 4.12), for example, the ν_{ij}^{RC} interaction parameters can be displayed as

ξ_1	ν_1	$\nu_1\nu_2$	$\nu_1\nu_2\nu_3$	$\nu_1\nu_2\nu_3\nu_4$
ν_1	ξ_2	ν_2	$\nu_2\nu_3$	$\nu_2\nu_3\nu_4$
$\nu_1\nu_2$	ν_2	ξ_3	ν_3	$\nu_3\nu_4$
$\nu_1\nu_2\nu_3$	$\nu_2\nu_3$	ν_3	ξ_4	ν_4
$\nu_1\nu_2\nu_3\nu_4$	$\nu_2\nu_3\nu_4$	$\nu_3\nu_4$	ν_4	ξ_5

Note that, in this formulation, we follow Goodman (1972) in fitting the diagonals exactly, as in the quasi-independence and quasi-symmetry models. Researchers may not want to fit the diagonal cells exactly for parsimony reasons (e.g., Mare 1991). In the loglinear form of Eq. 4.27, for cells $i \neq j$, the ν_{ij}^{RC} interaction parameters can be parameterized as the sum of the coefficients of the following four sets of design matrices:

$$
\begin{array}{ccccc}
0 & 1 & 1 & 1 & 1 \\
1 & 0 & 0 & 0 & 0 \\
1 & 0 & 0 & 0 & 0 \\
1 & 0 & 0 & 0 & 0 \\
1 & 0 & 0 & 0 & 0
\end{array}
\qquad
\begin{array}{ccccc}
0 & 0 & 1 & 1 & 1 \\
0 & 0 & 1 & 1 & 1 \\
1 & 1 & 0 & 0 & 0 \\
1 & 1 & 0 & 0 & 0 \\
1 & 1 & 0 & 0 & 0
\end{array}
\qquad
\begin{array}{ccccc}
0 & 0 & 0 & 1 & 1 \\
0 & 0 & 0 & 1 & 1 \\
0 & 0 & 0 & 1 & 1 \\
1 & 1 & 1 & 0 & 0 \\
1 & 1 & 1 & 0 & 0
\end{array}
\qquad
\begin{array}{ccccc}
0 & 0 & 0 & 0 & 1 \\
0 & 0 & 0 & 0 & 1 \\
0 & 0 & 0 & 0 & 1 \\
0 & 0 & 0 & 0 & 1 \\
1 & 1 & 1 & 1 & 0
\end{array}
$$

with the four matrices respectively corresponding to ν_1, ν_2, ν_3, and ν_4. With the diagonal cells blocked out by the ξ parameters, only $(I - 3)$ of the $(I - 1)$ ν parameters in Eq. 4.27 are identified. For our 5×5 example, only two ν parameters are identified. Goodman (1972) recommends normalizing the first and the last ν: $\nu_1 = \nu_{I-1} = 1$. Without the diagonals blocked, all $(I - 1)$ ν's are identifiable.

One interesting feature of the crossings model is that the local odds-ratios for adjacent rows and columns not involving diagonal cells satisfy local independence. For our 5×5 example, let us consider the odds-ratio involving cells in rows 4, 5, and columns 1, 2:

$$
\theta_{41} = \frac{F_{41} F_{52}}{F_{42} F_{51}} = \frac{(\nu_1 \nu_2 \nu_3)(\nu_2 \nu_3 \nu_4)}{(\nu_2 \nu_3)(\nu_1 \nu_2 \nu_3 \nu_4)} = 1.
$$

For Hauser's example of intergenerational mobility, the crossings model fits the observed data rather well. The G^2 statistic is 64.24 for 9 degrees of freedom ($BIC = -24.85$). The version not blocking out the diagonal cells has a G^2 statistic of 89.91 for 12 degrees of freedom ($BIC = -28.88$). Although the crossings model (in either version) is short of Hauser's topological model in pure goodness-of-fit, the crossings model yields estimates of parameters that may be easier to interpret. For the second version, for example, the crossings estimates in the log scale are (from the second occupational category to the last one) $(-0.4256, -0.3675, -0.2935, -1.403)$. Thus, of all the barriers separating adjacent categories, the last barrier separating lower manual occupations and farming is the most difficult to cross, and the next most difficult barrier is the one separating upper nonmanual and lower nonmanual occupations.

4.5   Models for Ordinal Variables

So far, we have treated the row and column variables as nominal variables (i.e., discrete variables with unordered categories). In substantive applications, it is often reasonable to assume that categories are ordinal, meaning that they are ranked on either an observed or latent scale. This additional information of ordering can be used to obtain parsimonious model specifications.

Typically, researchers use ordering information to specify the interaction terms only (i.e., μ_{ij}^{RC} of Eq. 4.20), leaving the marginal distributions fitted exactly. This is a conservative approach, for the ordinal information is used only for the association between the row and column variables. As shown before, for an $I \times J$ table, there are $(I-1)(J-1)$ degrees of freedom for interactions after the marginal totals are fitted. If ordering information is used, it may take few (sometimes just 1) degrees of freedom to describe the association. Note that the payoff to ordering information goes up as the numbers of categories increase.

4.5.1   Linear-by-Linear Association

Let x_i and y_j denote respectively the measured attributes (or indexes) of the row and column variables. They can be used in the specification of a linear-by-linear association, as

$$\log F_{ij} = \mu + \mu_i^R + \mu_j^C + \beta x_i y_j. \tag{4.28}$$

Compared to Eq. 4.20, the linear-by-linear association model replaces the μ_{ij}^{RC} term with a more parsimonious form $\beta x_i y_j$, where β can be seen as the association coefficient between x and y. For an odds-ratio involving any pair of rows (i and i') and any pair of columns (j and

j'), Eq. 4.24 simplifies to

$$\log \theta = \log \frac{F_{ij}F_{i'j'}}{F_{ij'}F_{i'j}} = \beta(x_i - x_{i'})(y_j - y_{j'}). \qquad (4.29)$$

That is, the log-odds-ratio is proportional to the product of the distances of the row and column variables in index scores. Multiple linear-by-linear terms can be used, so long as they are fewer than $(I-1)(J-1)$, changing Eq. 4.28 to

$$\log F_{ij} = \mu + \mu_i^R + \mu_j^C + \sum_m \beta_m x_{im} y_{jm}, \qquad (4.30)$$

where x_m and y_m are the row and column attributes for the mth linear-by-linear association. The same attribute for row (or column) may be used in combination with different attributes for column (or row). Examples using this approach are found in work by Hout (1984) and Lin and Xie (1998).

For example, in Lin and Xie's (1998) model of interstate migration, state-level economic growth rates (denoted as g's) are used to capture the "push" and "pull" forces of migration. The push force of origin is measured by $1/g_i$, the pull force of destination by g_j. The model is similar to 4.28 with $(1/g_i)g_j$ as an interaction term between origin and destination. Lin and Xie find the push-and-pull interaction to be highly significant in explaining interstate migration streams in the United States.

4.5.2   Uniform Association

The previous discussion presumes the existence of attribute (or index) variables for the row and column variables. In the absence of such index variables, what can the researcher do? There are two answers to this question. One is to impose an interval-score structure on the categories. The second is to estimate the latent score associated with the categories. We discuss the first approach in this subsection and leave the second approach to the Section 4.5.4, "Goodman's RC Model."

The easiest way to impose an interval structure is to assign consecutive integers to categories, if the categories form an ordinal scale and are correctly ordered. For the example of attitude toward premarital sex (full version, Table 4.8), we may assign the scores as follows. For the outcome variable, assign Always Wrong = 1, Almost Always Wrong = 2, Sometimes Wrong = 3, and Not Wrong at All = 4. For the explanatory variable of education, assign Less than H.S. = 1, High School = 2, Some College = 3, and College and Above = 4. This method of assigning scores basically assumes that the distance between any two adjacent categories is uniform across all possible values. We call this scoring method integer-scoring, and the resulting model the uniform association model. The particular values assigned are inconsequential, so long as they are uniformly spaced. That is, $(1, 2, 3, 4)$ yields the same model as $(-10, -8, -6, -4)$. As a convention, however, we use consecutive integers beginning with 1. That is, set $x_i = i$ and $y_j = j$. Substituting these imposed uniform scores to Eq. 4.28 yields

$$\log F_{ij} = \mu + \mu_i^R + \mu_j^C + \beta ij. \tag{4.31}$$

Consuming 1 degree of freedom for interactions, the uniform-association model has $(I-1)(J-1)-1$ degrees of freedom for residuals. A special feature of the uniform association model is that its odds-ratios involving two adjacent rows and columns are invariant. Using the constraint of Eq. 4.31 and solving for Eq. 4.9, we see that

$$\theta_{ij} = \frac{F_{ij} F_{(i+1)(j+1)}}{F_{i(j+1)} F_{(i+1)j}} = \exp(\beta) \tag{4.32}$$

and

$$\log \theta_{ij} = \beta.$$

In fact, this important property of Eq. 4.31 can be used to define the uniform association model (Goodman 1979). For an odds-ratio involving arbitrary pairs (i and i' for row, j and j' for column), the log-odds-ratio is simply

$$\beta(i - i')(j - j').$$

For our example of attitude toward premarital sex, the uniform association model yields a G^2 of 31.33 with 8 degrees of freedom. The estimate of β is 0.097 with a standard error of 0.013.

The uniform association model is a special case of the linear-by-linear model in which integer-scoring is used. More generally, other scoring methods may also be reasonable. For example, midpoints or weighted means may be used to "linearize" categories that were originally interval. For the education variable in the attitude example, one may wish to assign 10 to Less Than H. S., 12 to High School, 14 to Some College, and 17 to College and Above.

4.5.3 Row-Effect and Column-Effect Models

The uniform association model imposes integer-scoring to both the row and column variables. A less restrictive approach is to assume integer-scoring for either the row or the column variable, but not for both. When integer-scoring is used for the column variable, the resulting model is called the row-effect model. Conversely, when integer-scoring is used for the row variable, the model is called the column-effect model. These models were developed by Goodman (1979). For an innovative application, see Duncan's (1979) study of an 8×8 intergenerational mobility table.

For the row-effect model, Eq. 4.20 is simplified to

$$\log F_{ij} = \mu + \mu_i^R + \mu_j^C + j\phi_i, \qquad (4.33)$$

where ϕ_i can be seen as the row effect (or row score) *estimated* from the model. Assuming that the column categories are correctly ordered and approximately follow the integer-scoring scale, the row-effect model is a generalization of the uniform association model. Comparing Eq. 4.33 to Eq. 4.31 for the uniform association model, however, we see that there is no β for the row-effect model. This is due to the fact that the row effect (ϕ_i) is latent and needs to be normalized. In other words, it is not possible to separate β from $\beta\phi_i$ when ϕ_i is latent. So, we set $\beta = 1$ to normalize the scale of ϕ_i. In addition, we also need to normalize the location of ϕ_i. One convenient normalization is to use dummy-variable coding with the first category as the reference category so that $\phi_1 = 0$.

With $(I - 1)$ parameters for interactions between row and column, the row-effect model has $(I - 1)(J - 2)$ degrees of freedom. With these specifications for the R-C interactions, it is easy to see that, as a special variant of Eq. 4.29,

$$\log \frac{F_{ij}F_{i'j'}}{F_{ij'}F_{i'j}} = (\phi_i - \phi_{i'})(j - j'). \tag{4.34}$$

For the fundamental local log-odds-ratios,   ·

$$\log \theta_{ij} = \log\left(\frac{F_{ij}F_{(i+1)(j+1)}}{F_{i(j+1)}F_{(i+1)j}}\right) = \phi_{i+1} - \phi_i. \tag{4.35}$$

Likewise, we can define the column-effect model in a similar manner, which changes Eq.4.20 to

$$\log F_{ij} = \mu + \mu_i^R + \mu_j^C + i\varphi_j, \tag{4.36}$$

where φ_j is called the column-effect and requires a normalization. The column-effect model has $(I - 2)(J - 1)$ degrees of freedom. Note that the column-effect model presumes that the row categories are correctly ordered and approximately follow the integer-scoring scale. For the column-effect model, the LOR structure for any two pair of categories is

$$\log \frac{F_{ij}F_{i'j'}}{F_{ij'}F_{i'j}} = (\varphi_j - \varphi_{j'})(i - i'), \tag{4.37}$$

and the LOR for local subtables is

$$\log \theta_{ij} = \log\left(\frac{F_{ij}F_{(i+1)(j+1)}}{F_{i(j+1)}F_{(i+1)j}}\right) = \varphi_{j+1} - \varphi_j. \tag{4.38}$$

Hence, we see similarities and differences among the uniform association, the row effect, and the column effect models. The uniform association model can be viewed as a special case either of the row effect model or of the column effect model. They are far more parsimonious than the saturated model. The gain in parsimony increases rapidly with the dimension of a table. Like many parsimonious models, these three types of models can also be used in combination with the key feature of the quasi-independence model [i.e., blocking out diagonal cells (or any subsets of a table)].

We now apply the uniform association model and the row effect model to Hauser's mobility data, first by themselves and then after blocking out the diagonal cells. The row effect model is borrowed from Duncan (1979). To compare these models against alternative specifications, we also present the goodness-of-fit statistics from other models we have discussed. The results are provided in Table 4.15. The column denoted by G^2 is the likelihood-ratio chi-squared for residuals (e.g., Eq. 4.17), with degrees of freedom reported in the column labeled DF. With $n = 19,912$, BIC is calculated according to Eq. 4.18. As a purely descriptive measure of goodness-of-fit, we also use the Index of Dissimilarity (Shryock and Siegel 1976, p.131), denoted as Δ. The Index of Dissimilarity here can be interpreted as the proportion of misclassified counts according to the expected frequencies under a model.

As shown in Table 4.15, several models other than Hauser's topological model fit the data reasonably well. For example, the row-effect and the uniform-association models fit the data reasonably well ($BIC = -34.39, -25.98$) with diagonal cells blocked. The other two models that fit the data well are the quasi-symmetry ($BIC = -31.95$) and the crossings ($BIC = -28.88$) models.

4.5.4   Goodman's *RC* Model

If we further follow the path of generalization from the uniform association model to the row effect and column effect models, we may want to know what happens if we treat both the row and the column scores as unknown. In an influential paper published in the *Journal of the American Statistical Association* in 1979, Goodman addresses this question. Goodman's initial solution consists of two types of models, row-and-column-effects association model I and row-and-column-effects association model II (which was renamed as the *RC* model by Goodman (1981b) and is now commonly referred to by that name).

Goodman's association model I simplifies Eq. 4.20 into

$$\log F_{ij} = \mu + \mu_i^R + \mu_j^C + j\phi_i + i\varphi_j, \qquad (4.39)$$

Table 4.15: Goodness-of-Fit Statistics for Mobility Models

Model Specification	G^2	DF	BIC	Δ
Independence	6170.13	16	6011.74	20.07
Row effects	2080.18	12	1961.39	12.32
Uniform association (UA)	2280.69	15	2132.21	11.98
Quasi-independence	683.34	11	574.45	5.52
Row effect, diagonals deleted	34.91	7	−34.39	1.10
UA, diagonals deleted	73.01	10	−25.98	1.95
Hauser's topological model	66.57	12	−52.22	1.77
Quasi-symmetry	27.45	6	−31.95	1.13
Crossings (diagonals kept)	89.91	12	−28.88	2.12
Crossings (diagonals blocked)	64.24	9	−24.85	1.63

Note: Δ is the index of dissimilarity between observed and predicted frequencies (in percent).

where ϕ_i and φ_j are respectively row and column scores as in the row effect and column effect models. That is, model I can be seen as specifying the interaction term μ^{RC} of Eq. 4.20 as the sum of the interaction terms of the row effect and column effect models $(j\phi_i+i\varphi_j)$. However, it is necessary to add a scale normalization to either ϕ_i or φ_j, in addition to normalizing their locations. For example, one possible normalization is $\phi_1 = \varphi_1 = \varphi_J = 0$. The degrees of freedom for residuals equal $(I-2)(J-2)$. The general formula for LOR is

$$\log\left(\frac{F_{ij}F_{i'j'}}{F_{ij'}F_{i'j}}\right) = (\phi_i - \phi_{i'})(j - j') + (\varphi_j - \varphi_{j'})(i - i'), \qquad (4.40)$$

which is the sum of the weighted distances between the row scores and between the column scores. The reader should compare Eq. 4.40 to Eqs. 4.34 and 4.37. Similar to the row-effect and column-effect models, model I also assumes that the rows and columns are correctly ordered. This property means that the model is not invariant to positional changes in the categories of the row and column variables. If the researcher has no knowledge that the categories are correctly ordered, or in fact needs to determine the correct ordering of the categories, model I is of limited use. For this reason, Goodman's model II has received the most attention. It is of the form

$$\log F_{ij} = \mu + \mu_i^R + \mu_j^C + \phi_i \varphi_j, \qquad (4.41)$$

where ϕ_i and φ_j are respectively row and column scores collectively requiring three normalization constraints. One possible normalization is to set the location of both ϕ_i and φ_j (e.g., $\sum \phi_i = 0$ and $\sum \varphi_j = 0$) and the scale of either ϕ_i or φ_j (say $\sum \phi_i^2 = 1$). Model II has the same degrees of freedom as model I, $(I-2)(J-2)$, for only $I+J-3$ parameters are used to describe the row-column association. The model does not require the correct ordering of either the row or the column categories. The estimation of the scores (ϕ_i's and φ_j's) reveals the ordering of the categories implicit in the model. The LOR for any two pair of categories is

$$\log \left(\frac{F_{ij} F_{i'j'}}{F_{ij'} F_{i'j}} \right) = (\phi_i - \phi_{i'})(\varphi_j - \varphi_{j'}), \qquad (4.42)$$

which is the product of the distances between the row scores and between the column scores. Goodman's association model II is also called the log-multiplicative model (Clogg 1982), since two-way interaction is characterized by a multiplicative term involving two unknown parameters in Eq. 4.41. This creates some difficulty for estimation, which requires an iterative procedure, since ϕ_i and φ_j cannot be separated in a single estimation. The iterative procedure alternately treats one set of estimates (or initial values), say ϕ_i's, as known in updating the other set of estimates (or initial values), say φ_j's, until they stabilize.[3] Besides the GLIM macros available from this book's website, special-purpose computer packages for this type of model are also available (such as ASSOC and LEM).

The association models proposed by Goodman are parsimonious because the number of parameters for interactions increases by $(I+J-3)$ instead of $(I-1)(J-1)$ as in the saturated case. Obviously, the parsimony of these models can be achieved only with tables of a sufficiently large dimension. As a rule, the number of categories should be at least three for such models to be applicable.

---

[3]In standard packages such as GLIM, this procedure does not produce correct standard errors.

The dimensionality requirement is even clearer in light of interpretations of the estimated scores (ϕ_i's and φ_j's). As Clogg (1982) shows, the real meaning of the estimated scores lies in differences in intervals between two adjacent categories. Such differences in intervals are not meaningful for variables with less than three categories.

The log-multiplicative model of Eq. 4.41 can further be generalized to multiple dimensions, mimicking the case with multiple dimensions of observed attributes. This is called the $RC(m)$ model, extensively discussed by Goodman (1986) and Becker and Clogg (1989). In the multiple dimension case, it is convenient to reparameterize the unknown parameters differently by adding an unknown coefficient β and renormalizing

$$\log F_{ij} = \mu + \mu_i^R + \mu_j^C + \sum_m \beta_m \phi_{im} \varphi_{jm}, \qquad (4.43)$$

with

$$\sum \phi_{im} = 0; \qquad \sum \phi_{im}^2 = 1$$
$$\sum \varphi_{jm} = 0; \qquad \sum \varphi_{im}^2 = 1,$$

where β_m measures the strength of association for the mth dimension. For some applications, the researcher may wish to save degrees of freedom by constraining ϕ_{im} and φ_{jm} across m, and even between ϕ_{im} and φ_{jm} for square tables.

To illustrate the usefulness of the RC association model, let us take a look at one of Clogg's (1982) examples from the 1977 General Social Survey. The tabular data are reproduced in Table 4.16.

The row variable consists of patterns conforming to a Guttman scale measuring attitudes toward abortion. In parentheses are responses to questions asking whether legal abortion should be available to a woman under three different situations: (1) if she is not married and does not want to marry the man; (2) if the family has a very low income and cannot afford any more children; and (3) if a woman is married and does not want any more children. Given the varying severity of the three situations, most respondents fall into the patterns of approval of abortion under a more severe situation if they approve

Table 4.16: Attitudes Toward Abortion and Premarital Sex

Attitude	Attitude Toward Premarital Sex			
Toward Abortion	(1)	(2)	(3)	(4)
(1) Error	44	11	38	62
(2) (yes,yes,yes)	59	41	147	293
(3) (yes,yes,no)	23	11	13	27
(4) (yes,no,no)	27	8	16	27
(5) (no,no,no)	258	57	105	110

Note: For the column variable, (1) = Always Wrong; (2) = Almost Always Wrong; (3) = Sometimes Wrong; (4) = Not Wrong at All.

of abortion under a less severe situation. The first category of "Error" consists of respondents who do not neatly fall into the Guttman scale.

As is well known, Guttman scales yield only ordinal variables. That is, for our example, we only know that respondents in category (5) disapprove of abortion more strongly than those in category (4), and those in category (4) in turn disapprove of abortion more strongly than those in category (3), and so on. We do not know the relative distances separating the various categories. In addition, we do not know where the nonconforming respondents in category (1) belong.

Table 4.17: Estimated Scale Scores

	Row (Abortion)	Column (Premarital Sex)
(1)	0.075	−0.743
(2)	0.776	−0.127
(3)	−0.098	0.271
(4)	−0.155	0.598
(5)	−0.598	−

Clogg (1982) chose measured attitude toward premarital sex as an instrument in scaling the ordinal measure of the abortion attitude. To do this, Clogg applied the RC model to these data. We replicated Clogg's results using an iterative ML estimation procedure implemented as a GLIM macro, which is available from this book's website. We normalize the model using the convention in Eq. 4.43, thereby restricting both the location and scale of the row and column scores and freeing up an association parameter β. The estimated model fits the data very well ($G^2 = 5.55$ for 6 degrees of freedom; $BIC = -37.81$). The estimated scores are given in Table 4.17, with β estimated to be 1.308, which means a strong positive association between attitude toward abortion and attitude toward premarital sex.

These estimated parameters are essentially the same as those reported by Clogg, although they appear to be different due to different normalizations. The estimated scores should be interpreted in terms of relative distances. For example, the respondents in the first row category ("Error") are estimated to approve of abortion less strongly than those in category (2) but more strongly than those in other categories. It is important to emphasize that a shift of categories would not affect the estimation of the RC model. That is, although the RC model presumes the ordinal scale of the row and column variables, it does not require the correct ordering of the categories. Estimation reveals such ordering. For our data in Table 4.16, the column categories are correctly ordered. The row categories are not.

4.6   Models for Multiway Tables

Most studies in social science are concerned with relationships among variables, for such relationships often reveal underlying social processes. Two-way tables are the most basic form of representation relating observed variables to each other. In the last two decades, social researchers have fruitfully applied the loglinear models presented in the preceding sections in analyzing associations in two-way tables.

However, two-way tables are inherently limited because they contain little information. For example, two variables may be associated due to their common association with a third variable. When the third variable is controlled, the partial association between the two variables may be nil. To test for such "omitted-variable bias," it is necessary to bring other dimensions into a multivariate study.

Another common situation in which the researcher analyzes three-way or higher-way tables is when the key research interest lies in the variation of a two-way association along one or more dimensions. Examples include trend analysis and comparative analysis. We will review some examples in the sociological literature later in this section.

In the next section, we introduce loglinear models for the analysis of three- and higher-way contingency tables. We lump tables of three or higher dimensions under the general label of "multiway" tables. Although our discussion focuses only on models for three-way tables, generalization to higher-way models should be straightforward. It is also important to realize that the models for multiway tables are generalizations of the models presented earlier for two-way tables.

4.6.1   Three-Way Tables

Let R, C, and L respectively denote the row, column, and layer variables, with layer being the additional third variable. The three-way table of $R \times C \times L$ gives the detailed association among R, C, and L. In this three-way table, the researcher can obtain *partial* tables between any two variables (say R and C) while holding the third variable (L) constant at a given level. The R-C association in $R \times C$ partial tables is called the partial association. When the R-C partial association varies across different categories of L, it is said that there is three-way interaction involving R, C, and L. The researcher could also ignore the third variable (say L) and collapse the three-way table ($R \times C \times L$) into a two-way table, called the *marginal* table ($R \times C$), containing the marginal association between the two variables (R and C). In general, partial associations are different from marginal associations. Otherwise, the researcher would opt for simpler tables and model them statistically. In the next subsection, we will discuss conditions under which a partial association equals a marginal association.

In Table 4.18, we present a table pertaining to data on graduate admissions at the University of California-Berkeley. Table 4.18 involves three variables: sex of applicants (men versus women), admission outcome (admitted versus rejected), and major (A through F). The data came from a study looking into the allegation that graduate admission at the University of California-Berkeley was biased in favor of

Table 4.18: Graduate Admission Data from UC-Berkeley

| | Men | | Women | |
| | Number of | Percent | Number of | Percent |
Major	Applicants	Admitted	Applicants	Admitted
A	825	62%	108	82%
B	560	63%	25	68%
C	325	37%	593	34%
D	417	33%	375	35%
E	191	28%	393	24%
F	373	6%	341	7%

men against women (Bickel et al. 1975; Freedman, Pisani, and Purves 1978). For convenience, let us label sex R, admission outcome C, and major L. Although Table 4.18 presents the data in the form of proportions and counts for sex by major combinations, converting the table into frequencies by $R \times C \times L$ is easy.[4]

Table 4.18 shows clearly that the admission rate of women applicants is *not* appreciably lower than men applicants in any major. If there is a notable difference by sex, it is that women have a higher admission rate (at 82%) than men (at 62%) for major A. However, the relationship between sex and admission outcome looks very different if we collapse the data into a two-way marginal table over major. Table 4.19 is the resulting table.

Table 4.19: Collapsed Graduate Admission Data

Sex	No. of Applicants	% Admitted
Men	2691	45%
Women	1835	30%

Table 4.19 suggests that women have a much lower rate of admission (30%) than that of men (45%). Why do the two tables based on

---

[4]The converted frequency table is available from this book's website.

the same data tell us two different stories? Understanding this puzzle is essential to a multivariate analysis of tabular data.

4.6.2   The Saturated Model for Three-Way Tables

For the three-way table $R \times C \times L$, let f_{ijk} denote the observed frequency, and F_{ijk} the expected frequency for the cell indexed by the ith row, jth column, and kth layer. Analogous to Eq. 4.19, the saturated model for the three-way table can be written as

$$F_{ijk} = \tau \tau_i^R \tau_j^C \tau_k^L \tau_{ij}^{RC} \tau_{ik}^{RL} \tau_{jk}^{CL} \tau_{ijk}^{RCL}, \tag{4.44}$$

where the τ parameters are subject to usual normalization constraints. The loglinear form of the model is

$$\log F_{ijk} = \mu + \mu_i^R + \mu_j^C + \mu_k^L + \mu_{ij}^{RC} + \mu_{ik}^{RL} + \mu_{jk}^{CL} + \mu_{ijk}^{RCL}, \tag{4.45}$$

where the μ parameters are simply the logarithms of the τ parameters and are thus subject to the same normalization constraints. For the ANOVA-like normalization,

$$\prod_i \tau_i^R = \prod_j \tau_j^C = \prod_k \tau_k^L =$$
$$\prod_i \tau_{ij}^{RC} = \prod_j \tau_{ij}^{RC} = \prod_i \tau_{ik}^{RL} = \prod_k \tau_{ik}^{RL} = \prod_j \tau_{jk}^{CL} = \prod_k \tau_{jk}^{CL} =$$
$$\prod_i \tau_{ijk}^{RCL} = \prod_j \tau_{ijk}^{RCL} = \prod_k \tau_{ijk}^{RCL} = 1.$$
$$\tag{4.46}$$

Or, in terms of the μ parameters,

$$\sum_i \mu_i^R = \sum_j \mu_j^C = \sum_k \mu_k^L =$$
$$\sum_i \mu_{ij}^{RC} = \sum_j \mu_{ij}^{RC} = \sum_i \mu_{ik}^{RL} = \sum_k \mu_{ik}^{RL} = \sum_j \mu_{jk}^{CL} = \sum_k \mu_{jk}^{CL} =$$
$$\sum_i \mu_{ijk}^{RCL} = \sum_j \mu_{ijk}^{RCL} = \sum_k \mu_{ijk}^{RCL} = 0.$$
$$\tag{4.47}$$

Alternatively, we can use dummy-variable coding and set the following normalization constraints (with the first category as the reference):

$$
\begin{aligned}
\tau_1^R = \tau_1^C &= \tau_1^L = \\
\tau_{1j}^{RC} = \tau_{i1}^{RC} = \tau_{1k}^{RL} &= \tau_{i1}^{RL} = \tau_{1k}^{CL} = \tau_{j1}^{CL} = \\
\tau_{1jk}^{RCL} = \tau_{i1k}^{RCL} &= \tau_{ij1}^{RCL} = 1.
\end{aligned}
\tag{4.48}
$$

Or, in terms of the μ parameters,

$$
\begin{aligned}
\mu_1^R = \mu_1^C &= \mu_1^L = \\
\mu_{1j}^{RC} = \mu_{i1}^{RC} = \mu_{1k}^{RL} &= \mu_{i1}^{RL} = \mu_{1k}^{CL} = \mu_{j1}^{CL} = \\
\mu_{1jk}^{RCL} = \mu_{i1k}^{RCL} &= \mu_{ij1}^{RCL} = 0.
\end{aligned}
\tag{4.49}
$$

The τ^R, τ^C, and τ^L parameters in Eq. 4.44 (or μ^R, μ^C, and μ^L in Eq. 4.45) are called marginal parameters, τ^{RC}, τ^{RL}, and τ^{CL} (or μ^{RC}, μ^{RL}, and μ^{CL} in Eq. 4.45) two-way interactions, and τ^{RCL} (or μ^{RCL} in Eq. 4.45) three-way interactions. Since additive terms are easier to work with than multiplicative terms, the loglinear form of Eq. 4.45 is commonly used.

4.6.3   Collapsibility

Collapsibility is meaningful when research interest lies in the association between two particular variables. The question is whether the measured association differs before and after a table is collapsed from three-way to two-way. A three-way table is said to be collapsible if the partial association equals the marginal association when the three-way table is collapsed over the variable not involved in the association of primary interest. That is, a table is considered collapsible if marginal and partial relationships are identical.

To be more precise, let us say that we are primarily interested in the R-C association in the table of $R \times C \times L$. The table can be collapsed over L to the marginal two-way table of $R \times C$, if the marginal association in the $R \times C$ table is the same as the partial association between R and C conditional on L.

Conditions of collapsibility for the three-way table of $R \times C \times L$ into the two-way table of $R \times C$ follow:

1. There is no three-way RCL interaction: $\mu_{ijk}^{RCL} = 0$, for all i, j, and k.

2. *Either RL or CL* two-way interaction is nil: either $\mu_{ik}^{RL} = 0$ or $\mu_{jk}^{CL} = 0$, for all i, j, and k.

To appreciate these two conditions, let us review conditions for omitted variable bias in the linear regression context: an omitted variable may cause a bias to the estimated effect of the primary variable of interest on the dependent variable only if both of the following two conditions are true:

1. The omitted variable is (unconditionally) related to the primary variable of interest; and

2. The omitted variable affects the dependent variable.

When one of the two conditions is not met, there cannot be an omitted variable bias. For example, researchers can ignore other relevant explanatory variables in an experimental study because randomization ensures their independence with the primary variable of interest—experimental treatment.

By analogy, we can collapse a three-way table over the control variable if the control variable is unrelated either to the primary explanatory variable or to the outcome variable. Unlike the case for omitted variable bias in linear regressions, the condition of unrelatedness for collapsing contingency tables refers to partial association, not unconditional association. The collapsibility property is important in analysis of multiway contingency tables, for the researcher should always try to simplify the analysis whenever possible.

For our example of the admissions data, we can see that the two conditions of collapsibility do not hold if one attempts to collapse the data over major: Sex is related to major due to sex segregation by majors (i.e., $RL \neq 0$), and the proportion being admitted varies radically across majors (i.e., $CL \neq 0$). Given these conditions, collapsing results in a marginal association (as in Table 4.19) that is different from the partial association controlling for major (as in Table 4.18). As in the case of evaluating an omitted variable bias, we can infer the direction of the difference between the marginal association and the partial association. In our admissions example, RL and CL interactions are such that women applicants are poorly represented in majors where the proportion of being admitted is high (such as major A). This combination leads to a lower proportion of women being admitted if the three-way table is collapsed over the dimension of major.

One use of the collapsibility conditions is to purge rates of confounding effects of a third variable. Assuming no three-way interactions, Clogg (1978) proposed to purge the confounding factor of L in studying the association between R (primary explanatory variable) and C (outcome variable for the calculation of rates) by adjusting the frequencies according to

$$f^*_{ijk} = f_{ijk}/\tau^{RL}_{ik}, \qquad (4.50)$$

where f^* is the adjusted frequency to be used for calculating purged rates. This adjustment by Eq. 4.50 ensures that there is no partial association between R and L for the adjusted frequencies. Thus, the conditions of collapsibility are satisfied so that the third dimension L can be ignored in the adjusted table. Xie (1989) further proposed an alternative way to purge rates of confounding factors by meeting the conditions of collapsibility in a different way:

$$f^*_{ijk} = f_{ijk}/\tau^{CL}_{jk} \qquad (4.51)$$

(i.e., by eliminating the partial association between C and L). Clogg (1978) discussed ways to purge three-way interactions (τ^{RCL}) when present.

4.6.4   Classes of Models for Three-Way Tables

As in the case for two-way tables, the saturated model is seldom of research interest, for it simply parameterizes observed frequencies. Researchers often wish to construct more parsimonious models and test them against observed data. Let us now further simplify the saturated model of Eqs. 4.44 and 4.45 into the following special classes of models. From now on, we will use the loglinear notation of Eq. 4.45, although corresponding notation in terms of the multiplicative form of Eq. 4.44 can be easily obtained. We use a notation for models in which additive terms are separated by a comma, and interactions between variables are not separated. Unless explicitly stated, hierarchical structure of terms is maintained so that a higher-order interaction implicitly assumes the presence of lower-order interactions and marginal parameters. Thus, the saturated model of Eq. 4.45 can be denoted simply as (RCL).

Class 1: Let us first consider the "mutual independence" model, denoted as (R, C, L). The key feature of the model is that there are no interactions. Under this model, all two-way and three-way interactions are nil (i.e., $\mu^{RC} = \mu^{RL} = \mu^{CL} = \mu^{RCL} = 0$ for all i, j, and k). This model assumes that the three variables are independent of each other pairwise:

- R and C are independent;

- R and L are independent;

- C and L are independent.

Because there is no two-way interaction, the three-way table can be collapsed in all three dimensions. That is,

- marginal association = partial association = nil, for any pair of variables.

If the model holds true, it calls for a *univariate* analysis.

Class 2: Let us now consider the "joint independence" model, denoted as (R, CL), (RC, L), or (RL, C). This class of models allows only one two-way interaction. Hence, two sets of two-way interactions and the three-way interactions are nil. Let us use model (R, CL) as an illustration. In this case, $\mu^{RC} = \mu^{RL} = \mu^{RCL} = 0$ for all i, j, and k, so that R is independent with respect to the other two variables (C and L):

- R and L are independent;

- R and C are independent.

The three-way table is collapsible in all three dimensions. We have,

- marginal association = partial association, for any pair of variables. In addition,

- marginal RL and RC association = partial RL and RC = nil.

Class 3:   Let us further consider the model of "conditional independence," denoted as (RL, CL), (RC, CL), or (RC, RL). This class of models contains two two-way interactions. With (RL, CL) as our example, the conditional independence model means that R and C are independent of each other at each level of L:

- R and C are independent, given L.

The table is collapsible along R and C, but not along L. In other words,

- marginal RL and CL association = partial RL and CL association, but

- marginal RC association $\neq$ partial RC association (= nil).

This is an important model. It means that the marginal association (RC) may be spurious if one ignores a relevant variable (L), similar to an omitted-variable bias in linear regressions. As will be shown later, the graduate admission example fits this model rather well.

Class 4:   Finally, let us consider the "no three-way interaction" model (RC, RL, CL). This model allows for all three two-way interactions. It does not imply conditional independence. No three-way interaction implies homogeneous associations: partial two-way association does not vary with the third variable.

The table is not collapsible in any direction. That is,

- marginal two-way association $\neq$ partial two-way association, for any pair of variables.

Finally, when the (RC, RL, CL) model does not fit the data, partial two-way associations $(RC$, RL, and $CL)$ vary as a function of the third variable. This property is called heterogeneous association, which requires modeling of three-way interactions.

Table 4.20: Goodness-of-Fit Statistics of Models for Admission Data

Model	Parameter Terms	G^2	DF	BIC	Δ
(1)	(R, C, L)	2092.69	16	1958.01	25.98
(2)	(RL, C)	872.08	11	779.48	16.85
(3)	(RL, CL)	21.13	6	−29.37	1.66
(4)	(RL, CL, dummy)	2.81	5	−39.28	0.81

Note: R = sex, C = admission outcome, and L = major. Dummy refers to the cell where R = female, C = admitted, and L = major A. Δ is the index of dissimilarity between observed and predicted frequencies (in percent).

We now apply various models to the graduate admissions data earlier presented in Table 4.18. The data are of the dimension $2 \times 2 \times 6$ (for $R \times C \times L$), where R is sex, C is admission outcome, and L is major. Summary measures of fit for the various models are provided in Table 4.20. Model 1 is the mutual independence model, which does not fit the data ($G^2 = 2092.69$, for 16 degrees of freedom; $BIC = 1958.01$) but is presented here as a baseline for other models. Model 2 is a joint independence model allowing for the interaction between sex and major. In allowing for the interaction between sex and major, we bracket out the sex segregation of major as a pre-existing condition prior to the admission process. With $G^2 = 872.08$ for 11 degrees of freedom and $BIC = 779.48$, model 2 significantly improves upon model 1 in goodness-of-fit. In model 3, we further allow for the interaction between major and admission outcome and in effect specify conditional independence. There is no net association between sex and admission outcome conditional on major. Model 3 fits the data reasonably well

($G^2 = 21.13$ for 6 degrees of freedom, $BIC = -29.37$). Based on the BIC statistic, we may conclude that the data support the conditional independence hypothesis.

However, we observed earlier that female applicants seem to have an advantage in major A. Testing this specific three-way interaction, we add to model 4 a dummy variable denoting the cell where $R =$ female, $C =$ admitted, and $L =$ major A. As the goodness-of-fit statistics show, model 4 fits the data extremely well ($G^2 = 2.81$ for 5 degrees of freedom, $BIC = -39.28$). The final model means that conditional independence holds true for all majors except for major A, where there is a sex difference in admission rates. As shown in the estimated parameters presented in Table 4.21, the sex difference for major A is in favor of women, contrary to the criticism that the admission process at the University of California-Berkeley favors male applicants. From the parameter estimates, we also observe clearly that women applicants are underrepresented in majors A and B and overrepresented in majors C through F, and that the admission rate is higher in majors A and B than in other majors and is particularly low in major F.

Table 4.21: Estimates of Interaction Parameters of Model 4

Class of Parameters	Parameter	Estimate	(S.E)
Gender by Major	Female×Major A	–	–
	Female×Major B	−0.329	(0.311)
	Female×Major C	3.382	(0.244)
	Female×Major D	2.674	(0.244)
	Female×Major E	3.502	(0.250)
	Female×Major F	2.691	(0.245)
Admission by Major	Admitted×Major A	–	–
	Admitted×Major B	0.052	(0.112)
	Admitted×Major C	−1.106	(0.100)
	Admitted×Major D	−1.155	(0.104)
	Admitted×Major E	−1.572	(0.119)
	Admitted×Major F	−3.159	(0.168)
Dummy	Female, Major A, Admitted	1.027	(0.261)

4.6.5   Analysis of Variation in Association

The preceding subsection considered some common models for three-way tables. These models are primarily used to test the presence or absence of partial associations. From these tests, we are able to say whether a three-way table is collapsible over a dimension. We did not consider complicated cases beyond the no three-way interaction model.

What should we do if the no three-way interaction model does not fit the data? Fitting the saturated model is usually not a satisfactory answer, since the saturated model is not parsimonious. For the admissions example, we were able to identify a local three-way interaction by carefully examining the table.

We now consider a general situation where the research interest centers on the variation of a two-way association over a third dimension (or more generally a combination of other dimensions). Examples of this kind are plentiful in social science. For example, researchers studying comparative social mobility may be interested in whether the association between father's occupation and son's occupation varies systematically as a function of a nation's characteristics (Grusky and Hauser 1984). Family sociologists may be interested in whether educational assortative mating has strengthened over time (Mare 1991).

In this section, we recommend a "conditional" approach generalized from loglinear models for two-way tables for the analysis of variation in association. There are two advantages to this conditional approach. First, the researcher often can achieve parsimony. Second, parameters from such an approach are relatively easy to interpret.

Let us illustrate the approach with a three-way table of $R \times C \times L$ where the primary research interest lies in the analysis of R-C association over the dimension of L. Under the saturated model, the expected frequency is given in Eq. 4.44. Given the objective of analysis of variation in association over a third dimension, the researcher often wishes to begin with the model of conditional independence (RL, CL); that is,

$$F_{ijk} = \tau \tau_i^R \tau_j^C \tau_k^L \tau_{ik}^{RL} \tau_{jk}^{CL}, \qquad (4.52)$$

implying that there is no association between R and C given L. Compared to the saturated model of Eq. 4.44, we see that the baseline two-way interaction (τ^{RC}) and the three-way interaction (τ^{RCL}) are omitted in Eq. 4.52. The researcher typically focuses on the specification of τ^{RC} and τ^{RCL}. This is what we mean by a conditional approach, for the analysis of variation in association is now conditioned on Eq. 4.52. This point is made even clearer if we write out the local odds-ratio conditional on $L = k$ from the saturated model Eq. 4.44:

$$\theta_{ij|k} = \frac{F_{ijk}F_{(i+1)(j+1)k}}{F_{i(j+1)k}F_{(i+1)jk}} = \frac{\tau_{ij}^{RC}\tau_{(i+1)(j+1)}^{RC}}{\tau_{i(j+1)}^{RC}\tau_{(i+1)j}^{RC}}\frac{\tau_{ijk}^{RCL}\tau_{(i+1)(j+1)k}^{RCL}}{\tau_{i(j+1)k}^{RCL}\tau_{(i+1)jk}^{RCL}}. \qquad (4.53)$$

That is, the conditional odds-ratio depends only on the two-way interaction τ^{RC} parameters and the three-way interaction τ^{RCL} parameters.

There are many ways to parameterize τ^{RC} and τ^{RCL}. See Goodman (1986), Xie (1992), and Goodman and Hout (1998) for more thorough treatments of the subject. Note that both τ^{RC} and τ^{RCL} contain a R-C two-way association. The most common specification for τ^{RCL} is to interact a two-way R-C association pattern with layer. Let us say that τ^{RC} is modeled to follow a baseline association ω^{RC}, and τ^{RCL} is modeled by interacting a two-way cross-layer "deviation" association (ψ^{RC}) and layer (L). ω^{RC} and ψ^{RC} can be the same. With this notation, we will provide some general guidelines and illustrate them with a concrete example.

Recommendation 1:   It is desirable to have a simple model to reduce ω and ψ to just ψ. This is tantamount to specifying that the two-way R-C association has the same pattern across layers. When this is the case, we can set τ^{RC} to 1 and τ^{RCL} as interaction between ψ with L. This strategy requires that ψ be a more parsimonious specification than the full-interaction of R and C [i.e., consuming less than $(I - 1)(J - 1)$ degrees of freedom]. Otherwise, the resulting model is saturated. This strategy works because we only specify the same association function for the basic two-way association but allow the parameters for the function to differ across layers. For example, the researcher may specify a general RC association model at each layer and estimate the different RC parameters at different layers (Becker and Clogg 1989; Clogg 1982).

Recommendation 2: If it is necessary to give different specifications to the baseline association ω and the deviation association ψ, it is desirable to have a more parsimonious specification for ψ than for ω. This is intuitive because the number of parameters for the RCL three-way interaction (which is the interaction between ψ and L) multiplies quickly as the complexity of ψ increases. Researchers sometimes give a saturated model to ω in order to achieve a better fit. In Mare's (1991) study of trends in educational homogamy, for example, ω is the full interaction, but ψ is a crossings models with only four parameters. Interacting the four crossings parameters with time, Mare was able to show the trends in the strength of educational homogamy.

Recommendation 3: It is desirable to specify the log-multiplicative-layer specification between ψ and L rather than the simple interaction specification. This is particularly powerful if recommendation 1 is taken so that ψ and ω are the same. By the log-multiplicative-layer specification, we mean the following model (Xie 1992) (with $\omega = 1$):

$$F_{ijk} = \tau \tau_i^R \tau_j^C \tau_k^L \tau_{ik}^{RL} \tau_{jk}^{CL} \exp(\psi_{ij}\phi_k), \tag{4.54}$$

where the ψ parameters describe the R-C two-way deviation association, and ϕ's indicate the layer-specific deviations in the association. With this specification, the conditional local log-odds-ratio (from Eq. 4.53) is simplified to

$$\log(\theta_{ij|k}) = (\psi_{ij} + \psi_{(i+1)(j+1)} - \psi_{i(j+1)} - \psi_{(i+1)j})\phi_k$$
$$= \phi_k \log(\theta_{ij}),$$

where θ_{ij} is a function of the ψ parameters and can be thought of as the baseline odds-ratio. This log-multiplicative-layer model is parsimonious, for it only adds $(K - 1)$ degrees of freedom to test for three-way interactions, yielding a 1-degree-of-freedom test for each additional layer. In addition, at each layer, the R-C association follows the same pattern but with different strengths. See Goodman and Hout (1998) for a discussion of situations where $\omega \neq 1$.

We now provide an example where these three recommendations are put to practice. The example was drawn from a study of class mobility in three nations (England, France, and Sweden) conducted by Erikson, Goldthorpe, and Portocarero (1979). There are seven categories for both father's class and son's class, giving rise to a $7 \times 7 \times 3$ table. The same data were also analyzed by Hauser (1984) and Xie (1992). In Table 4.22, we present a series of models for these data. Both the data and the estimated models are available from this book's website.

Table 4.22: Models for Three-Nation Class Mobility Data

Model	Features	G^2	DF	BIC
CA	Conditional independence	4860.03	108	3812.57
FI_0	Homogeneous full-interaction	121.30	72	-577.01
FI_l	Heterogeneous full-interaction	0	0	0
FI_x	Log-multiplicative full-interaction	92.14	70	-586.77
H_0	Homogeneous levels model	244.34	103	-754.63
H_l	Heterogeneous levels model	208.50	93	-693.48
H_x	Log-multiplicative levels model	216.37	101	-763.20
RCQ_0	Homogeneous quasi-RC	337.86	76	-399.24
RCQ_l	Heterogeneous quasi-RC	271.97	54	-251.76
RCQ_x	Log-multiplicative quasi-RC	332.37	74	-385.34

In the first line of Table 4.22, we present the conditional independence model, which fits the data poorly ($G^2 = 4860.03$ for 108 degrees of freedom), as the null model. The second line is the homogeneous full-interaction model (FI_0), which is the same as the no three-way interaction model. Although model FI_0 fits the data reasonably well by the BIC statistic criterion, its heterogeneous form (simply interaction with layer) is the saturated model (FI_l). In the log-multiplicative-layer model with full-interaction as ψ (FI_x), we use 2 more degrees of freedom to test for systematic variation in the full-interaction across layer, providing a superior goodness-of-fit, by both the reduction in G^2 (29.16 for 2 degrees of freedom) and BIC (-586.77). The three H models are based on a topological pattern (with six levels). (The levels matrix is available from the book's website.) With this parsimonious baseline specification for the origin-destination association, the homogeneous levels model provides a reasonable fit to the data (notably $BIC = -754.63$) for 5 additional degrees of freedom beyond the CA model. Since the levels model is parsimonious, we can adopt the first recommendation and interact the levels matrix and layer, resulting in the heterogeneous levels model, H_l. Given the large sample size (16,297), Erikson, Goldthorpe, and Portocarero (1979) and Hauser (1984) choose to prefer model H_0 over model H_l, even though, strictly speaking, the chi-squared statistic between the two nested models (35.84 for 10 degrees of freedom) is significant. According to BIC, model H_0 has a lower negative value and thus fits the data better than model H_l. With the specification that the origin-destination association varies log-multiplicatively cross-nationally, model H_x is between models H_0 and H_l. By the log-likelihood-ratio chi-squared statistic, model H_x (G^2 of 216.37 with 101 degrees of freedom) fits the data significantly better than model H_0 ($\Delta G^2 = 27.97$ for 2 degrees of freedom) and not significantly worse than model H_l ($\Delta G^2 = 7.87$ with 8 degrees of freedom). Additionally, of all the models in Table 4.22, model H_x has the lowest BIC value and thus fits the data the best according to the BIC criterion.

In the last three lines of Table 4.22, we change the two-way association specification (ψ) from a levels model to an RC association model while blocking diagonals, called quasi-RC and denoted as RCQ. In this specification, the $\tau^{RC}\tau^{RCL}$ part of Eq. 4.44 becomes

$$\exp(\beta_k \phi_{ik} \varphi_{jk}) \quad \text{for } i \neq j.$$

Model RCQ_0 constrains all three parameters (β, ϕ, and φ) to be invariant across L, while RCQ_l allows them to vary freely with L. The log-multiplicative-layer version (RCQ_x) is intermediate in fixing the scores (ϕ and φ) but allowing the strength parameter β to vary by level. The results in Table 4.22 indicate that model RCQ_0 fits the data better than the other two versions of the RCQ model according to the BIC statistic.

One advantage of the log-multiplicative-layer model is that a simple parameter measuring the strength of association can be obtained for each table, subject to a global normalization. Xie (1992) capitalizes on this property to separate *levels* of mobility from *patterns* of mobility, the latter of which Xie assumes to be the same in all modern societies according to his revised interpretation of a classic hypothesis in the social mobility literature. We report these parameters for the three log-multiplicative models in Table 4.23. From these estimates, we can conclude a similar pattern regardless of model specification: the strength of the association between father's class and son's class is weaker in Sweden than in England and France but similar between England and France. This example shows that fine-tuning of two-way specifications (both baseline and deviation) sometimes has little consequence for the main research objective: detection of the variation in a two-way association along a third dimension.

Table 4.23: Nation-Specific ϕ Parameters

Model	ϕ_1 (England)	ϕ_2 (France)	ϕ_3 (Sweden)
FI_x	0.617	0.633	0.468
H_x	0.613	0.634	0.472
RCQ_x	0.652	0.575	0.495

4.6.6   Model Selection

In Table 4.22 we have selected models based on two criteria: the change in G^2 for nested models and BIC for nested as well as unnested models. We recommend using these and other goodness-of-fit criteria (including Pearson chi-squared statistic and the index of dissimilarity) in the course of model fitting.

The likelihood-ratio chi-squared test in terms of the change in G^2 is the most common method for selecting among competing nested models. The likelihood-ratio test has the advantage of having a familiar proportionate reduction in error interpretation, much like the F-test in OLS regression models and of being applicable to any model estimated with ML. The index of dissimilarity provides a descriptive measure, which is useful in assessing how well a model is able to reproduce the observed frequencies. The BIC statistic helps the researcher trade parsimony for goodness-of-fit in large samples, for which even a "good" model might be rejected by the G^2 statistic.

Chapter 5

Statistical Models for Rates

5.1 Introduction

This chapter outlines statistical models for analyzing change in a qualitative variable over time. The change from one qualitative status (or state) to another is referred to as a transition. Models for analyzing transitions come in many varieties and go by many names, such as event-history analysis, duration analysis, and hazard models. We use the term *transition rate* model or, simply, *rate* model.[1]

We distinguish between methods for nonrepeatable events and repeatable events. Data for the analysis of rates can come from cross-sectional or panel studies. Cross-sectional data are collected at one point in time but may convey retrospective information on the statuses of individuals at previous points in time. For example, a typical survey such as the National Longitudinal Survey of Youth provides information on timing of marriage and childbearing in any given survey year from which we can estimate marriage and fertility rates. Panel studies, with repeated measures on individuals at several points in time, provide prospective information on the status of individuals at different time points that can also be used to model transition rates.

---

[1]This chapter presents a condensed treatment of this subject matter. For a more complete review of this topic we refer the interested reader to any of the following sources: Allison (1984); Blossfeld, Hamerle, and Mayer (1989); Tuma and Hannan (1984); Yamaguchi (1991).

5.2   Log-Rate Models

An event may be defined as a change in status (or a transition from one qualitative state to another) within some specific interval of time. How transition rates are affected by other factors is of general interest to social scientists. For example, policy analysts may be interested in the correlates of exiting welfare for those initially on welfare or the determinants of leaving the labor force for those who are initially employed. Similarly, demographers may be interested in factors affecting life-course transitions such as birth, marriage, divorce, and death.

In its simplest form, a rate is defined as the number of individuals or observations possessing a particular characteristic divided by the total amount of exposure to the risk of having such characteristic. For example, a demographer computes the mortality rate as the ratio of the number of deaths that occur during a given year to the number of person-years lived by the population in a single year. Multiplying this by 1,000 yields the mortality rate per thousand persons in the population per year.

In this sense, the concept of a rate is not unlike that of a proportion. Despite the similarities, there are a number of conceptual differences. As outlined in Chapter 3, a proportion is defined as the number of events (successes) divided by the number of trials. The concept of rate, unlike that of proportion, is a dynamic one that depends critically on the concept of exposure, which for a given individual, is defined as the length of time that an initial state is occupied before a transition to another state occurs. The term *rate*, or *transition rate*, is a measure of the instantaneous probability (per unit of time) of an event occurrence.

When data can be grouped, it is often convenient to array events in the form of a contingency table. In the case of individual-level data and a single nonrepeatable event, the events are binary variables taking the value 1 if the event occurs and 0 otherwise. The same statistical procedures can be used with either grouped or ungrouped data.

In addition to events, an analysis of rates also involves a consideration of the duration (or waiting time) spent in the initial state. Individuals differ in the amount of time spent at risk, and this differential exposure is likely to be influenced by a number of explanatory factors.

Duration, or waiting time, is regarded as a continuous variable whose value is observed only when an event occurs. It is often the case that a portion of the population will not experience events within the observation period or will be removed from risk for other reasons. In such cases, event times are said to be censored on the right (or *right censored*). Methods for the analysis of event-histories are uniquely suited to take this aspect of the data into account. For example, suppose we are interested in modeling the risk of premarital birth using a random sample of young women with retrospective information on the dates and occurrence of first birth and first marriage. By definition, those who marry before giving birth are not at risk of premarital births. As a result, their event times are right censored at their marriage dates. Similarly, the waiting times for those who do not marry or experience a premarital birth by the time of the survey or last observation are right censored.

Researchers use individual-level or cross-classified data to model rates as functions of independent variables and interaction terms. Occurrence (event counts) and exposure (cumulative waiting time at risk) are two key concepts used in modeling rates.

5.2.1   The Role of Exposure

The concept of exposure plays a key role in the analysis of rates. Exposure necessarily involves both an accounting of the number of individuals at risk and their respective waiting times at risk. In the earlier example, the yearly mortality rate was expressed in terms of incidence per thousand persons per year. In this example, exposure consists of the number of person-years at risk. In examining yearly mortality rates, all individuals alive at the beginning of the year are at risk of dying over the period of one year, so there is only one year of accumulated risk per individual. In this case, the number of person-years of exposure is identical to the number of individuals exposed to risk. Demographers often make the assumption that exposure in an interval equals the number entering the interval minus half of those dying in an interval, thus assuming a uniform distribution of deaths throughout the interval.[2] In our example, we assume that events take place at the end of the interval.

Cross-sectional survey data may also yield retrospective individual-level information on the waiting times to events. This information, either in individual or tabular form, can be used to estimate transition rates. The following example illustrates how individual-level data may be aggregated and used to model rates.

Suppose we are interested in comparing completion rates for two academic programs using retrospective survey data. We will assume that students entered one of two programs, Track 1 or Track 2. Table 5.1 shows the number of months a student takes to complete the program, along with a binary variable indicating whether or not the student graduated. Reasons for failing to complete the program could include withdrawal or failure to "graduate" from the program in the observation period. The waiting times to completion for these individuals are right censored. Right censored times constitute unobserved or missing data insofar as we know only an individual's time at risk up to the time they were last observed. We require the simplifying assumption that the processes governing censoring and event occurrence are independent from one another.

At this point, we might consider carrying out an analysis using the binary variable for graduation. However, this would ignore information about the time spent in the program. Rather than focusing only on the binary variable for the event "Graduate," we need to focus on the duration variable (T), measured as months to completion of the program. How can we estimate the completion rate using data such as those in Table 5.1?

Statistical Concepts Underlying Rate Models

Considering the sample as a whole, let $t_1, t_2, \ldots, t_n$ denote the waiting times for n individuals, with distribution function $F(t) = \Pr(T < t)$ and probability density function $f(t)$. The hazard rate, transition rate, intensity function, or failure rate is denoted by $\lambda(t)$. The hazard

---

[2]Letting N denote the number entering the interval and D denote the number dying in an interval, the rate is calculated as $D/(N - 0.5D)$.

Table 5.1: Waiting Time to Program Completion

Program Track	Months to Completion	Graduate
1	12	Yes
1	24	No
1	6	Yes
1	13	No
1	16	Yes
1	24	No
2	5	Yes
2	18	Yes
2	20	No
2	8	Yes
2	10	Yes
2	17	No

rate can be viewed as the instantaneous probability of an event in the interval $[t, t+\Delta t]$, given that the event has not already occurred before the beginning of the interval. More formally, the hazard rate is the limit of a conditional probability (or transition probability),

$$\lambda(t) = \lim_{\substack{\Delta t \to 0 \\ \Delta t > 0}} \frac{1}{\Delta t} \Pr[t \le T < t + \Delta t | T \ge t]. \qquad (5.1)$$

The probability of surviving to time t is given by the survival function,

$$S(t) = \Pr[T > t] = 1 - F(t) = \int_t^\infty f(u)du, \qquad (5.2)$$

which is the complement of the cumulative distribution function [i.e., $S(t) = 1 - F(t)$].

In general, $F(t)$ could be a distribution function corresponding to any non-negative random variable, and we could derive the corresponding hazard and survivor functions. If we assume that waiting times follow an exponential distribution with density function $f(t) = \lambda \exp(-\lambda t_i)$, the expression for the survival function in Eq. 5.2 is

$S(t) = \exp(-\lambda t_i)$. The expression for the hazard rate of Eq. 5.1 can be defined as the ratio $\lambda(t) = f(t)/S(t) = \lambda$. The exponential distribution implies a constant hazard over time [i.e., $\lambda(t)$ does not depend on t].

Estimation with Censored Data

Estimates of the hazard rate (λ) can be obtained using several of the methods outlined in this book, such as maximum likelihood or iteratively reweighted least squares. For ML estimation, we consider the distinct contributions to the likelihood function when t represents an event time (i.e., t is observed) and when t represents a censoring time (i.e., t is missing). In the preceding example, if a student graduates, then t is an event time. If they fail to graduate, we know only that their event time is greater than t. The duration data for individuals who do not experience events are right censored. It is convenient to define an indicator variable $d_i = 1$ if t is an event time, and $d_i = 0$ if t is right censored. For the data in Table 5.1, this is the binary variable for "Graduate." Under the model of a constant hazard, the individual contributions to the likelihood function are then

$$L_i = \begin{cases} f(t) = \lambda \exp(-t_i \lambda) & \text{if } d_i = 1, \\ S(t) = \exp(-t_i \lambda) & \text{if } d_i = 0. \end{cases} \tag{5.3}$$

Combining this with the event/censoring indicator and taking the log results in a simpler expression for the ith individual's contribution to the log-likelihood function:

$$\log L_i = d_i \log \lambda - t_i \lambda. \tag{5.4}$$

The sample log-likelihood is

$$\log L = \sum_{i=1}^{n} \log L_i = \sum_{i=1}^{n} (d_i \log \lambda - t_i \lambda). \tag{5.5}$$

Solving the likelihood equation gives the MLE as $\hat{\lambda} = \sum d_i / \sum t_i = D/E = 7/173 = 0.0405$, the total number of events (D) divided by the total time "exposed to the risk" (E) of graduation. $\widehat{\lambda}$ is an estimate of the "central rate," which implies a completion rate of 4 students per 100 per month. The estimated variance of $\widehat{\lambda}$ is $\widehat{\lambda}^2 / \sum t_i = \widehat{\lambda}^2 / E = 0.0002$. This information can be used to construct a 95% confidence interval around λ, as

$$\lambda = \widehat{\lambda} \pm z_{\alpha/2} \sqrt{\mathrm{var}(\widehat{\lambda})}$$
$$= 0.0405 \pm 1.96(0.014) \tag{5.6}$$
$$= [0.0131, 0.0679].$$

With no loss of information, these data can be presented in the form of an occurrence-exposure matrix as in Table 5.2. Let D_j $(j = 1, 2)$ denote the total number graduating from each program. Similarly, let E_j denote the number of person-months at risk in each program.

The empirical rates are calculated as $\widehat{\lambda}_j = D_j / E_j$, $(j = 1, 2)$, giving estimated graduation rates $\widehat{\lambda}_1 = 0.0316$ for Track 1 and $\widehat{\lambda}_2 = 0.0513$ for Track 2.

Table 5.2: Occurrence-Exposure Matrix for Data in Table 5.1

	Program Track 1	Program Track 2
Occurrences (D_j)	3	4
Exposure (E_j)	95	78

More generally, the hazard rate for the ith individual (λ_i) can be expressed as a function of a set of K independent variables, $\mathbf{x}_i = (x_{i1}, x_{i2}, \ldots, x_{iK})'$ and unknown parameters, $\boldsymbol{\beta} = (\beta_1, \beta_2, \ldots, \beta_K)'$. Using the standard index-function notation, the hazard rate can be written as[3]

$$\lambda_i = \lambda_0 \exp\left(\sum_k \beta_k x_{ik}\right) \qquad k = 1, \ldots, K \tag{5.7}$$
$$= \lambda_0 \exp(\mathbf{x}_i' \boldsymbol{\beta}).$$

---

[3]This form of the hazard function guarantees that the estimated rate is always positive.

This expression shows that independent variables act multiplicatively on the baseline hazard, λ_0. With no loss of generality, the baseline hazard term (λ_0) can be absorbed into the intercept term as

$$\lambda_i = \exp(\sum_k \beta_k x_{ik}) \qquad k = 0, \dots, K$$
$$= \exp(\mathbf{x}_i'\boldsymbol{\beta}), \tag{5.8}$$

where x_{i0} is 1 for all individuals, accounting for the constant term. In this parameterization, covariates act additively on the log-rate, $\log \lambda_i$.[4]

With exponentially distributed waiting times, the likelihood from this model can be written as

$$L = \prod_{i=1}^{n} \lambda_i^{d_i} \exp(-t_i \lambda_i)$$
$$= \prod_{i=1}^{n} \exp(\mathbf{x}_i'\boldsymbol{\beta})^{d_i} \exp\{-t_i \exp(\mathbf{x}_i'\boldsymbol{\beta})\}. \tag{5.9}$$

When the independent variables are categorical (or can be treated as such), the data can be grouped as in Table 5.2. For a contingency table with J cells, the data likelihood can be expressed in terms of the cell-specific occurrences (D_j) and exposures (E_j) ($j = 1, \dots, J$) as

$$L = \prod_{j=1}^{J} \lambda_j^{D_j} \exp(-E_j \lambda_j). \tag{5.10}$$

5.2.2   Estimating Log-Rate Models

A general estimation approach outlined by Holford (1980) and Laird and Oliver (1981), which applies to situations involving either grouped

---

[4]Many statistical packages such as SAS and LIMDEP estimate accelerated failure time models in $\log t_i$, instead of $\log \lambda(t)$. The accelerated failure time exponential model is written as $\log t_i = \mathbf{x}_i'\boldsymbol{\beta} + \varepsilon_i$, where ε follows an extreme-value distribution. In this specification, covariates act to lengthen or shorten the time to the event. A covariate that increases the risk decreases the waiting time to the event. Thus, the estimated covariate effects from accelerated failure time models have signs opposite to those from hazard rate models.

data or ungrouped data, exploits the similarity between the distribution functions of exponential and Poisson variables. If events occur repeatedly over time, and if the times between events are independent exponential variables with mean $E(T) = 1/\lambda$ (i.e., a time-homogeneous Poisson process), then the probability of d events in a time interval of length t is given by the Poisson probability function,

$$\Pr(d \mid \lambda, t) = \frac{(t\lambda)^d \exp(-t\lambda)}{d!}. \tag{5.11}$$

The mean number of events in time interval t is $\mu = t\lambda$. For a sample of size n, we can model the *conditional* mean count as a function of independent variables, so that for the ith individual, the expected number of events in time interval t is

$$\mu_i = t_i \lambda_i = t_i \exp(\mathbf{x}_i'\boldsymbol{\beta}).$$

The likelihood is a product of the individual Poisson probabilities in Eq. 5.11 and is proportional to

$$L = \prod_{i=1}^{n} (t_i \lambda_i)^{d_i} \exp(-t_i \lambda_i). \tag{5.12}$$

To show the equivalence between Poisson regression and the exponential rate model, note that exponential likelihood in Eq. 5.9 can also be written as

$$L = \prod_{i=1}^{n} (t_i \lambda_i)^{d_i} \exp(-t_i \lambda_i) / \prod_{i=1}^{n} t_i^{d_i}, \tag{5.13}$$

where the term in the denominator does not depend on unknown parameters and can be ignored for the purposes of estimating $\boldsymbol{\beta}$. Thus, the likelihood for the exponential rate model factors into an expression that is proportional to the Poisson likelihood.[5] Therefore, maximizing

---

[5]For this statistical relationship to hold, the events must correspond to n independent, time-homogeneous Poisson processes with rates λ_i. The number of events for the ith process in a time interval of length t follows a Poisson distribution with mean $t_i \lambda_i$. The observed number of events (d_i) is not 0,1,2,3,..., but 0 or 1. This is equivalent to observing the ith process until either a *first* event occurs, or a fixed time, t_i, has elapsed without the event occurring. See Barlow and Proschan (1975:64) for a discussion on the relationship between Poisson models and exponential rate models.

Eq. 5.12 yields the same MLEs as maximizing Eq. 5.9.[6] This means that the exponential hazard *rate* model can be estimated using a Poisson regression model for *counts*. Taking logs of the Poisson mean $(\mu_i = t_i \lambda_i)$, we obtain the following loglinear regression model:

$$\log \mu_i = \log t_i + \log \lambda_i$$
$$= \log t_i + \mathbf{x}_i' \boldsymbol{\beta}. \tag{5.14}$$

The term $\log t_i$ appearing in this model has a fixed coefficient of one and is known as an offset. To fit these models using software for Poisson regression, we declare the log exposure as an offset term in the model.

IRLS Estimation

The log-rate model can be estimated as a standard loglinear model with an offset term equal to the logged exposure. Maximum likelihood estimation or iteratively reweighted least squares will result in identical parameter estimates. The generalized linear model technique is straightforward and is implemented in several statistical packages. Letting $\eta_i = \sum_{k=1}^K \beta_k x_{ik} = \mathbf{x}_i' \boldsymbol{\beta}$ denote the linear structural component of the model, iteratively reweighted least squares is applied to

$$\widehat{z}_i = \widehat{\eta}_i + (y_i - \widehat{\mu}_i)/\widehat{\mu}_i, \tag{5.15}$$

where $\widehat{\mu}_i = t_i \exp(\widehat{\eta}_i)$, and model weights are given by $\widehat{W}_i = \widehat{\mu}_i$. Applying the IRLS technique to the data in Tables 5.1 and 5.2, with $x_i = 1$ for Track 2 and 0 otherwise, yields the following estimates (standard errors): $\widehat{\beta}_0 = -3.456$ (0.577), $\widehat{\beta}_1 = 0.485$ (0.764).

5.2.3   Illustration

Extensions to higher dimensional tables are straightforward. Table 5.3 presents occurrence-exposure data on premarital births to young women in the NLSY from 1979 to 1988 by race (White/Nonwhite) and family structure (Intact/Nonintact). The data have been cross-classified by age at premarital birth or censoring. Three age intervals

---

[6]The $d!$ term appearing in the denominator of Eq. 5.11 does not depend on unknown parameters, so it can be effectively ignored for estimating $\boldsymbol{\beta}$.

are chosen to represent distinct periods of risk corresponding to early, middle, and late teenage years. The rate of premarital births is assumed to be constant within any age interval but may change over age intervals. Models of this type are known as piecewise constant rate models. Piecewise constancy offers a flexible way of accounting for changing rates over time and allows the researcher to incorporate covariates that change in value over some predetermined time intervals.[7]

Table 5.3: Teen Premarital Births by Age, Race, and Family Structure

| | Intact | | | | Nonintact | | | |
| | White | | Nonwhite | | White | | Nonwhite | |
Age	D	E	D	E	D	E	D	E
14–16	17	13220	33	13838	10	7332	68	12827
16–18	39	10266	104	9823	42	5417	160	8516
18–20	43	3552	112	3331	42	1599	128	2594

The cell-specific exposure, E_i, is in the form of person-months from age 14 to age at premarital birth or censoring. D_i denotes cell-specific number of events. Table 5.4 shows the same data expressed in column format suitable for input to standard computer packages.

A loglinear model (log-rate model) is fit to the observed counts, D_i, with $\log E_i$ as offset. The variables to be included in selected models include dummy variables for the age interval of first premarital birth, A ($A_2 = 1$ for ages 16–18, 0 otherwise; $A_3 = 1$ for ages 18–20, 0 otherwise), family structure, NI (coded 1 if nonintact, 0 otherwise), and race, NW (coded 1 if nonwhite, 0 otherwise). We fit two additional two-way interaction models. It is convenient to summarize selected models using an analysis of deviance as in Table 5.5. Programs for loglinear modeling typically report the deviance (or G^2 statistic). As outlined in Chapters 3 and 4, differences in G^2 values are distributed as χ^2 and are used to evaluate nested models.

Model 1 fits only the baseline age-specific (log) rates; model 2 adds the main effects of race and family structure. Models 3 and 4 fit two-

---

[7]We will provide a more detailed derivation of this model later in this chapter.

Table 5.4: Column-Formatted Data from Table 5.3

Number of Events (D)	Person-Months of Exposure (E)	Age Interval (A)	Family Structure (NI)	Race (NW)
17	13220	1	0	0
39	10266	2	0	0
43	3552	3	0	0
33	13838	1	0	1
104	9823	2	0	1
112	3331	3	0	1
10	7332	1	1	0
42	5417	2	1	0
42	1599	3	1	0
68	12827	1	1	1
160	8516	2	1	1
128	2594	3	1	1

way interaction terms. Model 4 is of particular interest as it tests for proportional covariate effects. That is, race and family structure may have different impacts on premarital birth rates in the early and late teen years. For example, do the effects of family structure diminish over adolescence, or do ascriptive factors such as race have constant effects over time? The analysis of deviance of nested models shows that the best model for these data is the main effects model. This model may be written as

$$\log \mu_i = \log E_i + \beta_0 + \beta_1 A_{2i} + \beta_2 A_{i3} + \beta_3 NI_i + \beta_4 NW_i. \qquad (5.16)$$

Estimates (and standard errors) from this model are given in Table 5.6. Note that we could have excluded the intercept term from this model. This feature is available in most programs for loglinear modeling. This reparameterization allows us to estimate the age effects directly, which is useful when calculating age-specific rates and their standard errors. The resulting model can be written as

$$\log \mu_i = \log E_i + \beta_1 A_{1i} + \beta_2 A_{2i} + \beta_3 A_{3i} + \beta_3 NI_i + \beta_4 NW_i. \qquad (5.17)$$

Table 5.5: Analysis of Deviance

Model	Description	G^2	DF
1	A	228.965	9
2	$A + NI + NW$	6.977	7
3	$A + NI + NW + NI \times NW$	6.352	6
4	$A + NI + NW + NI \times A + NW \times A$	5.461	3

These estimates are given in the second panel of Table 5.6.

Table 5.6: Estimated Effects on the Risk of Teen Premarital Births

Variable	$\widehat{\beta}$	$\exp(\widehat{\beta})$	$\widehat{\beta}$	$\exp(\widehat{\beta})$
Constant	−6.808	0.001	−	−
	(0.115)			
Age 14–15	−	−	−6.808	0.001
			(0.115)	
Age 16–18	1.350	3.857	−5.458	0.004
	(0.104)	(0.104)	(0.089)	
Age 18–20	2.433	11.393	−4.375	0.013
	(0.104)		(0.089)	
Nonintact	0.561	1.752	0.561	1.752
	(0.072)		(0.072)	
Nonwhite	0.905	2.472	0.905	2.472
	(0.083)		(0.083)	

5.2.4   Interpretation

Coefficients estimated from Poisson regression models with an offset term may be interpreted as additive effects on the log rate. In the teen premarital birth example of Table 5.6, the constant term represents the log rate of premarital birth for those aged 14–16. Exponentiating this term, we are able to retrieve the age-specific premarital birth rate for 14–16 year old Whites from intact families of $e^{-6.808} = 0.0011$ (or 11 per ten thousand per month). For those aged 16–18 and 18–20, the premarital birth rates, for the same race and family structure, are $e^{(-6.808+1.35)} = 0.0043$ (or 43 per ten thousand per month) and $e^{(-6.808+2.433)} = 0.0126$ (or 126 per ten thousand per month), respectively. Thus the relative risk of a premarital birth for those aged 16–18 is $e^{1.35} = 3.86$ times higher than for those aged 14–16. Similarly, the relative risk for women aged 18–20 is $e^{2.43} = 11.36$ times that for those aged 14–16. Net of age effects, nonwhite women face a risk that is $e^{.905} = 2.47$ times that of Whites. Similarly, young women from non-intact families face a risk that is 1.75 times higher than those residing with both biological parents at age 14.

A different normalization of the parameters using centered effects (ANOVA) coding would permit an alternative interpretation of the effects. Because centered effects coding constrains the sum of the effects over different "levels" of a categorical variable to be zero, we can estimate the extent to which the risk differs from the "average" risk.

5.3   Discrete-Time Hazard Models

We can extend the notion of log-rate models to encompass situations in which the exact timing of the event is unknown, as might occur with a panel data design. The methods used to model event occurrences or transition rates from panel data, or in instances where events take place at well-defined time points, have come to be known as discrete-time hazard models.[8] For example, it is often the case that events of interest to social scientists occur at fixed time points rather than at any possible time point along a continuum. Elections, for example, may take place every 2 or 4 years, and graduation generally takes place at the end of school terms. In other cases, the exact timing of events is unavailable due to inaccuracies in the way information is reported or recorded. For example, a panel study may record the status occupied at the survey date but may lack information on how long the state has been occupied. We may know that a person is employed, unemployed,

---

[8] For a more complete review of discrete-time hazard models, see Allison (1982).

or out of the labor force during the survey week in any survey year, but we might lack information about the duration in the initial state. Nevertheless, such data are used routinely to model events or transition probabilities.

5.3.1   Data Structure

Individual-level data can be used to construct discrete-time event-history models. The components for the discrete-time model using individual-level data consist of measurements of variables over two or more panel waves. Suppose that there are n observations followed over q points in time. Let T denote a discrete variable taking the values $t = 1, \ldots, q$. We let y_{it} $(i = 1, \ldots, n)$ denote a binary variable equal to 1 if an event occurs to the ith observation at time t, and 0 otherwise. This sequence of binary data represents the discrete-time event history, or sample path, for the ith individual. The conditional probability that an event occurs at time t given that it has not yet occurred is the discrete-time hazard rate

$$
\begin{aligned}
p_{it} &= \Pr(y_{it} = 1 \mid y_{it-1} = 0, y_{it-2} = 0, \ldots, y_{i0} = 0) \\
&= \Pr(T_i = t \mid T_i \geq t).
\end{aligned}
\tag{5.18}
$$

In most applications, either a logistic or complementary log-log transformation is used to ensure that predicted values of p_{it} lie in the $[0,1]$ range. Therefore, the discrete-time hazard for the ith individual in time period t can be written as a function of K fixed or time-varying independent variables, $\mathbf{x}'_{it} = (x_{i1t}, x_{i2t}, \ldots, x_{iKt})$, as either a logit model,

$$
p_{it} = \frac{\exp(\alpha_t + \mathbf{x}'_{it}\boldsymbol{\beta})}{1 + \exp(\alpha_t + \mathbf{x}'_{it}\boldsymbol{\beta})},
\tag{5.19}
$$

or a complementary log-log model,

$$
p_{it} = 1 - \exp\{-\exp(\alpha_t + \mathbf{x}'_{it}\boldsymbol{\beta})\}.
\tag{5.20}
$$

The α_t terms in these models allow for an intercept parameter for each distinct time point. These may be thought of as the baseline time-specific logged rates. It is also possible to introduce time dependence in other ways, such as with polynomials in t of the form

$$p_{it} = 1 - \exp\{-\exp(\alpha_1 t + \alpha_2 t^2 + \alpha_3 t^3 +, \cdots, +\alpha_q t^q + \mathbf{x}'_{it}\boldsymbol{\beta})\}. \quad (5.21)$$

5.3.2   Estimation

Estimation of the discrete-time model is simplified by arranging the data in the appropriate format. In order to account for exposure, the data are usually arranged in the form of person-years (assuming a yearly panel design). For example, suppose that we begin with a sample of individuals at risk of experiencing a particular event. Suppose there are n individuals at risk of becoming unemployed at the beginning of a five-year panel study. Let $y_{it} = 1$ if the individual is unemployed at time t, and 0 otherwise. The sequence of binary y-values that we might observe is given in Table 5.7.

Table 5.7: Sequences of Observed Binary Responses Over a Five-Wave Panel

	Year				
	1	2	3	4	5
Person	y_1	y_2	y_3	y_4	y_5
1	0	0	1	1	0
2	0	0	0	0	0
3	0	1	0	0	1
$\vdots$	$\vdots$	$\vdots$	$\vdots$	$\vdots$	$\vdots$
n	0	1	1	0	0

The first individual's sequence is characterized by 2 years of employment followed by 2 years of unemployment and 1 year more of employment. The remaining individuals' sequences could be similarly described. The main concern in an event-history analysis of a single event is not the overall pattern in the data, but rather the event occurrence and the accumulation of time at risk up to and including an event or censoring. In the hypothetical data in Table 5.7, the first and third individuals experienced unemployment in the third and second year, respectively.[9] The second individual's event time is right censored; we know only that he or she remained employed, or was observed as employed, for all five survey years.

To estimate the discrete-time model, we need to find the probability that an individual remains employed (i.e., survives) past time t given that they are employed until time t. Recall that p_{it} represents the conditional probability that an individual experiences an event (i.e., becomes unemployed) at time t having been employed up to time t. It follows that the conditional probability of surviving (i.e., being employed) until just after time t is given by

$$\Pr(T_i > t \mid T_i \geq t) = 1 - p_{it}. \tag{5.22}$$

The discrete-time survivor function can be expressed as the product of the conditional probabilities of having "survived" all previous time points or time intervals, as

$$S_{it} = \Pr(T_i \geq t) = \prod_{s=1}^{t-1}(1 - p_{is}). \tag{5.23}$$

The unconditional event probability (or probability of experiencing the event at time t) is the discrete-time analog of the continuous-time probability distribution function and may be written as

$$
\begin{aligned}
\Pr(T_i = t) &= \Pr(T_i = t \mid T_i \geq t)\Pr(T_i \geq t) \\
&= p_{it}S_{it} \\
&= p_{it}\prod_{s=1}^{t-1}(1 - p_{is}).
\end{aligned}
\tag{5.24}
$$

The likelihood function for the discrete-time model can be written by combining the various terms mentioned earlier. When t is an event time, the individual contribution to the likelihood is the discrete-time counterpart of the density function (pdf). Individuals censored just

---

[9]We will assume that individuals are at risk of the event up to but not including time t, although other assumptions about the period of risk are possible.

prior to t contribute S_{it}. Thus, the individual contribution to the sample likelihood can be summarized as

$$L_i = \begin{cases} \Pr(T_i = t) & \text{if } y_{it} = 1, \\ \Pr(T_i \geq t) & \text{if } y_{it} = 0. \end{cases} \tag{5.25}$$

Taking logs and using the preceding expressions, we can write the individual contribution to the log-likelihood as

$$\log L_i = y_{it} \log p_{it} + \sum_{s=1}^{t-1} \log(1 - p_{is})$$
$$= \sum_{s=1}^{t} [y_{is} \log p_{is} + (1 - y_{is}) \log(1 - p_{is})]. \tag{5.26}$$

The log-likelihood on the data is the sum of the individual contributions

$$L = \sum_{i=1}^{n} \sum_{s=1}^{t} [y_{is} \log p_{is} + (1 - y_{is}) \log(1 - p_{is})], \tag{5.27}$$

which, aside from the second summation sign, is the formula for the log-likelihood of a binary dependent variable.

Maximum likelihood estimates of the parameters of this model can be obtained by a number of computer packages. To make use of standard binomial modeling software, we need to account for accumulated risk implied by the extra summation sign. The easiest way to do this is by constructing an event-oriented or split-episode data file. In an event-oriented file based on the yearly panel in Table 5.7, the data would be arrayed as person-year observations (or *pseudo-observations*), which allow individuals to contribute a varying number of records to the likelihood expression in Eq. 5.27, depending on when and if they experience an event over the course of the panel. In our example, the first individual's event history would be represented by three pseudo-observations, while the second individual would contribute five pseudo-observations.

Table 5.8 illustrates how this particular data would be arranged. This arrangement of data allows both fixed and time-varying covariates. Variables like race/ethnicity and sex—that remain fixed over

Table 5.8: Layout of a Hypothetical Event-Oriented Data File

Case	y	Sex	Race	Marital Status	Age
1	0	Male	White	Married	35
1	0	Male	White	Divorced	36
1	1	Male	White	Divorced	37
2	0	Female	Black	Married	27
2	0	Female	Black	Married	28
2	0	Female	Black	Married	29
2	0	Female	Black	Married	30
2	0	Female	Black	Married	31
3	0	Male	White	Single	23
3	1	Male	White	Single	24

time—and variables such as marital status and age—that can change on a yearly basis—can be incorporated easily into an analysis. In this example, we see that marital status changes for case 1 but remains fixed for the remaining observations.

Application

Table 5.9 reports coefficients from a discrete-time hazard regression model based on a random sample of young White males from the NLSY. A complementary log-log link is used for this example. However, a logit link will give essentially the same results. The event of interest is the transition from employment (i.e., working during the week of the survey) to inactivity (not working or not in school during the survey week). The sample consists of 1,077 respondents who contributed 5,681 person-years of data, representing 7 survey years, from 1979 to 1985. Individuals aged 14–17 in 1979 were followed over time, thus allowing us to estimate up to 10 age-specific hazard rates. This example uses 5 two-year age intervals.

Several time-varying covariates are introduced, such as whether or not the individual graduated from high school in the year prior to the survey ($GRAD_{t-1}$), the unemployment rate in the local labor market ($UNEMP_t$), and whether the respondent left home by the survey date ($SPLIT_t$). The fixed covariates include nonintact family structure at age 14 (NONINT), father's high school or college education (FHS or FCOL), 1979 family income (INCOME), residence in the south (SOUTH), and standardized scores on the Armed Services Vocational Aptitude Battery test (ASVAB).

Table 5.9: Discrete-Time Hazard Model of Transition from Work to Inactivity

Age Effects	$\widehat{\alpha}_t$	$SE(\widehat{\alpha}_t)$	Baseline Hazards $1 - \exp\{-\exp(\widehat{\alpha}_t)\}$
Age 14–15	−4.092	(0.313)	0.017
Age 16–17	−3.334	(0.239)	0.035
Age 18–19	−2.727	(0.252)	0.063
Age 20–21	−2.989	(0.282)	0.049
Age 22–23	−3.858	(0.426)	0.021
Covariate Effects	$\widehat{\beta}$	$SE(\widehat{\beta})$	Relative Risks or Multiplicative Effects $\exp(\widehat{\beta})$
FHS	0.226	(0.157)	1.254
FCOL	0.087	(0.183)	1.091
$GRAD_{t-1}$	0.174	(0.182)	1.190
INCOME	−0.232	(0.131)	0.793
ASVAB	−0.450	(0.075)	0.638
NONINT	0.395	(0.154)	1.485
$UNEMP_t$	0.420	(0.168)	1.522
SOUTH	−0.530	(0.184)	0.589
$SPLIT_t$	−0.475	(0.188)	0.622
n	5681		
$\log L$	−1015.62		
Model χ^2	140.81		
DF	13		

Note: Data are in the form of person-years.

The age-specific hazards of entering a period of inactivity rise until about age 20 and decline thereafter. These rates are depicted graphically in Fig. 5.1.

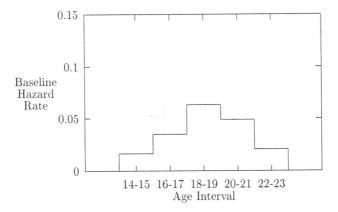

Figure 5.1: Estimated Age-Specific Rates of Work to Inactivity Transition

A complementary log-log link function is used in this example. To transform the additive estimates to probabilities depicted in Fig. 5.1, we substitute the estimated baseline log-rates into the following formula:

$$\widehat{p}_{it} = 1 - \exp\{-\exp(\widehat{\alpha}_t)\}, \qquad (5.28)$$

where $\widehat{\alpha}_t$ denotes the estimated baseline effect for the tth age group.

Fitting a logit model to the same data would yield a different set of baseline effects that would be transformed to probabilities as follows:

$$\widehat{p}_{it} = \frac{\exp(\widehat{\alpha}_t)}{1 + \exp(\widehat{\alpha}_t)}. \qquad (5.29)$$

In either the complementary log-log or the logit specification, the relative risks corresponding to categorical covariates are given by $e^{\widehat{\beta}}$. For example, the risk of a transition from work to inactivity is 1.49 times higher for those living in nonintact families compared to those from intact families. For continuously measured covariates, such as income, test scores, and unemployment rates, the relative risk interpretation gives way to a multiplicative effect interpretation. For example, a 1 point increase in the local unemployment rate yields a 52%

$[(e^{0.42} - 1) \times 100]$ increase in the risk of a work-to-inactivity transition, whereas a 1 point increase in standardized ASVAB test score yields a $[(1 - e^{-0.45}) \times 100]$ or 36% decrease in the risk of a work-to-inactivity transition.

5.4 Semiparametric Rate Models

The rate models we have discussed so far are identical to models for the analyses of event histories. An individual's event history is a representation of the statuses (or states) occupied and the duration in these statuses over some period of observation. An event history may be reconstructed retrospectively or may make use of longitudinal data collected over time. Throughout this chapter, we have considered the simple two-state (or single-event) models in which all individuals begin in a common origin state and are at risk of making a transition to a single common destination state. The state variable in this case is a binary variable coded 1 if a transition occurs and 0 otherwise. These models can be extended to competing-risk and multistate models. In this most basic form, an event history contains information about a single transition from a common origin state to a particular destination state. The data would consist of the state occupied at some initial point in time, the duration in the state, and an indicator of whether or not a destination state was entered (or the origin state was exited). Event-history data generally take the form:

Obs. No. (id)	Starting Time (st)	Starting Status (ss)	Ending Time (ft)	Ending Status (fs)	x-Variables (x)

Starting time is considered to be the beginning of an episode of risk for a particular transition. Starting state is the status at the beginning of an episode. Ending time is an event or censoring time. A transition (event) occurs with a change in status, while censoring occurs when there is no change (i.e., destination status = origin status). The ending status variable captures this change in status or exit from the origin state. This way of arranging the data offers a good deal of flexibility for handing multiple transitions (multistate and competing-risk models), as well as the incorporation of episode-specific values of time-varying independent variables.

We will discuss two flexible models for simple transitions involving a single event, the piecewise constant exponential model and the proportional hazard model of Cox (1972). The piecewise constant rate model that was used earlier for grouped data can be extended to accommodate individual-level data and time-varying independent variables. This model is semiparametric, making the assumption of an exponential hazard within predefined time periods but allowing the hazard to change over periods in a nonparametric way. We also consider the Cox proportional hazards model, which is also semiparametric. Rather than focusing on the discrete outcome or count, our focus in this section will be on the continuous (and possibly censored) random variable T representing duration.

5.4.1   The Piecewise Constant Exponential Model

The piecewise constant exponential model is an elaboration of the fundamental exponential waiting-time (or failure-time) model presented earlier. The grouped data version of the model can be derived from the individual-level model. The rationale for extending the basic exponential model in this way is to allow for simple forms of duration dependence (time dependency of the hazard) and nonproportional hazards.

The standard exponential hazard model is one of a few models that are in the class of proportional hazards models. Proportional hazards imply that the ratio of the hazards of two individuals with different constellations of covariate values is constant over time. Let x_1 and x_2 denote the covariate values corresponding to two individuals, and let λ_{x_1} and λ_{x_2} be the corresponding hazard rates. Since the hazards are constant over time, the hazard ratio is

$$\frac{\lambda_{x_1}}{\lambda_{x_2}} = \frac{\exp(\beta_0 + \beta_1 x_1)}{\exp(\beta_0 + \beta_1 x_2)}$$
$$= \exp\{\beta_1(x_1 - x_2)\}.$$

Thus, the hazards of two individuals are proportional (i.e., multiplicative in β_1).

A major drawback of this particular form of the hazard is that it is constant for all values of t. This may be a plausible assumption for certain phenomena, but many social and physical processes do not follow these simple rules; increasing, decreasing, or nonmonotonic hazards are commonplace. A variety of parametric models have been proposed to deal with this aspect of hazard modeling.[10]

We advocate a simple alternative in which the researcher chooses the number and length of the time intervals in advance, assuming constant hazards within time intervals, and allowing hazards to increase or decrease across intervals. This approach has been advocated by Holford (1980), Laird and Oliver (1981), and others. It is straightforward to introduce interaction terms to capture time-varying covariate effects. Fortunately, no special methods or software are required other than those used for the standard log-rate model. However, like the discrete-time model, the data must be arranged in a suitable event-oriented (or split-episode) format.

Illustration

Consider the data presented in Table 5.1. Suppose we are interested in whether or not the completion rates vary by time spent in the program. For ease of exposition, we will define two time periods of risk—one from 0 to 12 months and another from 12 to ∞ months. More generally, one defines $q + 1$ time intervals $[c_0, c_1), [c_1, c_2), \ldots, [c_{q-1}, c_q), [c_q, c_{q+1})$, where $c_0 = 0$ and $c_{q+1} = \infty$. The intervals define cutpoints in the duration variable T. In this example, we let $c_1 = 12$ and $c_2 = \infty$ define the endpoints for the two time periods. Omitting individual-level subscripts, the two-piece hazard may be now defined based on these cutpoints as follows:

---

[10]Discussions of these models and the pitfalls associated with making incorrect assumptions about the distributions of waiting times are presented in more detail in the work of Blossfeld, Hamerle, and Mayer (1989), Heckman and Singer (1984); Tuma and Hannan (1984).

$$\lambda_j = \begin{cases} \lambda_1 & \text{for } 0 < t \le c_1, \\ \lambda_2 & \text{for } c_1 < t \le \infty. \end{cases} \tag{5.30}$$

The extension to more than two time periods is straightforward.

$$\lambda_j = \begin{cases} \lambda_1 & \text{for } 0 < t \le c_1, \\ \lambda_2 & \text{for } c_1 < t \le c_2, \\ \vdots & \\ \lambda_q & \text{for } c_{q-1} < t \le c_q \\ \lambda_{q+1} & \text{for } c_q < t \le c_{q+1}. \end{cases} \tag{5.31}$$

We define a dummy variable, $d_1 = 1$, if the program is completed in the interval from 0 to 12 months, and 0 otherwise. Similarly, let $d_2 = 1$ if graduation occurs in the interval covering 12 or more months, and 0 otherwise. Stated in terms of the duration variable and the cutpoints,

$$d_j = \begin{cases} 1 & \text{if } c_{j-1} < t \le c_j \text{ (event in interval)}, \\ 0 & \text{otherwise (censored in interval)}. \end{cases} \tag{5.32}$$

If an individual experiences the event in the interval from 0 to 12 months, the event time is t. Right censored observations in this interval have censoring times of 12 months. If an individual experiences an event in the second interval, his/her ending time is equal to the amount of time he/she was exposed to risk in the first interval (12 months) plus the difference $(t - 12)$. Those who are right censored also accumulate 12 months of exposure in the first period and $(t - 12)$ months of exposure in the second period. It is convenient to define exposure (t_j) in the jth time interval in a more general way as follows:

$$t_j = \begin{cases} 0 & \text{for } t < c_{j-1}, \\ t - c_{j-1} & \text{for } c_{j-1} < t \le c_j, \\ c_j - c_{j-1} & \text{for } t > c_j. \end{cases}$$

The log-likelihood can now be written using these components:

$$\log L = \sum_{i=1}^{n} \sum_{j=1}^{q+1} d_{ij} \log \lambda_{ij} - \sum_{i=1}^{n} \sum_{j=1}^{q+1} t_{ij} \lambda_{ij}. \tag{5.33}$$

This expression can be shown to be the sum of $q + 1$ independent log-likelihoods—one for each time interval. This implies that each episode of risk for the ith individual could be treated as separate observations in a standard log-rate (Poisson regression) model.

Table 5.10 shows how the data can be arranged in the form of an event-oriented (or split-episode) data file using information on the status in each interval, d_j, and the starting and ending times in each interval. The starting times for each interval are given by the cutpoints c_{j-1}. The ending times could be event times or censoring times. Let $c_j^* = \min(t, c_j)$ (i.e., the smaller of t or c_j). Due to the common origin status, only the final or ending state needs to be recorded.

Table 5.10: Arrangement of Split-Episode Event History Data

	Program 1				Program 2		
Case	c_{j-1}	c_j^*	d_j	Case	c_{j-1}	c_j^*	d_j
1	0	12	1	7	0	5	1
2	0	12	0	8	0	12	0
2	12	24	0	8	12	18	1
3	0	6	1	9	0	12	0
4	0	12	0	9	12	20	0
4	12	13	0	10	0	8	1
5	0	12	0	11	0	10	1
5	12	16	1	12	0	12	0
6	0	12	0	12	12	17	0
6	12	24	0				

Using this data arrangement, we can define duration (exposure) as $t_j = c_j^* - c_{j-1}$. That is, we define an episode with starting time c_{j-1} and ending time c_j^* with duration t_j. The event/censoring indicator variable, d_j, is declared as a dependent variable in a Poisson regression with offset term $\log t_j$. With no loss of generality, we allow the hazard in the jth time interval to depend on fixed and time-varying covariates as follows:

$$\lambda_{ij} = \exp(\alpha_j + \mathbf{x}'_{ij}\boldsymbol{\beta}). \qquad (5.34)$$

With categorical covariates, it may be more convenient to work with grouped data, in which case the events (d_j) and durations (t_j) are *accumulated* within cells of a contingency table. Table 5.11 presents the data of Table 5.10 in an equivalent format obtained by aggregating events and durations.

Table 5.11: Cross-Classified Data from Table 5.10

Months to Completion	Program Track 1		Program Track 2	
	E	D	E	D
0–12	66	2	59	3
12–∞	29	1	19	1

Let T_2 denote a dummy variable indexing the time period, coded 1 if event/censoring takes place in the interval from 12–24 months and 0 otherwise. Let P_2 be a dummy variable denoting program 2, coded 1 if the student enters program 2 and 0 otherwise. We also include an interaction term $T_2 \times P_2$ to allow for nonproportional covariate effects. That is, not only are the baseline hazards permitted to shift over time, the covariate effects are permitted to shift as well. This ability to take account of nonproportional effects is a primary strength of the piecewise constant rate model. We fit the following model to the data:

$$\log \lambda_i = \beta_0 + \beta_1 T_{2i} + \beta_2 P_{2i} + \beta_3 [T_{2i} \times P_{2i}]. \qquad (5.35)$$

This model can be fitted as a loglinear model for the counts (D_i) with the logged exposure $(\log E_i)$ as an offset term. We can also use the split-episode individual-level data. We can see from Table 5.12 that neither the period effect nor the interaction effect reach statistical significance at conventional levels (panel A). In fact, as we found before, there is no difference in rates by type of program. Panel B of Table 5.12 estimates the period-specific baseline (log) rates directly by omitting the constant term from the model and fitting a term for T_1, a dummy variable that is complementary to T_2 (e.g., $T_1 + T_2 = 1$).

Table 5.12: Piecewise Constant Rate Model with Nonproportional Effects

	A		B	
	$\widehat{\beta}$	SE($\widehat{\beta}$)	$\widehat{\beta}$	SE($\widehat{\beta}$)
Constant	−3.367	1.00	−	−
T_1	−	−	−3.367	1.00
T_2	0.129	1.22	−3.497	0.71
P_2	0.518	0.91	0.518	0.91
$T_2 \times P_2$	−0.095	1.68	−0.095	1.68

5.4.2 The Cox Model

Probably the most frequently used model for duration data is the proportional hazards model proposed by Cox (1972). This model is attractive because it makes no distributional assumptions about the waiting times. As in the exponential model, the hazard rates for any two individuals with different covariate values are proportional. The most common applications of the Cox model involve continuous-time event data. When the measurement of the timing of the event is less precise, a discrete-time Cox model should be used.

The Continuous-Time Cox Model

Assuming a set of rank-ordered event times $t_1 < t_2 < \cdots < t_n$, the hazard rate in the Cox model depends on an unspecified baseline hazard rate, $\lambda_0(t)$, and a set of fixed or time-varying covariates $\mathbf{x}_i(t)$, as follows:

$$\lambda(t) = \lambda_0(t) \exp\{\mathbf{x}_i(t)'\boldsymbol{\beta}\}.$$

Estimation is based on the method of partial likelihood (Cox 1975), which is written as

$$L_p = \prod_{i \in \mathcal{D}} \frac{\exp\{\mathbf{s}_i(t)'\boldsymbol{\beta}\}}{\left[\sum_{l \in \mathcal{R}(t_i)} \exp\{\mathbf{x}_l(t)'\boldsymbol{\beta}\}\right]^{d_i}}, \tag{5.36}$$

where $\mathcal{D}$ denotes the set of all uncensored episodes, and $\mathcal{R}(t_i)$ denotes the risk set at ending time t_i of the ith episode in $\mathcal{D}$. The vector $\mathbf{s}_i$ denotes the sum of the covariate vector ($\mathbf{x}_i$) for individuals with tied failure times, and d_i is the number of tied failure times at t_i. The presence of ties will bias our estimate of $\boldsymbol{\beta}$ because information from individuals with different configurations of covariate values is being aggregated. Therefore, when there are many tied times, a discrete-time model or piecewise constant exponential model would be preferable.

The risk set $\mathcal{R}$ includes the set of all event times and censoring times with starting times less than t_i and ending times greater than or equal to t_i. That is, we look at the ending times for episodes ending in an event, and for each point in time we construct the risk set. The ratio in Eq. 5.36 represents the probability that the ith individual is the one who experiences an event at time t, given the set of individuals at risk of having an event at time t. Note that the ranks of the failure times are used to determine the risk set. Censored times enter into the calculation of the partial likelihood only through the risk set (i.e., as part of the denominator). Estimates obtained by maximizing the partial likelihood have properties similar to maximum likelihood estimates.

Illustration

Table 5.13 presents estimates from a Cox proportional hazards model of the transition to first marriage for a sample of young men from the NLSY. The risk of first marriage is assumed to depend on a number of family background factors including race (NONWHT= 1 if respondent is nonwhite, 0 otherwise), family structure (NONINT= 1 if not living with both biological parents at age 14, 0 otherwise), father's education (FCOL= 1 if father has more than 12 years of schooling, 0 otherwise), urban residence (URBAN= 1 if living in an urban area, 0 otherwise), respondent's family income (INCOME) in thousands of

Table 5.13: Cox Model for Transition to First Marriage

Variable	$\widehat{\beta}$	SE$(\widehat{\beta})$	exp$(\widehat{\beta})$
NONWHT	−0.283	0.044	0.754
NONINT	−0.141	0.047	0.869
FCOL	−0.212	0.053	0.809
URBAN	−0.360	0.048	0.697
INCOME	−0.058	0.041	0.994
FHH79	−0.223	0.060	0.800
$-2 \log L$	38814.99		
Model χ^2	180.40		
DF	6		
n	4687		
Number of Events	2424		
Percent Censored	48.28		

dollars adjusted by family size, and county-level female headship rate in 1979 (FHH79).

The interpretation of results from the continuous-time Cox model is the same as that from the models considered earlier. The exponentiated coefficients may be interpreted as relative risks for categorical covariates and as multiplicative effects for continuous covariates.

The Discrete-Time Cox Model

If the underlying event times are assumed to arise from a proportional hazards model, then it can be shown that the appropriate discrete-time estimator is the binomial response model (binary regression model), with a complementary log-log link (Aranda-Ordaz 1983; Candy 1984). To see this, we can consider the grouped data case where the number of events between the time points $t_0 < t_1 < \cdots < t_q$ is given by $y_1, y_2, \ldots, y_q$, and the number at risk at the beginning of each time interval is $n_1, \ldots, n_q$. Then y_i $(i = 1, \ldots, q)$ are binomial random variables with parameters p_{it} and n_i. We assume that the underlying continuous-time hazard function, $\lambda(t)$, is of the form

$$\lambda(t) = \exp\{\alpha(t) + \mathbf{x}'_{it}\boldsymbol{\beta}\},$$

where $\alpha(t)$ denotes any arbitrary time-dependence, such as piecewise constancy or a parametric function (e.g., a polynomial in t) about p_{it},

$$p_{it} = 1 - \exp\{-\int_{t_{i-1}}^{t_i} \lambda(t)dt\}.$$

This integral can be approximated as

$$p_{it} = 1 - \exp\{-\Delta_i\lambda(t)\},$$

where $\Delta_i = t_i - t_{i-1}$ is the length of the time interval.

Therefore, if we have information on the length of the time interval for each individual, we can account for differential exposure by writing the hazard as

$$p_{it} = 1 - \exp[-\Delta_i \exp\{\alpha(t) + \mathbf{x}'_{ik}\boldsymbol{\beta}\}],$$

where Δ_i denotes difference in the ending and starting times of the ith interval.

Adjusting the model in this way has little effect on the estimates of $\boldsymbol{\beta}$ when the interval length is small or n_i is large. However, the estimates of the baseline effects will be more similar to those from a continuous-time proportional hazards model. This model would be estimated using standard binomial modeling software, using a complementary log-log link function and declaring $\log \Delta_i$ as an offset.

5.5   Models for Panel Data

In this section, we consider repeated measures of a binary response variable over time from a sample of n respondents.[11] The unique char-

---

[11] These methods are developed more fully in Hsiao (1986). For a more concise review, see Maddala (1987).

acteristics of longitudinal data with repeatable events allow one to
control for unobserved individual characteristics. As in the discrete-
time event-history models, we assume that data on a binary variable
(or state variable) are available over $T > 1$ panels. That is, we observe
values of a binary state variable, y_{i1}, $y_{i2}, \ldots, y_{iT}$, as a sequence of zeros and ones, as depicted earlier in Table 5.7. Instead of modeling the
transition from an origin to a destination state as in the discrete-time
model, our concern here is in estimating the probability of a sequence
of states conditional on a set of covariates that may also vary over
time.

We assume that the observations are independent across individuals, but not necessarily across waves. Independence across waves would
imply that this joint (conditional) probability could be expressed as a
product of (conditional) probabilities. We could then easily estimate
separate cross-sectional models for each panel or pool over panels to
estimate a single cross-sectional model. When observed values are not
independent across waves, this joint probability cannot be easily evaluated. Rather than assuming independence, we can exploit the unique
features of panel data to gain some insight into the serial correlation
of the state variable across waves.

There are two major sources of serial correlation in the dependent
variable over panel waves: state dependence, and unobserved heterogeneity. State dependence implies that the past history of states occupied by an individual affects an individual's current status. Individuals
who have experienced an event in the past are more likely to experience
that event in the future; that is, a previous event induces a change in
individual behavior. Unobserved heterogeneity implies that individuals differ in certain unobserved behavioral characteristics that cannot
be included in the model but affect their probability of experiencing
an event. As a result, even when conditioning on measured variables,
the values of the state variables are not independent across waves. As
we shall see, more reliable predictions of the sequence of transitions
can be obtained when controlling for unobserved heterogeneity.

In the discussion that follows, our interpretation focuses on unobserved heterogeneity as a component of the model error. We discuss
the fixed effect logit model and two varieties of random effects probit
models.

5.5.1   Fixed Effects Models for Binary Data

The fixed effect model for binary panel data was proposed by Andersen (1970) and developed further by Chamberlain (1980, 1984). The basic formulation is

$$\Pr(y_{it} = 1 \mid \alpha_i) = \frac{\exp(\mathbf{x}'_{it}\boldsymbol{\beta} + \alpha_i)}{1 + \exp(\mathbf{x}'_{it}\boldsymbol{\beta} + \alpha_i)}, \tag{5.37}$$

where y_{it} is the binary state variable for the i th individual in the tth wave ($t = 1, \dots, T$). This depends on a set of individual covariates that vary across waves and an individual-specific heterogeneity term, α_i. In other words, a separate intercept is included for each cross-sectional unit but remains fixed across panel waves. The model proposes that the probability of the sequence $y_{i1}, \dots, y_{iT}$ is

$$\Pr(y_{i1}, \dots, y_{iT} \mid \alpha_i) = \prod_{t=1}^{T} \frac{[\exp(\mathbf{x}'_{it}\boldsymbol{\beta} + \alpha_i)]^{y_{it}}}{1 + \exp(\mathbf{x}'_{it}\boldsymbol{\beta} + \alpha_i)}. \tag{5.38}$$

This model suffers from the so-called incidental parameter problem because there is a unique α_i term for each individual. This term can be factored out by considering only those binary sequences in which a change in y occurs.

More formally, eliminating the α_i term requires finding a minimal sufficient statistic that is independent of the structural parameters ($\boldsymbol{\beta}$). A conditional density function, without the α_i term, may then be written for each observation. The product of these densities yields a conditional likelihood that may be maximized using conventional methods. The estimates of the structural parameters have the desirable properties of ML estimates.

A sufficient statistic, h_i, for this model is obtained by summing over y_{it} (an individual's binary sequence), $h_i = \sum_{i=1}^{T} y_{it}$. If $h_i = 0$ or $h_i = T$, an individual's sequence consists entirely of zeros or ones, and no transition has occurred. Only cases in which a change in status occurs will contribute information to the likelihood (i.e., $h_i > 0$ and $h_i < T$).

As an example, consider the following observed sequences in a two-wave panel $(T = 2)$:

Sequence	y_1	y_2	h
A	0	0	0
B	0	1	1
C	1	0	1
D	1	1	2
E	1	1	2
F	0	1	1
G	1	0	0

When $y_1 = y_2$ (as in cases A, D, and E), the conditional probability $\Pr(y_1, y_2 \mid h) = 1$. That is, $\Pr(0, 0 \mid h = 0) = 1$ and $\Pr(1, 1 \mid h = 2) = 1$. Thus, only observations B, C, F, and G will contribute to the conditional log-likelihood. For the (0,1) sequences (cases B and F), we have (using basic rules for conditional probabilities):

$$\Pr(0, 1 \mid h = 1) = \frac{\Pr(0, 1) \cap \Pr(h = 1)}{\Pr(h = 1)} = \frac{\Pr(0, 1)}{\Pr(0, 1) + \Pr(1, 0)}. \quad (5.39)$$

After substituting Eq. 5.37 and applying some algebra, the α_i terms can be factored out to yield the conditional probability for the (0,1) sequence

$$\Pr(0, 1 \mid h = 1) = \frac{\Pr(0, 1)}{\Pr(0, 1) + \Pr(1, 0)}$$

$$= \frac{\dfrac{1}{D_{i1}} \times \dfrac{\exp(\mathbf{x}_{i2}'\boldsymbol{\beta} + \alpha_i)}{D_{i2}}}{\dfrac{1}{D_{i1}} \times \dfrac{\exp(\mathbf{x}_{i2}'\boldsymbol{\beta} + \alpha_i)}{D_{i2}} + \dfrac{\exp(\mathbf{x}_{i1}'\boldsymbol{\beta} + \alpha_i)}{D_{i1}} \times \dfrac{1}{D_{i2}}}$$

$$= \frac{\exp(\mathbf{x}_{i2}'\boldsymbol{\beta})}{\exp(\mathbf{x}_{i1}'\boldsymbol{\beta}) + \exp(\mathbf{x}_{i2}'\boldsymbol{\beta})},$$

$$(5.40)$$

where $D_{i1} = 1 + \exp(\mathbf{x}_{i1}'\boldsymbol{\beta} + \alpha_i)$ and $D_{i2} = 1 + \exp(\mathbf{x}_{i2}'\boldsymbol{\beta} + \alpha_i)$. The conditional likelihood is the product of these terms for all observations with (0,1) sequences (observations B and F, in this case). The same approach would be applied to the (1,0) sequences. The product of the analogous term (cases C and G) would be included in the conditional likelihood. Assembling all terms, the conditional likelihood is

$$
L_c = \frac{\exp(\mathbf{x}_{i2}'\boldsymbol{\beta})}{\exp(\mathbf{x}_{i1}'\boldsymbol{\beta}) + \exp(\mathbf{x}_{i2}'\boldsymbol{\beta})} \times \frac{\exp(\mathbf{x}_{i2}'\boldsymbol{\beta})}{\exp(\mathbf{x}_{i1}'\boldsymbol{\beta}) + \exp(\mathbf{x}_{i2}'\boldsymbol{\beta})}
$$
$$
\times \frac{\exp(\mathbf{x}_{i1}'\boldsymbol{\beta})}{\exp(\mathbf{x}_{i1}'\boldsymbol{\beta}) + \exp(\mathbf{x}_{i2}'\boldsymbol{\beta})} \times \frac{\exp(\mathbf{x}_{i1}'\boldsymbol{\beta})}{\exp(\mathbf{x}_{i1}'\boldsymbol{\beta}) + \exp(\mathbf{x}_{i2}'\boldsymbol{\beta})}.
$$

(5.41)

In the case of two time periods, the conditional likelihood can be simplified by noting that the last line in Eq. 5.40 can be written as

$$
\Pr(0, 1 \mid h = 1) = \frac{\exp(\mathbf{x}_{i2}'\boldsymbol{\beta})}{\exp(\mathbf{x}_{i2}'\boldsymbol{\beta}) + \exp(\mathbf{x}_{i1}'\boldsymbol{\beta})}
$$
$$
= \frac{\exp[(\mathbf{x}_{i2} - \mathbf{x}_{i1})'\boldsymbol{\beta}]}{1 + \exp[(\mathbf{x}_{i2} - \mathbf{x}_{i1})'\boldsymbol{\beta}]},
$$

(5.42)

which has the same form as a probability in a standard logit model. This means that, when $T = 2$, computer programs for estimating standard binary logit models can be readily applied to estimate the fixed effects model with the following steps:

1. Delete cases for which there is no change in the dependent variable.

2. Transform the dependent variable to z so that the $0 \rightarrow 1$ change in y is coded as 1, and the $1 \rightarrow 0$ change in y is coded as 0.

3. Take differences between time-varying independent variables at times 2 and 1 to obtain $\Delta\mathbf{x}$.

4. Regress the newly coded binary dependent variable z on $\Delta\mathbf{x}$.

The estimated coefficients of $\Delta\mathbf{x}$ can be interpreted as the structural coefficients for the original model.

These steps can also be illustrated by considering the latent variable formulation of the fixed-effects logit model:

$$
y_{it}^* = \mathbf{x}_{it}'\boldsymbol{\beta} + \alpha_i,
$$

(5.43)

$$y_{i1} = 0, y_{i2} = 1 \iff y_{i2}^* > y_{i1}^* \iff \Delta y_i^* > 0,$$
$$y_{i1} = 1, y_{i2} = 0 \iff y_{i2}^* < y_{i1}^* \iff \Delta y_i^* < 0. \tag{5.44}$$

From the structural equation,

$$\begin{aligned}
\Delta y_i^* &= y_{i2}^* - y_{i1}^* \\
&= (\mathbf{x}_{i2}'\boldsymbol{\beta} + \alpha_i) - (\mathbf{x}_{i1}'\boldsymbol{\beta} + \alpha_i) \\
&= (\mathbf{x}_{i2}' - \mathbf{x}_{i1}')\boldsymbol{\beta} \\
&= \Delta\mathbf{x}_i'\boldsymbol{\beta}.
\end{aligned} \tag{5.45}$$

Now, let us recode a new dependent variable z so that

$$\begin{aligned}
z = 1 &\quad \text{if } y_{i1} = 0 \text{ and } y_{i2} = 1, \\
z = 0 &\quad \text{if } y_{i1} = 1 \text{ and } y_{i2} = 0.
\end{aligned} \tag{5.46}$$

Again, the problem becomes one of estimating a logit model with z as the dependent variable and $\Delta\mathbf{x}$ as the independent variables.

In fact, use of the fixed effects model does not require panel data. As long as the data are hierarchical, and the unobserved heterogeneity terms are assumed to be constant at a higher level than the individual observations (assumption of fixed effects), the model is identified. For example, the fixed effects model can be applied to cross-sectional data to study how the difference in binary outcomes depends on factors that differ between siblings. In this way, all shared factors (genetic and environmental) are controlled.

Advantages and Disadvantages of This Approach: This approach has the advantage of being conservative because we make no assumptions about the distribution of unobserved heterogeneity (i.e., it is nonparametric). However, this advantage comes at the expense of losing many cases, thus it is less efficient than an approach that uses all the data. Moreover, because the fixed effects cancel out, it does not allow estimation of the effects of variables that remain constant over time.

Although the preceding demonstration is restricted to cases for which there are only two repeated observations per individual, it can be extended to situations with more than two repeated observations.

More generally, as suggested by Chamberlain (1980), a conditional likelihood that does not depend on α_i may be written as

$$L_c = \Pr(y_{i1}, \dots, y_{iT} \mid h_i) = \prod_{i=1}^{n} \frac{\exp(\sum_{t=1}^{T} y_{it}\, \mathbf{x}_{it}'\boldsymbol{\beta})}{\sum_{d_{it} \in \mathcal{D}_i} \exp(\sum_{t=1}^{T} d_{it}\, \mathbf{x}_{it}'\boldsymbol{\beta})}, \quad (5.47)$$

where $\mathcal{D}_i$ is the set of d_{it} such that, given h_i, any sequence of h_i events is found in that set. That is,

$$\mathcal{D}_i = \{(d_{i1}, \dots, d_{iT}) \mid d_{it} = 0 \text{ or } 1 \text{ and } \sum_t d_{it} = h_i\}. \quad (5.48)$$

Although this is an attractive model for the analysis of panel data for the reasons outlined earlier, the process of conditioning-out the unobserved heterogeneity also eliminates covariates that do not change across waves. Thus, the effects of fixed covariates are not estimable. Of course, it would be possible to stratify the sample by fixed covariates and estimate separate models. Next, we consider random effects models that can incorporate both fixed and time-varying covariates.

5.5.2   Random Effects Models for Binary Data

There are several varieties of the random effects probit model. Here we consider the random effects probit model of Heckman and Willis (1976). This model can be written as the following latent variable model:

$$y_{it}^* = \mathbf{x}_{it}'\boldsymbol{\beta} + \varepsilon_{it}. \quad (5.49)$$

The error term ε_{it} represents a combination of permanent and transitory processes, such that $\varepsilon_{it} = v_i + u_{it}$. The v_i term represents time-invariant unobserved heterogeneity (i.e., a single random effect for $t = 1, \dots, T$). The u_{it} term represents time-varying stochastic error, or error due to factors inherent to the process other than measured or unmeasured covariates. Both v_i and u_{it} are assumed to be normally distributed with mean zero and variances σ_v^2 and σ_u^2, respectively. Moreover, v_i and u_{it} are assumed to be independent and uncorrelated with the independent variables (i.e., $\sigma_{uv} = \sigma_{ux} = \sigma_{vx} = 0$).

However, the assumption that u_{it} and $\mathbf{x}_{it}$ are uncorrelated may be relaxed in certain variants of the basic random effects model.

Like the latent variable models discussed in Chapter 3, the observed binary dependent variables are assumed to be the result of a threshold-crossing process, where

$$y_{it} = \begin{cases} 1 & \text{if } y_{it}^* \geq 0, \\ 0 & \text{otherwise.} \end{cases} \tag{5.50}$$

The probability of an event for the ith individual can be written as a joint probability of y_{it},

$$\Pr(y_{i1}, \ldots, y_{iT}) = \int_{a_{i1}}^{b_{i1}} \ldots \int_{a_{iT}}^{b_{iT}} \phi(\varepsilon_{i1}, \ldots, \varepsilon_{iT}) d\varepsilon_{iT} \ldots d\varepsilon_{i1}, \tag{5.51}$$

where $a_{it} = -\mathbf{x}_{it}'\boldsymbol{\beta}$, $b_{it} = +\infty$ if $y_{it} = 1$, and $a_{it} = -\infty$, $b_{it} = -\mathbf{x}_{it}'\boldsymbol{\beta}$ if $y_{it} = 0$, and $\phi(\cdot)$ is the standard T-variate normal density function. Conditioning on the permanent component, v_i, this expression can be written as

$$\int_{a_{i1}}^{b_{i1}} \ldots \int_{a_{iT}}^{b_{iT}} \int_{-\infty}^{+\infty} \phi(u_{i1}, \ldots, u_{iT} \mid v_i)\phi(v_i) dv_i du_{i1} \ldots du_{iT}. \tag{5.52}$$

Because the transitory components are independent conditional on v_i, this expression can be simplified. In terms of model quantities, Eq. 5.51 can be written as

$$\Pr(y_{i1}, \ldots, y_{iT}) = \int_{-\infty}^{+\infty} \prod_{t=1}^{T} \Phi(\mathbf{x}_{it}'\boldsymbol{\beta} \mid v_i)^{y_{it}} \Phi(-\mathbf{x}_{it}'\boldsymbol{\beta} \mid v_i)^{1-y_{it}} \phi(v_i) dv_i, \tag{5.53}$$

where $\Phi(\cdot)$ is the cumulative standard normal distribution function.

The product of this expression over all individuals is a marginal likelihood (or integrated likelihood). The integral in this expression is the only thing that differentiates it from the likelihood for a standard probit model for panel data. We eliminate the random effect term by "integrating it out" of the expression for the marginal likelihood. The resulting likelihood function is then maximized in terms of the structural parameters (β) only. Some simplification is obtained by using a numerical method known as Hermite-quadrature to reduce this integral to a sum. This procedure is described by Butler and Moffitt (1982) and is implemented in a number of computer packages (e.g., LIMDEP, TDA, and HotzTran [Avery and Hotz 1985]).

The variance-covariance matrix of the equation error terms is of particular interest, as it captures the autocorrelation in the equation error terms. Due to the normalization of the probit model, ε_{it} is normally distributed with mean 0 and variance $\sigma_\varepsilon^2 = 1$. For any two distinct waves (t and t'), the error covariance or autocorrelation is $\text{cov}(\varepsilon_{it}, \varepsilon_{it'}) = \sigma_v^2$. Output from this model includes an estimate of σ_v, typically called ρ.

A possible extension to this model would allow wave-specific unobserved heterogeneity, in which case we replace v_i with v_{it}. In this case, the preceding single integral would be replaced by a T-fold integral. This can be reduced to a single integral providing we assume a product-correlation structure (Dunnett 1989). That is, for any two distinct waves (t and t'), the error covariance, $\text{cov}(\varepsilon_{it}, \varepsilon_{it'}) = \rho_t \rho_{t'}$.

Illustration

We apply each of the preceding random effects models to data on employment patterns of nonwhite men, ages 21–24 in 1986, from the 1986–1988 waves of the NLSY. Omitting those youth who are enrolled in school in any given year, we end up with a sample of 1,971 respondents over three survey waves. The state variable, y_{it}, equals 1 if the respondent's observed major activity during the survey week was employed or serving in the military, and 0 otherwise. The set of independent variables includes fixed measures, including family structure (NONINT), urban residence (URB), residence in the northcentral United States (NC), and standardized test scores (TEST). We also include the unemployment rate in the local labor market as a time-varying covariate (UNEMP$_t$).

Table 5.14 presents results from several models. Column (1) provides estimates from a pooled panel model that assumes independence of y_{it} conditional on $\mathbf{x}_{it}$. These are consistent (but inefficient) estimates. Columns (2) and (3) present estimates from random effects models with common (I) and wave-specific (II) heterogeneity.

We can see that there is a significant improvement in fit (as indicated by the likelihood ratio χ^2 values) when we consider the random effects models; however, model II offers only a marginal improvement in fit over model I at conventional significance levels ($p > 0.05$). The substantive interpretation of the covariate effects from these models is about the same. The estimated autocorrelation from model I is $\widehat{\rho}^2 = 0.58$. The implied autocorrelations under model II are $\widehat{\rho}_{12} = \widehat{\rho}_1\widehat{\rho}_2 = 0.57$, $\widehat{\rho}_{23} = \widehat{\rho}_2\widehat{\rho}_3 = 0.66$, and $\widehat{\rho}_{13} = \widehat{\rho}_1\widehat{\rho}_3 = 0.51$. Another way to assess the performance of these models would be to compare the predicted binary sequences generated under various models with the observed sequences in the data. For a three-way panel, this involves 2^T or 8 possible combinations.

Table 5.14: Probit Models for Panel Data

Variable	Pooled Panel (1) $\widehat{\beta}$	$\frac{\widehat{\beta}}{\mathrm{SE}(\widehat{\beta})}$	Random Effects I (2) $\widehat{\beta}$	$\frac{\widehat{\beta}}{\mathrm{SE}(\widehat{\beta})}$	Random Effects II (3) $\widehat{\beta}$	$\frac{\widehat{\beta}}{\mathrm{SE}(\widehat{\beta})}$
Constant	2.09	22.17	1.99	18.07	1.97	17.87
NONINT	-0.26	-6.08	-0.27	-4.95	-0.26	-4.78
TEST	0.40	17.04	0.39	13.11	0.39	12.95
URB	-0.31	-5.17	-0.29	-3.90	-0.28	-3.84
NC	-0.23	-4.47	-0.20	-3.04	-0.18	-2.75
UNEMP$_t$	-0.51	-6.72	-0.42	-4.74	-0.42	-4.71
ρ			0.76	43.44		
ρ_1					0.66	17.07
ρ_2					0.86	21.40
ρ_3					0.77	18.85
$-2\log L$	-2292.17		-2086.51		-2080.90	
χ^2			5.66		5.61	
DF			1		2	
p-value χ^2			0.02		0.06	

Table 5.15: Observed and Expected Frequencies of Binary Sequences

Observed Sequences	Observed Frequencies	Expected Frequencies Model (1)	Expected Frequencies Model (2)	Expected Frequencies Model (3)
(0,0,0)	106	279	92	89
(0,0,1)	44	13	61	58
(0,1,0)	32	1	45	35
(1,0,0)	51	5	56	68
(1,1,0)	100	4	93	92
(1,0,1)	88	2	96	87
(0,1,1)	138	16	110	126
(1,1,1)	1412	1651	1418	1416

Table 5.15 shows how these models compare in predicting the observed binary sequences. The predicted data sequences are obtained by inserting model estimates into the following index function:

$$y_{it} = \begin{cases} 1 & \text{if } \mathbf{x}_{it}'\widehat{\boldsymbol{\beta}} + \widehat{\varepsilon}_{it} \geq 0, \\ 0 & \text{otherwise,} \end{cases} \tag{5.54}$$

where $\widehat{\varepsilon}_{it}$ is the *predicted* random error term.

The three models make different assumptions about the way that error, $\widehat{\varepsilon}_{it}$, and the predicted sequences are generated. For the probit model without heterogeneity, the random error term is $\widehat{\varepsilon}_{it} = z_i$, where z_i is a vector of standardized normal variates (z-scores) that are unique to each individual.

For the type I random effects model, the error term used to generate the predicted sequence is the sum of a fixed (or stationary) component and a changing (or transitory) component (i.e., $\widehat{\varepsilon}_{it} = \sqrt{1 - \widehat{\rho}^2}z_{it} + z_i$, where $\widehat{\rho}$ is the square root of the estimated autocorrelation, z_{it} is a wave-specific standard normal variate, and z_i is an individual-specific standard normal variate that does not change over T).

For the type II random effects model, the error term used to generate the predicted sequences is obtained as $\widehat{\varepsilon}_i = \sqrt{1 - \widehat{\rho}_t^2}z_{it} + \widehat{\rho}_t z_i$, where the definitions of z_{it} and z_i are the same as before. Since the model allows for wave-specific heterogeneity, the $\widehat{\rho}_t$ terms can be used to estimate the autocorrelations for any two waves. From the results in Table 5.15, we find that the model without random effects does not come as close to predicting the data as models that allow for autocorrelation in equation errors.

There are a number of alternative specifications of qualitative response models with panel data. A long-standing concern in the statistical literature is how robust these models are to the assumptions of normally distributed error terms. One possible solution is to approximate the error distribution using a discrete-mixing distribution (Davies 1987). It is assumed that ε_{it} follows a q-point discrete distribution with masspoints $\alpha_1, \ldots, \alpha_q$ and associated probabilities $\pi_1, \ldots, \pi_q$, with $\sum_{j=1}^{q} \pi_j = 1$. The researcher starts with a small value of q, say $q = 2$ [a 2-point heterogeneity (mover-stayer) distribution] and increases the number of masspoints until the fit of the model fails to improve significantly. The method is straightforward in principle, however, it has yet to be implemented in most standard statistical modeling packages.

5.6 Unobserved Heterogeneity in Event-History Models

There are many ways that unobserved heterogeneity, or *frailty*, might arise in duration models. As in the usual regression case, unobserved heterogeneity may be due to omitted variables. In the OLS regression model, this would not present a problem. However, in duration models, this can change the profile of the risk over time.

Consider, for example, a population characterized by two groups, one of which experiences an event at a constant hazard rate of $\lambda_1 = 0.1$, and another with a constant hazard rate of $\lambda_2 = 0.5$. Suppose that each group initially constitutes half of the population. At time t, the overall hazard, $\bar{\lambda}$, in the population is expressed as the average of the two group's density functions divided by the average of their survival functions, or

$$\bar{\lambda} = \frac{\lambda_1 \exp(-\lambda_1 t_i) + \lambda_2 \exp(-\lambda_2 t_i)}{\exp(-\lambda_1 t_i) + \exp(-\lambda_2 t_i)}. \tag{5.55}$$

Figure 5.2 shows that although the underlying hazards are constant, the overall hazard rate decreases over time, exhibiting negative duration dependence. There is some truth and deception in the overall picture. The overall hazard actually does decline over time. However, to interpret this as time dependency is invalid. The observed declining hazard is due to the fact that the more frail members of the population fail earlier and are removed from the risk set. This leaves a subset of more resilient individuals who are characterized by lower average hazard rates.

As another example, consider a population comprised of two groups. One group experiences a constant hazard rate over time while a more frail group experiences an increasing hazard rate over time. The overall hazard rate in the population will be a mixture of these two processes that depends on the composition of the population in terms of the frail and nonfrail over time. In this case, we will observe an overall hazard rate that increases and then decreases with time. Unless we can control for the variable or variables that distinguish these two groups, we will find that the overall hazard misrepresents what is actually occurring in the population. There are many other examples of this kind of behavior in natural populations. An excellent review of the problem is given by Vaupel and Yashin (1985).

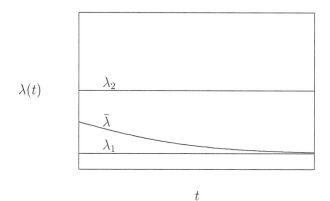

Figure 5.2: The Effect of Unobserved Heterogeneity on the Observed Hazard Rate

In this section we discuss methods for accounting for unobserved heterogeneity in hazard rate models. However, we caution the reader that the emerging literature remains undecided about the extent to which it is possible to compare models that control for unobserved heterogeneity against alternative models without unobserved heterogeneity (Hoem 1990; Trussel and Rodríguez 1990). For example, Trussel and Rodríguez (1990) show that an identification problem exists in the sense that a model specification with unobserved heterogeneity can be observationally equivalent to a model specified without unobserved heterogeneity, even though the two models appear to be conceptually distinct.

Recent applications have focused on estimating the variance in shared unmeasured factors that are common to paired or clustered observations (see, e.g., Guo and Rodríguez 1992). In the context of clustered data, the random effects model is a natural way to accommodate unobserved heterogeneity that is due to common unmeasured sources of variation within sibships, families, neighborhoods, communities, or other kinds of clusters. First, we discuss a general version of the gamma mixture model for individual-level data, which can be estimated by many programs for event-history analysis. Later, we will show how to extend this model to account for cluster-level heterogeneity.

5.6.1   The Gamma Mixture Model

We assume that the hazard rate depends on a set of covariates, $\mathbf{x}_i$, in addition to an unobserved stochastic term v_i. Moreover, the observed sources of heterogeneity ($\mathbf{x}_i$) are uncorrelated with the unobserved sources of heterogeneity (the v_i term). The hazard may be written in the usual way as the ratio of the density and survivor functions[12]:

$$\lambda(t \mid v) = \frac{f(t \mid v)}{S(t \mid v)}.$$

---

[12]The dependence of the hazard on $\mathbf{x}_i$ is assumed, so we omit this from the remaining expressions to reduce some cumbersome notation.

We assume that, conditional on v, the hazard rate is a product of an underlying hazard $\lambda(t)$ and the multiplicative frailty,

$$\lambda(t \mid v) = \lambda(t)v,$$

and that frailty (v) follows a gamma distribution,

$$g(v) = \frac{\alpha^{\alpha}v^{\alpha-1}}{\Gamma(\alpha)} \exp(-\alpha v) \qquad \text{where } \alpha > 0,$$

with mean $E(v) = 1$ and $var(v) = 1/\alpha = \phi$.

This distribution is termed the "mixing" distribution. Although the gamma is a flexible distribution, it is chosen mainly for convenience in this context.[13] A distribution that combines the characteristics of an underlying distribution with those of a mixing distribution is referred to as a "mixture" distribution. To remove the heterogeneity term from the mixture distribution, we must integrate over the range of v, obtaining the unconditional distribution

$$f(t)_m = \int_0^{\infty} f(t \mid v)g(v)dv, \tag{5.56}$$

where the subscript m serves to distinguish the unconditional (mixed) distribution from the underlying (unmixed) distribution. A similar expression can be found for the survival function:

$$S(t)_m = \int_0^{\infty} S(t \mid v)g(v)dv. \tag{5.57}$$

The density and survival functions obtained from the mixture distribution may be viewed as the expected values of the conditional distributions with respect to v (i.e., averaged over v). The choice of the gamma density simplifies the integration so that the resulting survivor function can be expressed in terms of the underlying (unmixed) distribution and parameters of the mixing distribution (α)

---

[13] In Bayesian terminology, the gamma distribution is the conjugate prior distribution for a number of other distributions in the exponential family.

$$S(t)_m = \int_0^\infty \exp\left\{-vH(t)\right\} g(v)dv$$
$$= \{1 + \frac{1}{\alpha}H(t)\}^{-\alpha}, \tag{5.58}$$

where $H(t) = \int_0^t \lambda(u)du$ is the underlying integrated hazard function.

The unconditional density function may be found by differentiating the negative of the unconditional survival function, $-S(t)_m$, yielding

$$f(t)_m = \lambda(t)\{1 + \frac{1}{\alpha}H(t)\}^{-\alpha-1}. \tag{5.59}$$

The hazard rate of the mixture distribution, $\lambda(t)_m$, is obtained as the ratio $f(t)_m/S(t)_m$ as

$$\lambda(t)_m = \lambda(t)\{1 + \frac{1}{\alpha}H(t)\}^{-1}. \tag{5.60}$$

For ease of exposition, we assume an underlying exponential distribution for waiting time, T (i.e., $f(t)$ is an exponential density function). Extensions to other distributions are also possible and follow the same logic. For the exponential model, the conditional hazard rate is

$$\lambda(t \mid v) = \exp(\mathbf{x}_i'\boldsymbol{\beta})v_i. \tag{5.61}$$

The underlying hazard rate is $\lambda(t) = \exp(\mathbf{x}_i'\boldsymbol{\beta})$, whereas the integrated hazard is $H(t) = t_i \exp(\mathbf{x}_i'\boldsymbol{\beta})$. With these terms, the mixture distribution can be described by the following functions

$$S(t)_m = \{1 + \phi H(t)\}^{-1/\phi},$$
$$f(t)_m = \lambda(t)\{1 + \phi H(t)\}^{-\frac{1}{\phi}-1}, \tag{5.62}$$
$$\lambda(t)_m = \lambda(t)\{1 + \phi H(t)\}^{-1},$$

where $\phi = 1/\alpha$ is the variance of v.

The nature of the time dependence of the mixture distribution can be seen by examining its hazard rate. For values of $\phi > 0$, the hazard rate, $\lambda(t)_m$, decreases over time.[14]

---

[14]The density function for an exponential model with gamma heterogeneity can

Illustration

Table 5.16: Modeling Unobserved Heterogeneity

	Model 1	Model 2
	Estimate	Estimate
Variable	(t-Ratio)	(t-Ratio)
Constant	-4.84	-1.83
	(-59.28)	(-8.59)
x	1.35	1.16
	(20.88)	(6.54)
$\log \phi$	$-$	0.84
		(6.13)
$-2 \log L$	-867.71	-681.93

Table 5.16 reports results using simulated data that are generated according to an exponential-gamma mixture model

$$\lambda(t \mid v) = \exp(\beta_0 + \beta_1 x_i) v_i,$$

where x is a standard random normal variable, and v follows a gamma distribution with shape parameter $\alpha = 0.4$ ($\phi = 1/\alpha = 2.5$), $\beta_0 = -2.0$, and $\beta_1 = 1.0$. The sample consists of $n = 200$ observations, 25% of which are randomly right censored.

Model 1 fits a standard exponential model to the simulated data, whereas Model 2 controls for unobserved heterogeneity by fitting an exponential-gamma mixture model. As might be expected, the mixture model gives estimates closer to the parameters used to generate the data. The estimated variance in heterogeneity ($\widehat{\phi}$) is $\exp(0.84) = 2.31$. This estimate can be used to compare hypothetical individuals at different points of the frailty distribution. For example, letting

---

be shown to be identical to a variant of a Pareto probability distribution function. This is similar to the consequences of using a gamma mixing distribution for a Poisson process resulting in a negative binomial model. In both cases, the mixture distribution is a naturally occurring distribution.

$G^{-1}(\alpha, p)$ denote the inverse of the cumulative gamma distribution function evaluated at the pth percentile, we find that the most frail (90th percentile) face a risk that is over seven times that of the risk faced by those of average frailty (50th percentile), or

$$\frac{G^{-1}(0.432, 0.9)}{G^{-1}(0.432, 0.5)} = \frac{2.787}{0.393} = 7.094.$$

Figure 5.3 compares the hazard rate (net of x) from Model 1 to the rate obtained when controlling for unobserved heterogeneity (Model 2).

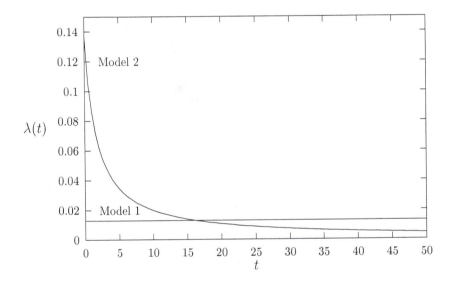

Figure 5.3: The Effect of Unobserved Heterogeneity on the Hazard Rate

Nonparametric Mixing Distributions

There has been a good deal of concern in the literature with the problems of specifying the underlying hazard model in the presence of unobserved heterogeneity. Heckman and Singer (1984) showed that

estimates from hazard models are sensitive to the assumed distribution of the unobserved heterogeneity. To address this concern, they proposed a nonparametric method to account for unobserved heterogeneity using a discrete mixing distribution. This approach assumes that v is an additive rather than a multiplicative heterogeneity term and follows a q-point discrete distribution with masspoints $v_1, \ldots, v_q$ and associated probabilities $\pi_1, \ldots, \pi_q$, with $\sum_{j=1}^{q} \pi_j = 1$. The masspoints (or support points) correspond to q latent classes. Associated with each latent class is a probability, π_j, that represents the proportion of the population falling into the jth latent class. The researcher begins with a few points, say $q = 2$ for a 2-point frailty *mover-stayer* distribution and increases q until the model fit fails to improve. The likelihood function for the Heckman-Singer correction for unobserved heterogeneity in hazard models is

$$L = \prod_{i=1}^{n} \sum_{j=1}^{q} \lambda(t \mid v_j)^{d_i} S(t \mid v_j) \pi_j. \tag{5.63}$$

For the exponential model, this takes the form

$$L = \prod_{i=1}^{n} \sum_{j=1}^{q} \exp(\mathbf{x}_i'\boldsymbol{\beta} + v_j)^{d_i} \exp\{-t_i \exp(\mathbf{x}_i'\boldsymbol{\beta} + v_j)\} \pi_j. \tag{5.64}$$

In principle, the method is straightforward; however, it has yet to be implemented in most hazard-modeling software. Moreover, this approach requires a parametric specification for the underlying hazard distribution.[15] Trussel and Richards (1985) show that misspecification of the underlying hazard distribution affects maximum likelihood estimates from the Heckman-Singer model. If both the conditional hazard and the heterogeneity are misspecified, the situation becomes even worse since it is generally not possible to distinguish misspecification of the duration distribution with misspecification of the unobserved heterogeneity.

---

[15] A piecewise constant distribution is also possible.

Models for Cluster-Level Frailty

Recent approaches to the problem of unobserved heterogeneity have adopted a semiparametric underlying distribution combined with gamma or nonparametric mixing distributions using clustered data (see e.g., Guo and Rodríguez 1992).

These methods integrate many of the ideas of "multilevel" modeling and hazard modeling. Assuming that individuals (level-1 units) are members of clusters (level-2 units) (i.e., families, sibships, etc.), these techniques identify and estimate the variance in the cluster-level random effect. In this case, random effects modeling provides a natural way to account for the within-cluster correlation in outcomes. Moreover, the variance in the random effect (ϕ) provides additional information about the risk of individuals in clusters (or cluster-level frailty) that we could not obtain using individual-level data alone. The random effects model provides a natural way to account for unmeasured heterogeneity that is common to members of clusters. This approach is very similar to multilevel modeling. However, the disturbance is multiplicative rather than additive and follows a gamma instead of a normal distribution. We provide a brief illustration modeling the risk of premarital birth using sisters in the NLSY as clusters.

Suppose that there are n_i individuals belonging to the ith cluster. The conditional hazard for the jth individual in the ith cluster can be written as

$$\lambda(t \mid v) = \lambda_0(t_{ij}) \exp(\mathbf{x}'_{ij}\boldsymbol{\beta})v_i, \qquad (5.65)$$

where v_i is now a cluster-level random effect as opposed to an individual-level random effect. Like the models described earlier, frailty is distributed as gamma with $E(v) = 1$ and $var(v) = 1/\alpha = \phi$.

Guo and Rodríguez (1992) and Lancaster (1995) suggest using an EM-algorithm to fit this model. The EM (expectation maximization) algorithm is useful in situations involving missing data (v in this case) and considers the simpler problem of estimating a hazard model if the frailty were known. For example, if v_i were known and the underlying hazard was a piecewise constant, we could simply include $\log v_i$ as an additional component of the offset term in a standard Poisson regression model (i.e., $\log t_i + \log v_i$). The EM approach finds an estimate (conditional on the data) of the frailty for each unit of analysis (individual or cluster). We can estimate α in one step and use this to estimate v_i. We can then incorporate this estimate $(\widehat{v}_i)$ in the offset term of a proportional hazards model. This process is repeated until the difference in successive estimates of α are negligible.

When frailty is distributed as gamma, the *estimated* frailty in the ith cluster is

$$\widehat{v}_i = \frac{d_{i+} + \widehat{\alpha}}{H(t_{i+}) + \widehat{\alpha}}, \tag{5.66}$$

where $d_{i+} = \sum_{j=1}^{n_i} d_{ij}$ denotes the total number of events in the ith cluster, and $H(t_{i+})$ denotes the sum of the integrated hazards over the n_i individuals in the ith cluster. Lancaster (1990) suggests using a Cox proportional hazards model to estimate $H(t)$, whereas Guo and Rodríguez estimate $H(t)$ using a piecewise constant exponential model. Our example uses a Cox proportional hazards model to estimate $\boldsymbol{\beta}$ [and hence $H(t)$] and a Newton-Raphson algorithm to estimate α. Standard errors of the estimates are obtained using the method described by Louis (1982).

Interpretation: The β's from the cluster-level frailty model have the usual interpretation as logged relative risks or additive effects on the logged hazard rates. The estimate of ϕ can be interpreted as a multiplier of the risk of an event at time t for a hypothetical individual if one cluster member were to experience an event at time t'. When $\phi = 0$, observations are mutually independent. When $\phi > 0$, the relative risk of an event for one cluster member given that another cluster member has experienced an event is $1 + \phi$ and is constant over time. That is, an event by one cluster member raises our estimate of the risk for a hypothetical individual in that cluster by $\phi \times 100\%$ relative to what it would have been if no individual in the cluster had experienced an event. For example, if $\widehat{\phi} = 1$, knowledge that one cluster member experienced an event increases our estimate of the risk for a hypothetical individual in that cluster by 100%. Stated in terms of relative risks, our estimate of that individual's risk is *doubled*. There is also a close relationship between ϕ and the intracluster rank correlation (τ), in that $\tau = \phi/(2 + \phi)$.

Illustration

We illustrate this model for a sample of non-Hispanic White women in the NLSY. The risk of first premarital birth is modeled as a function of several covariates taken from past research such as: nonintact family structure (NONINT), low mother's education (MED< 12) , family income (INCOME), number of older siblings (NSIBS), residence in the south (SOUTH), urban residence (URBAN), fundamentalist Protestant upbringing (FUNDPROT), Catholic (CATHOL), weekly church attendance (WEEKLY), traditional sex role attitude score (PROFAM), and self esteem score (SELFEST).

Table 5.17: Models for Cluster-Level Frailty

Variable	Cluster-Level Frailty Model		Standard Proportional Hazard Model	
	$\exp(\widehat{\beta})$	$\mid \widehat{\beta}/\text{SE}(\widehat{\beta}) \mid$	$\exp(\widehat{\beta})$	$\mid \widehat{\beta}/\text{SE}(\widehat{\beta}) \mid$
NONINT	1.99	4.55	2.14	5.40
MED< 12	1.92	4.27	2.24	5.80
INCOME	0.99	2.82	0.99	3.25
NSIBS	1.03	0.94	1.03	1.00
SOUTH	0.57	2.89	0.52	3.76
URBAN	1.16	0.79	1.25	1.33
FUNDPROT	1.82	3.39	1.90	3.89
CATHOL	0.84	0.93	0.78	1.47
WEEKLY	0.75	1.61	0.71	2.16
PROFAM	1.61	3.04	1.60	2.96
SELFEST	0.44	7.31	0.38	5.90
ϕ	1.19	3.10	—	—
Partial log L	-1587.55		-1573.85	

Table 5.17 compares the relative risks and multiplicative effects from the cluster-level frailty and the standard proportional hazard models. We find that the substantive interpretation remains about the same between the two models. However, we find modest differences in several effects, and one case—the effect of WEEKLY church attendance—where the effect is statistically significant in the standard model but not in the cluster-level frailty model. The estimate of ϕ implies that knowledge that one sibling experiences a premarital birth more than doubles (or increases by 119%) our estimate of the risk of a premarital birth for a hypothetical woman in that family. It follows that knowledge that two premarital births occur in a cluster increases our estimate of the risk by 238% (or $2\phi \times 100\%$). The estimated intracluster rank correlation is $\hat{\tau} = 1.19/(2 + 1.19) = 0.37$.

5.7   Summary

This chapter provides an overview of methods for the analysis of event histories. The approaches we advocate are extensions of the binary models of Chapter 3 (discrete-time models) and loglinear models of Chapter 4 (continuous-time models). Using the concepts of occurrence and exposure, we can derive the empirical rates from contingency tables and estimate hazard models using familiar loglinear modeling techniques. With individual-level data, a binary event/censoring indicator variable defines occurrence while exposure is represented by a duration variable (t). The empirical rate does not apply in this case, but the loglinear (Poisson regression) model still applies. When duration can be partitioned into episodes of constant risk, a piecewise-constant hazards model can be estimated simply by applying Poisson regression to split-episode (or stacked) data. As the number of time intervals increases, these models are essentially semiparametric, thus providing an alternative to parametric duration models.[16] We found that estimating discrete- and continuous-time models is straightforward once the data have been arrayed in a suitable split-episode format. We also intro-

---

[16]Unfortunately, few programs can automatically estimate this model (TDA is an exception). Programs like SAS and LIMDEP offer only parametric and semiparametric (Cox) models.

duced methods for handling correlations in binary responses over time and ways to handle unobserved heterogeneity in hazard rate models.

Chapter 6

Models for Ordinal Dependent Variables

6.1 Introduction

Many social phenomena of interest are measured by ordered categorical (or simply ordinal) variables. Typically, ordered categorical variables assume numerical values to denote the *rank order* of a particular attribute. These rankings, however, do not necessarily represent the actual magnitudes on a substantive scale. That is to say, the distance between two adjacent categories of an ordinal variable is not necessarily the same across different segments of its distribution. Ordinal variables can be viewed as somewhere between nominal variables on the one hand and continuous variables on the other hand in the following sense: Ordinal variables are more general than continuous variables in allowing for varying distances across adjacent values but more restricted than nominal variables in containing ordinal information. Examples of ordinal qualitative data include the Likert scale, in which responses on questions take such categories as strongly disagree, disagree, neutral, agree, or strongly agree. Other examples of ordered categorical data include discrete measures of years of schooling (less than 8 years, 8–11 years, 12 years, and 13 or more years) (Winship and Mare 1984) and property division among the elderly (none, part, and all) (Li, Xie, and Lin 1993).

As outlined in Chapter 1, ordinal variables are fundamentally categorical. Treating outcomes as ordered as opposed to nominal is a choice the researcher must make depending on the goals of the research. Sometimes, a given outcome can be treated either as a nominal variable or as an ordinal variable. If differences in outcomes and the effects of independent variables on these differences are the primary concerns, methods for unordered multinomial responses would be appropriate. These methods are discussed in detail in Chapter 7. If the primary interest lies in the understanding of how explanatory variables affect the conceptual dimension represented by the ordinal variable, ordinal models are appropriate. As will be shown, an ordinal dependent variable can also be treated as a continuous variable under a particular assumption. This chapter presents an overview of some common statistical methods and models for the analysis of ordered qualitative variables.

6.2   Scoring Methods

The fundamental problem facing a researcher analyzing an ordinal dependent variable is one of incomplete information. An ordinal variable reveals the rank order of its different values but not their magnitudes on a substantively meaningful scale. To resolve this difficulty, researchers have naturally resorted to various ways to recover the information pertaining to the magnitudes by assigning numerical scores to them. We call them "scoring methods." Scoring is perhaps the most widely used solution for analyzing ordinal dependent variables. Under certain circumstances, scoring methods work well. In this section, we provide a brief review of various scoring methods as the background for more advanced models.

6.2.1   Integer Scoring

The simplest and perhaps most popular method of scoring is integer scoring. The method assigns integers to represent the rank order. For a typical Likert-scaled question, one may assign the following: strongly disagree = 1, disagree = 2, neutral = 3, agree = 4, and strongly agree

= 5. As a concrete illustration, let us refer to an earlier example on attitudes toward premarital sex (Table 4.8). We can assign Always Wrong = 1, Almost Always Wrong = 2, Sometimes Wrong = 3, and Not Wrong at All = 4, with higher numbers representing greater levels of tolerance toward premarital sex.

The crucial assumption underlying integer scoring is that the distances between adjacent categories are all equal. Researchers who use integer scoring are not always conscious of and sensitive to this assumption. Instead, they use integer scoring mainly out of convenience.

Given that the latent scale is unobservable, there are infinitely many other scoring methods that will give results equivalent to integer scoring, so long as they satisfy the equal distance assumption. For example, for Likert-scaled responses, $(-2, -1, 0, 1, 2)$ scoring yields results indistinguishable from $(1, 2, 3, 4, 5)$ scoring. Similarly, for the education example, $(2, 4, 6, 8)$ scoring is functionally equivalent to $(1, 2, 3, 4)$ scoring. As is true with all latent variables, both the *location* and the *scale* of scores need to be normalized. The integer scoring method conveniently sets the location to begin at 1 and scale to be 1 for each increment in the category.

6.2.2   Midpoint Scoring

Sometimes ordinal variables result from categorical measures of variables that are conceptually continuous. In the example of attitudes toward premarital sex, education was originally collected as years of schooling in the General Social Surveys but was collapsed into four categories: Less Than High School (0–11 years), High School (exactly 12 years), Some College (13–15 years), and College and Beyond (16 or more years).

When an ordinal variable is a discretized version of a continuous variable, the researcher knows the cutpoints that bound the interval of each category. It is thus possible—and sometimes appealing—to impute the midpoint between the cutpoints for each interval to be the "average" value representing all cases falling in the interval. In fact, this is a commonly used method for resolving the aggregation problem in applied work.

There are two potential problems with the method of midpoint scoring. First, if the distribution is highly skewed within an interval, midpoints are poor estimates of the true values. For example, for respondents falling in the category "less than 12 years of schooling" in the GSS survey, 5.5 would be a severe underestimate of their mean years of schooling. Second, the last category is often open-ended. For the education example, the last category means college and beyond. One would need to make an assumption or use auxiliary information to come up with a reasonable midpoint for such open-ended categories. These two problems lead to our recommendation for a transformation rule based on an assumed distribution of the data.

6.2.3   Normal Score Transformation

As discussed in Chapter 1, one prominent approach in categorical data analysis, represented by Karl Pearson and his followers, is that categorical variables are manifestations of underlying, normally distributed variables. In the present context, this viewpoint dictates that ordinal variables are simply discretized versions of normally distributed variables. In a contingency table context, when both variables are ordinal, Goodman (1981b) shows a close relationship between the bivariate normal distribution model, which yields the tetrachoric correlation model, and the RC association model. As will be shown in the next section, the RC association model can be viewed as the adjacent category logit model. See Clogg and Shihadeh (1994) for a more detailed treatment of this topic.

Although the normal distribution assumption should ideally be invoked for the *conditional* distribution of the latent dependent variable after controlling for explanatory variables, it may be fruitful for some applications to capitalize on the marginal distribution of the dependent variable to derive normal scores. To assign normal scores to intervals based on marginal distributions, we take the following steps: (1) calculate the sample proportion in each category, (2) accumulate proportions across categories, (3) for each category, find the cumulative proportion that corresponds to its midpoint (50th percentile within category), and (4) transform the cumulative proportion to a z-

score based on the standardized normal distribution.[1] These steps are demonstrated in detail with the example of attitudes toward abortion in Table 6.1.

Table 6.1: Normal Score Transformation for the Attitude Example

	Always Wrong	Almost Always Wrong	Sometimes Wrong	Not Wrong at All
Frequency	1020	386	825	1573
Proportion	0.268	0.101	0.217	0.414
Cumulative Prop.	0.268	0.370	0.586	1.000
Mid-Point	0.134	0.319	0.478	0.793
Z-Score	-1.107	-0.471	-0.055	0.818

One interesting finding that emerges from the table is that, if we normalize scores on marginal distributions, the second category (Almost Always Wrong) is substantively much closer to the first category (Always Wrong) than the last one (Not Wrong at All). It appears that the third category (Sometimes Wrong) is a neutral position.

6.2.4   Scaling with Additional Information

The aforementioned scoring methods are internal within the same ordinal dependent variable. A more complicated, but preferred, approach is to utilize auxiliary information either from different variables in the same dataset or even from different data sources. This falls in a broader literature on scaling and will not be discussed at length here. A classic example is Duncan's (1961) construction of the socioeconomic status index. A more recent example utilizing "instrumental" variables for scaling is Clogg's (1982) use of Goodman's (1979) RC model to obtain numerical scales for ordinal measures. As mentioned in Chapter 4, one attractive feature of the RC model as a scaling method is that it does not necessarily assume the correct rank order of the categories.

---

[1]Recall that z is the inverse of a standard cumulative normal probability distribution [i.e., $z = \Phi^{-1}(p)$].

It can instead estimate the magnitudes as well as the rank order of the categories.

6.3   Logit Models for Grouped Data

In Chapter 3, which covers regression models for a dichotomous dependent variable (y), we define the logit as

$$\log\left(\frac{p}{1-p}\right) = \log\left[\frac{\Pr(y=1)}{\Pr(y=0)}\right]. \tag{6.1}$$

That is, the logit can be seen as the logged ratio of two probabilities. In general, for an outcome variable (y) with multiple responses $(j = 1, \ldots, J)$, the logit transformation takes the form of

$$\log\left[\frac{\Pr(y=j)}{\Pr(y=j')}\right] = \log\left(\frac{p_j}{p_{j'}}\right), \tag{6.2}$$

where p_j and $p_{j'}$ are respectively probabilities for categories j and j'. In addition, logits can be constructed using cumulative probabilities. Thus, many potentially interesting logits exist for a response variable with multiple outcomes. Of the many logits for a J-category response variable y $(y = 1, \ldots, J)$, however, only $J-1$ logits are nonredundant. Once we understand a set of nonredundant logits, knowledge of other logits can be deduced. In this section, we will present three ways to define nonredundant logits and discuss the relationships among them.

6.3.1   Baseline, Adjacent, and Cumulative Logits

Let us first introduce the baseline logit. The idea is to contrast all other response categories with a baseline category. With no loss of generality, we can use the first category as the baseline. The baseline logit for the jth category $(j = 2, \ldots, J)$ is

$$BL_j = \log\left[\frac{\Pr(y=j)}{\Pr(y=1)}\right] = \log\left(\frac{p_j}{p_1}\right), \quad j = 2, \ldots, J. \tag{6.3}$$

Of course, the choice of the first category as the baseline is entirely arbitrary, in the same sense that the choice of a reference category to construct a set of dummy variables for a nominal independent variable is arbitrary. Logit models for unordered, multiple-category dependent variables (i.e., multinomial logit models) commonly take the form of baseline logits and will be covered in Chapter 7.

Now let us turn to the adjacent logit. The basic idea is to contrast a pair of adjacent categories. Let us define it as

$$AL_j = \log\left[\frac{\Pr(y = j)}{\Pr(y = j - 1)}\right] = \log\left(\frac{p_j}{p_{j-1}}\right), \quad j = 2, \ldots, J. \quad (6.4)$$

As will be shown later, this logit formulation has a close connection with the local log-odds-ratios that play a central role in loglinear models (Chapter 4). Because of this, adjacent logit models are commonly used for grouped data so that interpretation draws on the loglinear modeling framework.

Finally, we can use cumulative probabilities to form the cumulative logit. Let us define

$$CL_j = \log\left[\frac{\Pr(y \leq j)}{\Pr(y > j)}\right] = \log\left(\frac{\sum_{k=1}^{j} p_k}{\sum_{k=j+1}^{J} p_k}\right) \quad (6.5)$$

to be the cumulative logit that the probability is less than or equal to j versus greater than j. This formulation plays an important role in ordinal logit models and will receive extensive discussion in this chapter.

From the preceding formulas, it is clear that

$$BL_j = \sum_{k=2}^{j} AL_k. \quad (6.6)$$

The relationship between cumulative logits and adjacent/baseline logits is nonlinear and will not be further explored here.

6.3.2   Adjacent Category Logit Model

The aforementioned three types of logits give rise to three types of logit models. The baseline logit model will be discussed in Chapter

7, and the cumulative logit model will be the focus of the remainder of this chapter. In this and the next subsections, we will explore the properties of the adjacent category logit model. Assuming one categorical independent variable x ($x = 1, \ldots, I$), the adjacent category logit model takes the form

$$\log \left(\frac{p_j}{p_{j-1}} \right) = \beta_{ij}, \quad i = 1, \ldots, I; \quad j = 2, \ldots, J . \qquad (6.7)$$

In fact, all the sufficient statistics for this model are contained in the $y \times x$ contingency table. If we take the contingency table as input, the resulting adjacent category logit model (Eq. 6.7) is simply a saturated model. In Table 6.2, we show the results for the example of predicting attitudes toward premarital sex based on educational attainment. The input data are taken from the 4×4 table of Table 4.8. In this model specification, we treat education as a nominal explanatory variable. The results are essentially the same as the odds-ratios reported in Table 4.9. The main differences are: (1) the entries in Table 6.2 contrast dependent outcomes within a category of the independent variable, whereas those in Table 4.9 are odds-ratios involving contrasts of both the dependent and the independent variables; and (2) the entries in Table 6.2 are in the logit scale, whereas those in Table 4.9 are in the odds-ratio scale.

Table 6.2: Education and Attitude Toward Premarital Sex

	Attitude toward Premarital Sex		
Education	C: 2 versus 1	C: 3 versus 2	C: 4 versus 3
Less than H.S.	−1.210	0.354	0.791
High School	−0.886	0.693	0.621
Some College	−0.827	0.919	0.663
College and Above	−0.908	1.075	0.546

If we assume that the explanatory variable is an interval-level variable, model 6.7 can be simplified to

$$\log \left(\frac{p_j}{p_{j-1}} \right) = \alpha_j + \beta_j x_i, \quad i = 1, \ldots, I, \quad j = 2, \ldots, J. \qquad (6.8)$$

Since we estimate $J - 1$ coefficients for any explanatory variable in Eq. 6.8, we still have not utilized the ordinal information in the dependent variable. If we further assume that the dependent variable can be scaled into an interval variable, y_j, model 6.8 can be further simplified to

$$\log \left(\frac{p_j}{p_{j-1}} \right) = \alpha_j + \beta(y_j - y_{j-1})x_i, \quad i = 1, \ldots, I, \quad j = 2, \ldots, J.$$
(6.9)

As a special case, if integer scoring is applied to both y and x, Eq. 6.9 is reduced to

$$\log \left(\frac{p_j}{p_{j-1}} \right) = \alpha_j + \beta i, \quad i = 1, \ldots, I; \quad j = 2, \ldots, J. \quad (6.10)$$

6.3.3   Adjacent Category Logit Models and Log-linear Models

Adjacent category logit models shown in the previous subsection are in essence loglinear models. The loglinear equivalent of model 6.7 is the saturated model. The loglinear equivalent of Eq. 6.8 is the following "generalized" column effects model:

$$\log F_{ij} = \mu + \mu_i^R + \mu_j^C + x_i \nu_j, \quad (6.11)$$

where x_i is the imputed score for the ith category of the explanatory variable. We use the term *generalized* because column effects models typically use integer scoring for the row variable, whereas here we allow a more general scale for the row variable. Given 6.11, it follows that the adjacent logit can be written as

$$\log \left(\frac{p_j}{p_{j-1}} \right) = \log \left(\frac{F_{ij}}{F_{i(j-1)}} \right) = \mu_j^C - \mu_{j-1}^C + x_i(\nu_j - \nu_{j-1}), \quad (6.12)$$

the same form as Eq. 6.8, with $\alpha_j = \mu_j^C - \mu_{j-1}^C$ and $\beta_j = \nu_j - \nu_{j-1}$ as the estimated coefficient of x for the j versus $j - 1$ logit contrast. If the underlying score of the dependent variable is known as y_j, βy_j can substitute for ν_j and reduces Eq. 6.12 to Eq. 6.9. As a special case, a uniform association model for the contingency table specifies that $x_i = i$ and $y_j = j$. This corresponds to integer scoring and reduces Eq. 6.12 to Eq. 6.10. These types of adjacent category logit models can be estimated with existing computer software for loglinear models.

We apply these models to the example of attitudes toward premarital sex. We first assign integer scores to the education variable so that $x_i = i$ and estimate model 6.8, which is equivalent to the column effects model. Our estimation yields a G^2 of 14.22 with 6 degrees of freedom ($BIC = -35.24$). The three adjacent category logit coefficients are 0.112, 0.343, 0.281 (with standard errors of 0.057, 0.045, and 0.039), respectively, for the contrasts of categories 2 vs. 1, 3 vs. 2, and 4 vs. 3 of the dependent variable. These estimates indicate that education is associated with higher tolerance toward premarital sex. This education effect appears to be weaker at the low end of tolerance than at the high end. To test the hypothesis that the education effect is the same across the spectrum of the response variable, we further assign integer scores to be y_j, and estimate Eq. 6.10, which is effectively the uniform association model. The model does not fit the data as well as the previous model, with G^2 of 31.33 for 8 degrees of freedom ($BIC = -34.62$). Note that scoring methods other than that of integer scoring can be used. For example, we can assign integer scores to x_i but normal scores to y_j (Table 6.1). The model however does not fit better than the uniform association model ($G^2 = 39.69$ for 8 degrees of freedom, $BIC = -26.26$).

6.4   Ordered Logit and Probit Models

This section considers ordered probability models for individual-level data (e.g., models with continuous explanatory variables). These models are commonly referred to as ordered (or ordinal) logit and probit models. The logit version can be seen as being based on cumulative logits.

There are two approaches to extending the binary logit and probit models discussed in Chapter 3 to the case of ordered outcomes. The first approach makes use of the logits or probits of cumulative probabilities. This approach might be preferred when the categories are ordered but the analyst is unwilling to assume that the outcome represents a recoded or collapsed version of a continuous variable that could possibly be measured more finely. The second approach assumes the existence of an underlying continuous latent variable, akin to the random-utility regression-type models for binary responses presented in Chapter 3. Regardless of which approach is used, the statistical properties of the models are the same.

6.4.1   Cumulative Logits and Probits

Let us now change notation and denote the ith observation in a sample by subscript i. Given that the response variable y_i assumes the values $1, 2, \ldots, J$ $(J \geq 3)$, which correspond to ordered responses, a general probability model can be written in terms of cumulative probabilities. The cumulative probability $\Pr(y_i \leq j)$ is the probability that y is less than or equal to a particular value j. Cast in this way, the cumulative probability has the familiar interpretation as a long-run cumulative relative frequency of a discrete random variable. The cumulative probability for the ith individual up to response level j, denoted as $C_{i,j}$, can be written as

$$C_{i,j} = \Pr(y_i \leq j) = \sum_{k=1}^{j} \Pr(y_i = k), \qquad j = 1, \ldots, J . \qquad (6.13)$$

By definition, the cumulative probabilities must sum to one when $j = J$, meaning that $C_{i,J} = 1.0$, for all i. This constraint implies that only $J - 1$ cumulative probabilities (or functions of them) are uniquely identified.

We now let the cumulative probability be a function of a vector of independent variables, $\mathbf{x}_i$, as follows:

$$C_{i,j} = F(\alpha_j + \mathbf{x}_i'\boldsymbol{\beta}), \qquad j = 1, \ldots, J - 1 , \qquad (6.14)$$

where $F(\cdot)$ is a suitable cumulative distribution function. In most cases, this is a symmetric distribution. The ordered logit model is obtained when $F(\cdot)$ follows a cumulative logistic distribution. Choosing a cumulative standard normal distribution for $F(\cdot)$ leads to the ordered probit model. In this specification, there are $(J-1)$ α_j parameters, which can be thought of as cutpoints, thresholds, or separate intercepts, corresponding to the ordered categories of the dependent variable. Defining the cumulative probabilities in this way means that $C_{i,j} > C_{i,j-1}$ so that $F(\cdot)$ increases with j as depicted in Fig. 6.1. Thus, the α_j parameters are necessarily nondecreasing in j.

Different parameterizations of this basic model are possible. For example, we could have defined $C_{i,j} = \Pr(y_i > j)$. In a symmetric distribution, this is equal to $1 - \Pr(y_i \leq j)$, so this model reverses the signs of the coefficients from the standard parameterization based on cumulative probabilities. It is important to know which parameterization is implemented in a particular software package when estimating these models. The cumulative probability parameterization is used in the SAS Proc Logistic procedure (SAS Institute 1990) and outlined by Agresti (1990). Section 6.4.4 discusses different parameterizations.

The conditional probabilities of the ordered outcomes can be written in terms of the cumulative probabilities as follows:

$$\Pr(y_i = j \mid \mathbf{x}_i) = \begin{cases} F(\alpha_1 + \mathbf{x}_i'\boldsymbol{\beta}) & j = 1, \\ F(\alpha_j + \mathbf{x}_i'\boldsymbol{\beta}) - F(\alpha_{j-1} + \mathbf{x}_i'\boldsymbol{\beta}) & 1 < j \leq J-1, \\ 1 - F(\alpha_{J-1} + \mathbf{x}_i'\boldsymbol{\beta}) & j = J. \end{cases}$$

$$(6.15)$$

In this way, the predicted probabilities associated with a response can be retrieved from the model.

6.4.2   The Ordered Logit Model

The cumulative probability of the ordered logit model is written as

$$C_{i,j} = \Pr(y_i \leq j \mid \mathbf{x}_i) = \frac{\exp(\alpha_j + \mathbf{x}_i'\boldsymbol{\beta})}{1 + \exp(\alpha_j + \mathbf{x}_i'\boldsymbol{\beta})}. \qquad (6.16)$$

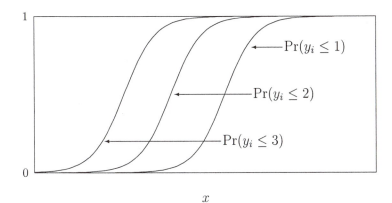

Figure 6.1: Cumulative Probabilities Corresponding to a Four-Category Response.

Like the models in Chapter 3, this model is linear in the logistic scale. Letting $l_j(x_i)$ denote the *cumulative logit* of $y \leq j$ versus $y > j$,

$$l_j(\mathbf{x}_i) = \log \left[\frac{\Pr(y_i \leq j \mid \mathbf{x}_i)}{\Pr(y_i > j \mid \mathbf{x}_i)} \right] \tag{6.17}$$
$$= \alpha_j + \mathbf{x}_i'\boldsymbol{\beta}.$$

This model is often called the *proportional odds* model. Given two covariate vectors $\mathbf{x}_{i1}$ and $\mathbf{x}_{i2}$, the odds of a response $y_i \leq j$ versus $y_i > j$ are proportionally higher or lower across the two situations $\mathbf{x}_i = \mathbf{x}_1$ and $\mathbf{x}_i = \mathbf{x}_2$. Letting $\omega(\mathbf{x}_h)$ $(h = 1, 2)$ denote the *cumulative odds* associated with covariate values, one obtains the *cumulative odds-ratio* as

$$\frac{\omega(\mathbf{x}_1)}{\omega(\mathbf{x}_2)} = \frac{\Pr(y \leq j \mid \mathbf{x}_1)/\Pr(y > j \mid \mathbf{x}_1)}{\Pr(y \leq j \mid \mathbf{x}_2)/\Pr(y > j \mid \mathbf{x}_2)}$$
$$= \frac{\exp(\mathbf{x}_1'\boldsymbol{\beta})}{\exp(\mathbf{x}_2'\boldsymbol{\beta})} = \exp\{(\mathbf{x}_1 - \mathbf{x}_2)'\boldsymbol{\beta}\}, \tag{6.18}$$

which is proportional to the distances between the values of the explanatory variables. The key to the proportionality property is that the effects of $\mathbf{x}$ are invariant with respect to outcome categories. That is, $\boldsymbol{\beta}$ is not indexed by j.

The log of the cumulative odds-ratio, or *cumulative log-odds-ratio* is

$$\log \left[\frac{\omega(\mathbf{x}_1)}{\omega(\mathbf{x}_2)} \right] = l_j(\mathbf{x}_1) - l_j(\mathbf{x}_2) = (\mathbf{x}_1 - \mathbf{x}_2)'\boldsymbol{\beta}. \qquad (6.19)$$

Equation 6.19 is also invariant with respect to j.

For J ordered categories and a single covariate, the fitted logits correspond to $J - 1$ parallel lines. It is also possible to test for equal slopes.[2]

In the preceding parameterization for a given covariate x_k, when $\beta_k > 0$, the cumulative logits increase as x_k increases. This means that y tends to be smaller for higher values of x_k. Similarly, when β_k is negative, increases in x_k are associated with higher levels of y. An alternative parameterization in which $C_{i,j} = \Pr(y_i > j)$ results in the usual interpretation associated with regression-type estimates. That is, for $\beta_k > 0$, higher values of x_k are associated with higher levels of y.

6.4.3   The Ordered Probit Model

Similarly, the ordered probit model can be obtained by specifying the following conditional cumulative probabilities:

$$C_{i,j} = \Pr(y_i \leq j \mid \mathbf{x}_i) = \Phi(\alpha_j + \mathbf{x}_i'\boldsymbol{\beta}), \qquad (6.20)$$

where $\Phi(\cdot)$ denotes the cumulative standard normal distribution function. The ordered logit and ordered probit are special cases of *cumulative link* models, which are closely related to the latent variable models in Section 6.4.4. Letting $F(\cdot)$ denote the cumulative distribution function of a continuous random variable, the inverse link function, $F^{-1}(p)$

---

[2]A chi-squared score test of proportionality can be used to test the equal slopes (probit) or proportional odds (logit) assumption. This test requires expressions for the vector of first and second partial derivatives of the log-likelihood function with respect to the parameters. The SAS software package provides this test as part of the output.

translates the cumulative probabilities, $\Pr(y_i \leq j)$, to the real line. Link functions other than the logit or probit would be suitable for variables following other distributions. For example, the complementary log-log link function introduced in Chapter 2 and Chapter 5 would be appropriate when the distribution is left-skewed [or when $\Pr(y_i \leq j)$ approaches 1.0 at a faster rate than it approaches 0.0].

The ordered probit model is very similar to the ordered logit model. The difference between the two is largely historical, as they were developed independently of each other in separate disciplines, with the probit model in social science (McKelvey and Zavoina 1975) and the logit model in biostatistics (McCullagh 1980). A choice between the two should be inconsequential in practice. Covariate effects (logits and probits) will have similar interpretations. However, in the ordered probit model, there is no natural odds-ratio interpretation for the effects of categorical independent variables.

6.4.4   The Latent Variable Approach

An alternative approach to setting up the same models is cast in terms of latent variables. This approach underlies the early development of the ordered probit model by McKelvey and Zavoina (1975). The latent variable approach is motivated by assuming an underlying continuous latent variable y^* that would represent the response if it could be measured more accurately. In the language of structural equations, we can view the relationship between latent and observed variables as constituting a measurement model (Xie 1989). Let us assume a set of unknown threshold values

$$\delta_0 < \delta_1 < \cdots < \delta_{J-1} < \delta_J, \tag{6.21}$$

where $\delta_0 = -\infty$ and $\delta_J = \infty$. The relationship between the latent variable and the realized outcome is

$$y_i = j \quad \text{if} \quad \delta_{j-1} < y_i^* \leq \delta_j. \tag{6.22}$$

This relationship is depicted in Fig. 6.2 for four ordered outcomes. We find, for example, that a realized ordered outcome of $y_i = 4$ corresponds to a continuous latent variable $y_i^* > \delta_3$.

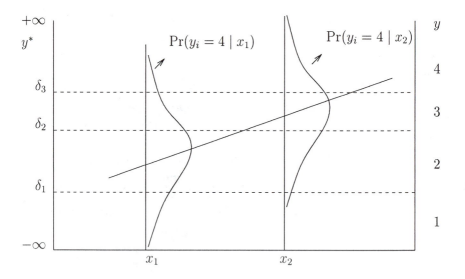

Figure 6.2: The Relation Between Latent Variables and Realized Outcomes

The latent variable approach places emphasis on the "structural" model for y_i^*,

$$y_i^* = \mathbf{x}_i'\boldsymbol{\beta} + \varepsilon_i, \tag{6.23}$$

where ε has mean zero and follows a symmetric distribution (i.e., normal or logistic). Just as with the latent variable models for binomial responses considered in Chapter 3, the location and scale of y^* are arbitrary and cannot be identified. Thus, we assume that for the probit model, the variance $\text{var}(\varepsilon)$ is 1 and for the logit, $\text{var}(\varepsilon) = \pi^2/3$.

The latent variable model for y_i^* can be written as a cumulative probability model. The equivalence is based on the following relationship between the observed discrete response and the continuous latent variable:

$$\Pr(y_i \leq j) = \Pr(y_i^* \leq \delta_j). \tag{6.24}$$

Substituting this expression for y^*, the cumulative probabilities are written as

$$C_{i,j} = \Pr(y_i \leq j \mid \mathbf{x}_i) = \Pr(\mathbf{x}_i'\boldsymbol{\beta} + \varepsilon_i \leq \delta_j). \tag{6.25}$$

Rearranging terms, we find that

$$C_{i,j} = \Pr(\varepsilon_i \leq \delta_j - \mathbf{x}_i'\boldsymbol{\beta}) = F(\delta_j - \mathbf{x}_i'\boldsymbol{\beta}), \tag{6.26}$$

where $F(\cdot)$ is the distribution function for ε. This parameterization reverses the signs of β from the cumulative probability model so that $\beta > 0$ has the familiar interpretation as a positive effect of x on y^*.

The cutpoints (δ_j's) for the latent variable approach are similar to α_j's for the cumulative probability approach in that they function to fit exactly the marginal distribution of outcome categories. For this reason, there is usually no intercept term in the structural equation (6.23). Some statistical packages, such as LIMDEP, include an intercept for the structural equation but then add a constraint to the measurement model of Eq. 6.21, such that $\delta_0 = 0$.

The cumulative probabilities under the latent variable model (without the intercept) take the form

$$\Pr(y_i = j \mid \mathbf{x}_i) = \begin{cases} F(\delta_1 - \mathbf{x}_i'\boldsymbol{\beta}) & j = 1, \\ F(\delta_j - \mathbf{x}_i'\boldsymbol{\beta}) - F(\delta_{j-1} - \mathbf{x}_i'\boldsymbol{\beta}) & 1 < j \leq J - 1, \\ 1 - F(\delta_{J-1} - \mathbf{x}_i'\boldsymbol{\beta}) & j = J. \end{cases}$$

$$\tag{6.27}$$

6.4.5   Estimation

Maximum likelihood estimation of the parameters of ordered probability models is straightforward. Newton-Raphson is the default method for obtaining ordered probits and ordered logits in many programs, and our experience shows this algorithm converges faster than other methods. The goal is to find estimates of $\boldsymbol{\beta}$ and α_j or δ_j that maximize the joint probability of obtaining the observed values. Because observations are independent, the joint probability factors into the product of marginal probabilities. The probability of observing $y = j$ is the difference between the cumulative probabilities

$$\Pr(y_i = j \mid \mathbf{x}_i) = \Pr(y_i \le j \mid \mathbf{x}_i) - \Pr(y_i \le j - 1 \mid \mathbf{x}_i).$$

The contribution to the likelihood for the ith observation depends on which value of j is observed. For each of the J values of the ordered response, we take the product over all observations for which $y = j$ and write the likelihood as

$$L = \prod_{i=1}^{n} \prod_{j=1}^{J} \Pr(y_i = j \mid \mathbf{x}_i)^{d_{ij}}, \qquad (6.28)$$

where $d_{ij} = 1$ if $y_i = j$, and 0 otherwise. Thus, the d_{ij} define a set of J dummy variables, only one of which is equal to 1 for any observation.

For the cumulative logit and probit models, the log-likelihood can be written in terms of model quantities as

$$\log L = \sum_{i=1}^{n} \sum_{j=1}^{J} d_{ij} \log \left[F(\alpha_j + \mathbf{x}_i' \boldsymbol{\beta}) - F(\alpha_{j-1} + \mathbf{x}_i' \boldsymbol{\beta}) \right]. \qquad (6.29)$$

For the latent variable model, the log-likelihood is

$$\log L = \sum_{i=1}^{n} \sum_{j=1}^{J} d_{ij} \log \left[F(\delta_j - \mathbf{x}_i' \boldsymbol{\beta}) - F(\delta_{j-1} - \mathbf{x}_i' \boldsymbol{\beta}) \right]. \qquad (6.30)$$

They yield the same parameter estimates for $\boldsymbol{\beta}$ but with opposite signs.

Numerical Example

As an illustration, we consider traditional sex role attitudes in a sample of 3,705 young non-Hispanic White women from the NLSY dataset. The ordered outcome is derived from the respondent's agreement or disagreement with the statement: "A woman's place is in the home not in the workplace." The possible responses are $1 =$ Strongly Disagree (40%), $2 =$ Disagree (45.2%), $3 =$ Agree (11.3%), and $4 =$ Strongly Agree (3.5%).

Table 6.3: Ordered Logit Estimates Under Alternative Parameterizations

Variable	Ordered Logit I		Ordered Logit II	
	Estimate	t-Value	Estimate	t-Value
AGE	0.036	(2.57)	−0.036	(−2.57)
NONINT	0.182	(2.43)	−0.182	(−2.43)
MWORK	0.224	(3.50)	−0.224	(−3.50)
MEDUC	0.084	(6.25)	−0.084	(−6.25)
INCOME	0.013	(2.29)	−0.013	(−2.29)
NSIBS	−0.046	(−3.07)	0.046	(3.07)
FUNDPROT	−0.479	(−6.69)	0.479	(6.69)
CONSTANT $(-\delta_1)$	–	–	2.041	(6.47)
α_1	−2.041	(6.47)	–	–
α_2	0.196	(0.62)	–	–
α_3	1.774	(5.52)	–	–
$\delta_2 - \delta_1$	–	–	2.234	(45.42)
$\delta_3 - \delta_1$	–	–	3.815	(41.50)
Log-Likelihood	−3947.3		−3947.3	
Model χ^2	178.1		178.1	
DF	7		7	

The model fit to the data includes the effects of age (AGE), non-intact family structure at age 14 (NONINT), mother's employment at age 14 (MWORK), mother's education (MEDUC), family income (INCOME), number of siblings (NSIBS), and fundamentalist Protestant upbringing (FUNDPROT).[3]

The results from an ordered logit model using two different parameterizations are presented in Table 6.3.[4] Ordered Logit I corresponds to the cumulative logit model whereas Ordered Logit II corresponds to the latent variable model.

---

[3]A score test for proportional odds yields a χ^2 of 11.78 with 14 degrees of freedom, which provides no evidence against this assumption.

[4]These results are obtained using SAS and LIMDEP. Note that LIMDEP sets $\delta_0 = 0$ and includes a constant term in the model. The threshold parameters reported by LIMDEP (μ_j) correspond to differences in the δ parameters, such that, $\mu_0 = \beta_0 = -\delta_1$ is the model intercept and $\mu_j = \delta_{j+1} - \delta_1$ ($j = 1, \ldots, J-2$).

Based on the first parameterization (Ordered Logit I), one finds higher levels of agreement with the statement "a woman's place is in the home" to increase with family size (NSIBS) and with fundamentalist Protestant upbringing (FUNDPROT). Lower levels of agreement tend to be associated with age, nonintact family structure, mother's education, work outside the home, and family income. For example, conditional on the other covariates, the odds that sex role attitude is less than or equal to a given level j versus greater than j is estimated to be $e^{-0.479} = 0.62$ times as high for respondents with fundamentalist Protestant upbringing as those from other religious backgrounds. In contrast, having a working mother is associated with an estimated 25% increase in the odds ($e^{0.224} = 1.25$).

The second parameterization (Ordered Logit II) provides an alternative interpretation of the same results. The latent variable, y_i^*, represents a tendency toward conservative sex roles. This tendency shifts upward by 0.479 for those with fundamentalist Protestant backgrounds. A unit change in mother's education is associated with a 0.084 decrease in the tendency toward conservative gender roles, holding other variables constant.

The two parameterizations simply reflect different ways of thinking about the data. The cumulative logit approach is based on a conventional definition of a cumulative probability. The results are interpreted as effects on the log-odds of a response being *less* than or equal to any level, j. The latent variable approach uses an analogy to linear regression, where covariate effects are interpreted as changes in a latent variable associated with unit changes in $\mathbf{x}$.

6.4.6 Marginal Effects

Within the latent variable approach, the effects of independent variables are interpreted in the usual regression sense as changes in y^* associated with changes in $\mathbf{x}$. Unfortunately, y^* is unobserved, so alternative interpretations would be desirable. In the ordered logit model, a natural interpretation occurs in the form of the odds-ratios expressed in Eq. 6.17. For the ordered probit model, however, there is no analogous odds-ratio interpretation. However, *partial* marginal effects representing changes in $\Pr(y_i = j \mid \mathbf{x}_i)$ provide a convenient way to express results. The *partial* marginal effects of x_k are given by

$$
\frac{\partial \Pr(y_i = j \mid \mathbf{x}_i)}{\partial x_{ik}} = \begin{cases} -f(\delta_1 - \mathbf{x}_i'\boldsymbol{\beta})\beta_k & j = 1, \\ [f(\delta_{j-1} - \mathbf{x}_i'\boldsymbol{\beta}) - f(\delta_j - \mathbf{x}_i'\boldsymbol{\beta})]\,\beta_k & 1 < j \leq J - 1, \\ f(\delta_{J-1} - \mathbf{x}_i'\boldsymbol{\beta})\beta_k & j = J. \end{cases}
$$

$$(6.31)$$

From these expressions, we find that the marginal effect has the opposite sign of β for $j = 1$ and the same sign as β for $j = J$ because the density, $f(\cdot)$, is nonnegative. However, the sign of the marginal effects for the intermediate categories will depend on the densities for j and $j - 1$ ($j = 2, \ldots, J - 1$) and cannot be determined from the estimates alone. For this reason, we urge caution when interpreting marginal effects and favor the simpler odds-ratio approach in the case of logit models.

Table 6.4: Ordered Probit Estimates and Marginal Effects

Variable	$\widehat{\beta}$	t-Value	$\dfrac{\partial \Pr(y_i = j \mid x_i)}{\partial x_i}$ Ordered Outcome			
			1	2	3	4
AGE	−0.021	−2.43	0.008	−0.003	−0.003	−0.014
NONINT	−0.100	−2.33	0.038	−0.016	−0.015	−0.007
MWORK	−0.139	−3.70	0.053	−0.023	−0.021	−0.010
MEDUC	−0.048	−6.16	0.019	−0.008	−0.007	−0.003
INCOME	−0.008	−2.37	0.003	−0.001	−0.001	−0.001
NSIBS	0.027	3.05	−0.010	0.004	0.004	0.002
FUNDPROT	0.278	6.67	−0.107	0.045	0.042	0.019
δ_1	−1.200	6.43				
δ_2	0.134	0.75				
δ_3	0.922	5.38				
Log L	−3947.2					
Model χ^2	178.4					
DF	7					

Table 6.4 shows the parameter estimates and marginal effects from an ordered probit model for the sex role attitude data. The marginal effects have been evaluated at the means of the independent variables, so that $\mathbf{x}_i'\boldsymbol{\beta}$ in the preceding expression is replaced by $\bar{\mathbf{x}}'\widehat{\boldsymbol{\beta}}$. The marginal effects are interpreted as a change in the probability that y equals a given level per unit change in x, conditional on other covariates. For dummy independent variables, this formulation of the marginal effects is not entirely correct, and alternative formulas are available. However, in practice, it is often easier to use the formula in Eq. 6.31 from the computational standpoint.

6.5   Summary

This chapter provides a review of several models for ordered responses. We have shown how the association models of Chapter 4 can be extended to encompass ordered responses in the context of loglinear modeling. For individual-level data, cumulative probabilities provide the basis for constructing and modeling cumulative logit and probit models. These models can be motivated by treating ordered responses simply as category rankings, or more abstractly, as representing an underlying (latent) continuous variable. We showed that, although the estimates may differ due to the particular normalization, the models lend themselves to the same substantive interpretation.

Chapter 7

Models for Unordered Dependent Variables

7.1 Introduction

Many substantively interesting phenomena are measured as unordered qualitative (or *polytomous*) variables. For example, sociologists and economists are interested in labor-force status (employed, unemployed, or out of the labor force), political scientists in party affiliation (Republican, Democratic, and Independent), and geographers and demographers in regions of residence (Northeast, Midwest, South, and West). We discuss statistical models with such unordered qualitative measures as dependent variables in this chapter. These models have a long tradition in the economics of consumer choice. For example, commuters may choose among alternative modes of transportation (train, bus, or car). As in the binary choice models covered in Chapter 3, the modeling framework for polytomous variables can also be derived from assuming a latent continuous variable, or a utility function, that underlies the individuals' preferences associated with their manifested choices. The models derived from this approach are generally referred to as *discrete-choice* models.

It should be emphasized at the outset that the values of unordered qualitative variables are truly nominal in the sense that they only classify individual members in a population into a mutually exclusive classification scheme. Unlike values for ordered categorical variables, numerical values for polytomous variables have no substantive meaning. Given this, one can easily reassign values to different categories without any loss or change of information, so long as mutual exclusiveness is maintained.

As illustrated in Chapter 6, ordered response models with categorical independent variables can be cast as loglinear models. Similarly, we show in this chapter that grouped-data models for polytomous dependent variables can be estimated in the familiar loglinear modeling framework.

7.2   Multinomial Logit Models

The multinomial logit model is one of the most commonly used methods for analyzing unordered categorical response variables in social science research. We can cite some reasons for its popularity: (1) it is a natural generalization of the binomial logit model; (2) it is equivalent to the loglinear model with grouped data; and (3) statistical software for estimating the model is widely available. In this section, we introduce the multinomial logit model by drawing on its close connection to the binomial logit model.

7.2.1   Review of the Binary Logit Model

For the ordinary logit model, the dependent variable is dichotomous: $y = 0, 1$. Although we have two outcome possibilities, we are only interested in either $\Pr(y = 1)$ or $\Pr(y = 0)$, since $\Pr(y = 0) = 1 - \Pr(y = 1)$. With $\Pr(y = 1)$ as the outcome of interest for the dependent variable, the binary logit model can be obtained as follows:

$$\log\left[\frac{\Pr(y = 1)}{1 - \Pr(y = 1)}\right] = \log\left[\frac{\Pr(y = 1)}{\Pr(y = 0)}\right] = \sum_{k=0}^{K} \beta_k x_k, \qquad (7.1)$$

where x_k denotes the kth independent variable ($x_0 = 1$) with coefficient β_k. From Eq. 7.1, it follows that

$$\Pr(y = 1) = \frac{\exp(\sum_{k=0}^{K} \beta_k x_k)}{1 + \exp(\sum_{k=0}^{K} \beta_k x_k)},$$
$$\Pr(y = 0) = \frac{1}{1 + \exp(\sum_{k=0}^{K} \beta_k x_k)}. \tag{7.2}$$

We can think of two sets of β's, one associated with outcome $y = 1$ (i.e., β_{1k}) and another associated with outcome $y = 0$ (i.e., β_{0k}). β_{1k} is the usual β in Eqs. 7.1 and 7.2, whereas β_{0k} is normalized to be zero. Noting that $\exp(0) = 1$, Eq. 7.2 can therefore be rewritten as

$$\Pr(y = 1) = \frac{\eta_1}{\eta_0 + \eta_1},$$
$$\Pr(y = 0) = \frac{\eta_0}{\eta_0 + \eta_1}, \tag{7.3}$$

where $\eta_j = \exp(\sum_{k=0}^{K} \beta_{jk} x_k)$, $j = 0, 1$, and $\beta_{0k} = 0$ for all k.

7.2.2 General Setup for the Multinomial Logit Model

When we say that a qualitative variable is unordered, we mean that each category is unique in comparison with other categories. There is no added advantage in locating a category in relation to other categories. The basic idea behind the multinomial logit model is to compare two outcomes at one time. In Chapter 6 (Section 6.3.1) we introduced the baseline and adjacent logits. Although both would provide the basis for constructing the multinomial logit model, the baseline logit is more commonly used.

Without any loss of generality, for an outcome variable (y) with J categories ($j = 1, \dots, J$), let us contrast the jth ($j > 1$) category with the first or "baseline" category, deriving the baseline logit for the jth category,

$$BL_j = \log\left[\frac{\Pr(y = j)}{\Pr(y = 1)}\right] = \log\left(\frac{p_j}{p_1}\right), \qquad j = 2, \dots, J, \tag{7.4}$$

where p_j and p_1 denote the probabilities for the jth and first categories. The choice of using the first category as the baseline is arbitrary. Any other category can be the baseline.

In the transformation framework, we can regress the baseline logit specified in Eq. 7.4 as a linear function of x. However, the situation here is different from that of Eq. 7.1 since the baseline logit (BL) in Eq. 7.4 is subscripted by j. Thus, it is necessary to specify the contrast category (i.e., j) as well as the baseline category (1 in this case) when we model unordered qualitative outcomes. There are $J - 1$ nonredundant baseline logits for an outcome variable with J categories.

Let us now consider the case of having only one independent variable x with a limited number of categories (i.e., $x = 1, \ldots, I$). This case is equivalent to a two-way contingency table. At each value of x ($x = i$), the baseline logit is

$$\log \left[\frac{\Pr(y = j \mid x = i)}{\Pr(y = 1 \mid x = i)} \right] = \log \left(\frac{p_{ij}}{p_{i1}} \right) = BL_{ij}. \tag{7.5}$$

Since in this context we have specified a saturated model, the estimation of Eq. 7.5 can be easily obtained as

$$\log \left(\frac{F_{ij}}{F_{i1}} \right) = \log \left(\frac{f_{ij}}{f_{i1}} \right), \tag{7.6}$$

where f_{ij} and F_{ij}, as defined in Chapter 4, are the observed and expected frequencies in the ith row and the jth column for the classified table of $x \times y$. We can easily rewrite the result in the form of a generalized linear model:

$$BL_{ij} = \sum_{i=1}^{I} \log \left(\frac{F_{ij}}{F_{i1}} \right) I(x = i), \tag{7.7}$$

where $I(\cdot)$ is the indicator function, $I = 1$ if true, 0 otherwise. With dummy-variable coding and the first category as reference, Eq. 7.7 is usually written as

$$BL_{ij} = \alpha_j + \sum_{j=1}^{J} \beta_{ij} I(x = i), \qquad x > 1, \tag{7.8}$$

where α_j is the baseline logit for $x = 1$, and β_{ij} is the difference in the baseline logit between $x = i$ and $x = 1$. In this simple case, α_j and β_{ij} can be estimated separately for all i and j. Simultaneous estimation will result in an equivalent model in this case. For models other than the saturated model, separate and simultaneous estimations generally yield different results.

7.3   The Standard Multinomial Logit Model

Let us now turn to the more general situation with individual data and change the notation so that i now represents the ith individual. Let y_i denote the polytomous outcome variable with categories coded from $1, \ldots, J$. Associated with each category is a response probability, $(P_{i1}, P_{i2}, \ldots, P_{iJ})$, representing the ith respondent's chances of falling into particular categories. Just as in the case for binary outcomes in Chapter 3, we assume the presence of a vector of measured characteristics of the respondent, $\mathbf{x}_i$ (including 1 as its first element) as predictors of the response probabilities.

Using the usual index-function notation, we allow the response probabilities to depend on nonlinear transformations of the linear function $\mathbf{x}_i'\boldsymbol{\beta}_j = \sum_{k=0}^{K} \beta_{jk} x_{ik}$, where K is the number of the predictors.[1] It is important to note that, unlike the cases for binary and ordered logit models, parameters in multinomial logit models vary across outcome categories.

The multinomial logit model can be viewed as an extension of the binary logit model, expressed by Eqs. 7.2 and 7.3, to situations where the outcome variable has multiple unordered categories. For example,

---

[1] In this notation, the first parameter β_0 is the intercept term, the same as the α parameter in Eq. 7.8.

in the case of three categories $(J = 3)$, we can write the probabilities as

$$\Pr(y_i = 1 \mid \mathbf{x}_i) = P_{i1} = \frac{1}{1 + \exp(\mathbf{x}_i'\boldsymbol{\beta}_2) + \exp(\mathbf{x}_i'\boldsymbol{\beta}_3)},$$

$$\Pr(y_i = 2 \mid \mathbf{x}_i) = P_{i2} = \frac{\exp(\mathbf{x}_i'\boldsymbol{\beta}_2)}{1 + \exp(\mathbf{x}_i'\boldsymbol{\beta}_2) + \exp(\mathbf{x}_i'\boldsymbol{\beta}_3)}, \qquad (7.9)$$

$$\Pr(y_i = 3 \mid \mathbf{x}_i) = P_{i3} = \frac{\exp(\mathbf{x}_i'\boldsymbol{\beta}_3)}{1 + \exp(\mathbf{x}_i'\boldsymbol{\beta}_2) + \exp(\mathbf{x}_i'\boldsymbol{\beta}_3)},$$

where $\boldsymbol{\beta}_2$ and $\boldsymbol{\beta}_3$ denote the covariate effects specific to the second and third response categories with the first category as the reference. Note that the equation for P_{i1} is derived from the constraint that the three probabilities sum to 1. That is, $P_{i1} = 1 - (P_{i2} + P_{i3})$.

Analogous to Eq. 7.3, the probabilities of Eq. 7.9 can be expressed in terms of the exponential function of the linear terms $\eta_{ij} = \exp(\mathbf{x}_i'\boldsymbol{\beta}_j)$:

$$P_{i1} = \frac{\eta_{i1}}{\eta_{i1} + \eta_{i2} + \eta_{i3}},$$

$$P_{i2} = \frac{\eta_{i2}}{\eta_{i1} + \eta_{i2} + \eta_{i3}}, \qquad (7.10)$$

$$P_{i3} = \frac{\eta_{i3}}{\eta_{i1} + \eta_{i2} + \eta_{i3}},$$

with the normalization that $\boldsymbol{\beta}_1 = \mathbf{0}$ so that $\eta_{i1} = 1$.

In general, for an outcome variable with J categories, the probability P_{ij} can be modeled as:

$$P_{ij} = \frac{\eta_{ij}}{\sum_{j=1}^{J} \eta_{ij}} = \frac{\exp(\mathbf{x}_i'\boldsymbol{\beta}_j)}{\sum_{j=1}^{J} \exp(\mathbf{x}_i'\boldsymbol{\beta}_j)}, \qquad (7.11)$$

with the requirement that $\sum_{j=1}^{J} P_{ij} = 1$ for any i. With the usual normalization that $\boldsymbol{\beta}_1 = \mathbf{0}$ so that $\eta_{i1} = 0$, Eq. 7.11 means that

$$\Pr(y_i = j \mid \mathbf{x}_i) = P_{ij} = \frac{\exp(\mathbf{x}_i\boldsymbol{\beta}_j)}{1 + \sum_{j=2}^{J} \exp(\mathbf{x}_i'\boldsymbol{\beta}_j)}, \qquad \text{for } j > 1$$

and

$$\Pr(y_i = 1 \mid \mathbf{x}_i) = P_{i1} = \frac{1}{1 + \sum_{j=2}^{J} \exp(\mathbf{x}_i'\boldsymbol{\beta}_j)}. \qquad (7.12)$$

Thus, for a model with K covariates, a total of $(K+1) \times (J-1)$ parameters must be estimated. We can see that the multinomial logit model subsumes the binary logit model: when $J = 2$, we estimate a single set of parameters corresponding to the outcome $y = 2$ with the first category ($y = 1$) as the reference category. This close relationship between the binary logit model and the multinomial logit model may be obscured by the fact that the binary dependent variable is often coded as $(0, 1)$ instead of $(1, 2)$. Beyond the coding difference, the binary logit model can be seen as a special case of the multinomial logit model.

One alternative way to code a polytomous response variable is to code the categories $0, \ldots, J - 1$ instead of $1, \ldots, J$, thus making the multinomial logit model more closely resemble the binary logit model. This coding scheme is adopted by Greene's LIMDEP package. With $0, \ldots, J - 1$ coding, we can still follow the convention of setting the first category ($y = 0$) as the reference category so that $\boldsymbol{\beta}_0 = \mathbf{0}$. Recall, however, that the choice of the first category as the reference category is just a convenient normalization convention. In principle, any other category can serve as the reference category. As will be shown in Section 7.3.2, when the first category is used as the reference category, all parameter estimates of $\boldsymbol{\beta}_j$ are in reference to it. Changes of the reference category result in apparent changes in normalized parameter estimates but not in substantive results.

7.3.1   Estimation

Estimation is carried out iteratively using maximum likelihood. It is convenient to define a set of J dummy variables: $d_{ij} = 1$ if $y_i = j$ and 0 otherwise. This results in one and only one $d_{ij} = 1$ for each observation. The log-likelihood is[2]

$$\log L = \sum_{i=1}^{n} \sum_{j=1}^{J} d_{ij} \log P_{ij}. \tag{7.13}$$

---

[2] A programming example showing the details of the ML estimation technique is provided on this book's website.

7.3.2 Interpreting Results from Multinomial Logit Models

Odds and Odds-Ratios

Odds and odds-ratios play an important role in multinomial models just as they do in binary response and loglinear models described in chapters 3 and 4. In the multinomial logit model framework, the odds between categories j and 1 for a given i are simply

$$\frac{P_{ij}}{P_{i1}} = \frac{\eta_{ij}}{\eta_{i1}} = \exp(\mathbf{x}_i'\boldsymbol{\beta}_j) \qquad j = 2, \ldots, J. \tag{7.14}$$

The log-odds, or logit, is then a linear function of $\mathbf{x}_i$:

$$\log\left(\frac{P_{ij}}{P_{i1}}\right) = \mathbf{x}_i'\boldsymbol{\beta}_j, \qquad j = 2, \ldots, J. \tag{7.15}$$

Given the $J - 1$ baseline odds of Eq. 7.14, the interpretation of multinomial logit coefficients is straightforward. A positive coefficient for an independent variable (x_k) implies an increased odds of observing an observation in category j rather than category 1 as x_k increases, holding other covariates constant; a negative coefficient implies that the chances of being in the baseline category are higher relative to category j as x_k increases. If x_k is a 0,1 coded dummy variable, then β_{jk} is a log-odds-ratio:

$$\log\left[\frac{(P_j \mid x_k = 1)/(P_1 \mid x_k = 1)}{(P_j \mid x_k = 0)/(P_1 \mid x_k = 0)}\right] = \beta_{jk}, \tag{7.16}$$

since other terms in Eq. 7.15 are cancelled out in Eq. 7.16. Interpretation of β_{jk} as a log-odds-ratio when x_k is a continuous variable requires that one compare $x_k = x_k^0 + 1$ and $x_k = x_k^0$, where x_k^0 is any arbitrary value of x_k:

$$\log\left[\frac{(P_j \mid x_k = x_k^0 + 1)/(P_1 \mid x_k = x_k^0 + 1)}{(P_j \mid x_k = x_k^0)/(P_1 \mid x_k = x_k^0)}\right] = \beta_{jk}. \tag{7.17}$$

The preceding relationships concern the contrast between category j and the baseline category 1. They can be easily extended to a contrast between any two categories j and j' by taking into account the coefficients for both the j and j' categories. Equation 7.14, for example, can be extended to

$$\frac{P_{ij}}{P_{ij'}} = \frac{\eta_{ij}}{\eta_{ij'}} = \exp\left[\mathbf{x}_i'(\boldsymbol{\beta}_j - \boldsymbol{\beta}_{j'})\right]. \tag{7.18}$$

Thus, for any given explanatory variable, x_k, the difference in coefficients $(\beta_{jk} - \beta_{j'k})$ determines the direction of the change in the odds between categories j and j'. A positive difference means that as x_k increases, there is a greater odds of observing alternative j rather than j'. This is tantamount to changing the baseline category so that we can assess the relative change in odds between any two categories. If we want information on how probabilities respond to changes in x_k, we need to compute marginal effects.

Marginal Effects

Since the multinomial logit model is a nonlinear model, the impact of x_k on P_{ij} is not constant over the range of x_k. In general, the marginal effect of a change in x_k on P_{ij} is complicated but can be calculated as (assuming $j = 1$ as reference)[3]

$$\frac{\partial P_{ij}}{\partial \mathbf{x}_{ik}} = P_{ij}\left(\boldsymbol{\beta}_j - \sum_{j=2}^{J} P_{ij}\boldsymbol{\beta}_j\right). \tag{7.19}$$

Although this is analogous to the case for binary logit models, the marginal effects are less useful for multinomial logit models than they are for binary logit models. The marginal effects for binary models are unambiguous, as a positive coefficient implies a positive change in the probability as x_k increases. However, in multinomial response models, a change in $\Pr(y_i = j)$ does not necessarily have the same sign as β_{jk}. For example, it would be possible to find that the change in $\Pr(y_i = 2)$ is decreasing with x_k even when β_{2k} is positive. Therefore, we urge caution when interpreting marginal effects from multinomial response models and recommend the simpler interpretation based on odds and odds-ratios.

---

[3]These calculations can be carried out using LIMDEP macros, and they can be requested directly in LIMDEP 7.0.

Illustration

Table 7.1 provides results from a multinomial logit model applied to individual-level data on a sample of 978 young men aged 20–22 from the NLSY. The outcome of interest is whether a youth's reported major activity in 1985 is (1) working, (2) in school, or (3) inactive. We use the last category (inactivity) as the reference category. A youth's major activity is assumed to depend on a dummy variable for race (BLACK = 1, 0 otherwise), nonintact family structure (NONINT = 1, 0 otherwise), a dummy variable indicating if the respondent's father has a college (or some college) education (FCOL = 1, 0 otherwise), 1979 family income in thousands (FAMINC), the local unemployment rate in 1980 (UNEMP80), and standardized scores on the Armed Services Vocational Aptitude Battery Test (ASVAB).

From the results of Table 7.1 we find, for example, that the odds of young Black males reporting working vs. inactive as a major activity are $\exp(-0.444) = 0.64$ times those of Whites and others. Stated differently, the odds of working (vs. inactive) for Whites are 1.56 times as great as those for Blacks. The odds of being in school (vs. inactive) for young men from intact families are $1/\exp(-0.547) = 1.73$ times as high as the odds for those from nonintact families. Interpretation of the effects of continuous variables is straightforward. We find, for example, that the odds of a person working or attending school increase with family income (FAMINC) and test score (ASVAB). Specifically, a 1 standard deviation change in the ASVAB test score increases the odds of working by 36% i.e., $[\exp(0.308) - 1] \times 100\%$ and increases the odds of being in school by 19%. This latter effect, however, is only marginally significant.

We can assess model fit using the methods outlined in Chapter 3. Tests of individual coefficients can be carried out using t-tests, whereas tests of nested models can be carried out using likelihood-ratio tests. The BIC statistic can also be used. However, since multinomial models estimate parameters for all but one alternative, a test that a particular variable is irrelevant is actually a test that the $J - 1$ parameters associated with the variable are all zero. In principle, a Wald test could be used to test linear constraints on a subset of the parameters. That is, coefficients for some alternatives may be zero, whereas those

Table 7.1: Multinomial Logit Results

Variable	Estimate	Std. Error	t-Ratio
Working			
Constant	0.726	0.347	2.091
BLACK	−0.444	0.219	−2.032
NONINT	−0.134	0.192	−0.699
FCOL	0.179	0.241	0.745
FAMINC	0.407	0.211	1.930
UNEMP80	−0.071	0.037	−1.903
ASVAB	0.308	0.110	2.794
In School			
Constant	0.359	0.333	1.078
BLACK	0.229	0.196	1.166
NONINT	−0.547	0.186	−2.941
FCOL	0.241	0.236	1.025
FAMINC	0.268	0.209	1.283
UNEMP80	0.012	0.035	0.361
ASVAB	0.177	0.106	1.658
$\log L$	−1017.2		
Model χ^2	69.7		
DF	12		

for other alternatives may be nonzero.[4] Unfortunately, few commercial packages that we are aware of can actually estimate multinomial logit models where covariate effects for some choices are constrained to zero, constrained to equal the corresponding parameters associated

---

[4]This would require obtaining model estimates and their variance-covariance matrix. One would then define the appropriate constraint matrix and calculate the Wald statistic using the matrix procedures outlined in Chapter 3. For testing differences in coefficients across categories j and j', we can use the general formula

$$z = \frac{\widehat{\beta}_j - \widehat{\beta}_{j'}}{\sqrt{\text{var}(\widehat{\beta}_j) + \text{var}(\widehat{\beta}_{j'}) - 2\text{cov}(\widehat{\beta}_j, \widehat{\beta}_{j'})}}.$$

with other choices, or modeled as functions of additional *scale* parameters to be estimated. DiPrete (1990) provides an extension to the basic multinomial model for modeling intragenerational mobility that allows constraints of this kind.[5]

7.4   Loglinear Models for Grouped Data

7.4.1   Two-Way Tables

Loglinear models provide a flexible tool for modeling multinomial response models with categorical explanatory variables (grouped data). When all covariates are categorical or can be treated as such, the baseline logits described earlier can be parameterized in terms of expected cell frequencies from a loglinear model for a contingency table. Let us first consider the case of a two-way contingency table with row (R) being the explanatory variable and column (C) being the response variable. In this case, the loglinear equivalent to the single explanatory variable model of Eq. 7.7 is a saturated model that can be written as

$$\log F_{ij} = \mu + \mu_i^R + \mu_j^C + \mu_{ij}^{RC}, \qquad (7.20)$$

where F_{ij} denotes the expected frequency. Let us normalize the parameters with dummy-variable coding and use the first categories of C and R as references so that $\mu_1^R = \mu_1^C = \mu_{1j}^{RC} = \mu_{i1}^{RC} = 0$. It is easily shown that

$$\log \left(\frac{p_{ij}}{p_{i1}} \right) = \log \left(\frac{F_{ij}}{F_{i1}} \right) = (\mu_j^C - \mu_1^C) + (\mu_{ij}^{RC} - \mu_{i1}^{RC}) = \mu_j^C + \mu_{ij}^{RC}, \qquad (7.21)$$

which has the same form as Eq. 7.8, with μ_j^C representing the baseline logit for $R = 1$ and μ_{ij}^{RC} representing the difference in the baseline logit between $R = i$ and $R = 1$ for $i \neq 1$. Note the one-to-one

---

[5]This follows Anderson's (1984) more general approach known as the Stereotypical Ordered Response (SOR) model, which can be viewed as a mixture of ordered and unordered multinomial response models.

correspondence between μ_j^C in Eq. 7.21 and α_j in Eq. 7.8, and μ_{ij}^{RC} in Eq. 7.21 and β_{ij} in Eq. 7.8. The terms that describe the marginal distribution of the explanatory variable, μ and μ_i^R, do not factor in the logit analysis.

7.4.2   Three- and Higher-Way Tables

Now let us extend the loglinear equivalent of the multinomial logit model to three- and higher-way contingency tables. We first illustrate the equivalence with a three-way table setup. Let f_{ijk} be the observed frequency, F_{ijk} be the expected frequency, for a three-way table of $R \times C \times L$. As before, the response variable is C. The saturated loglinear model for this three-way table is

$$\log F_{ijk} = \mu + \mu_i^R + \mu_j^C + \mu_k^L + \mu_{ij}^{RC} + \mu_{ik}^{RL} + \mu_{jk}^{CL} + \mu_{ijk}^{RCL}, \qquad (7.22)$$

and is commonly denoted by the notation $(R, C, L, RC, RL, CL, RCL)$.

An important requirement for the equivalence between a loglinear model and a multinomial logit model is that the joint distribution among all explanatory variables is left unmodeled and thus saturated. In the terminology of loglinear modeling, this requirement is tantamount to including $\mu, \mu_i^R, \mu_k^L, \mu_{ik}^{RL}$ in *all* models. This requirement means that the fitted marginal distribution of the explanatory factors must be equal to the observed marginal distribution. To implement the requirement, we fix the joint distribution among the explanatory variables by including the highest-order interaction of all the explanatory variables plus all the lower-order interactions and the main effects. That is, the loglinear model of (R, C, L, RL) is equivalent to the logit model of Eq. 7.8 in which all β parameters are constrained to zero.

To estimate the logit coefficients, we add interactions of the explanatory variables and the response variable. Each main effect is represented by a two-way interaction parameter. Interaction effects are estimated by including higher-order interaction terms. We can summarize the preceding discussion on the equivalence between the loglinear form and the multinomial logit form in Table 7.2.

To demonstrate the equivalence, let us elaborate the third model (C on R, L). Eliminating μ_{ijk}^{RCL} in Eq. 7.22, substituting it into Eq. 7.6

Table 7.2: Equivalence Between Multinomial Logit and Loglinear Models for Three-Way Tables

Multinomial Logit Model	Loglinear Model
C on L	(R, C, L, RL, CL)
C on R	(R, C, L, RL, RC)
C on R, L	(R, C, L, RL, RC, CL)
C on R, L, RL	(R, C, L, RL, RC, RCL)

(adding the subscript for L), normalizing it with dummy-variable coding, and simplifying, for $j > 1$,

$$
\begin{aligned}
\log\left(\frac{F_{ijk}}{F_{i1k}}\right) &= (\mu_j^C - \mu_1^C) + (\mu_{ij}^{RC} - \mu_{i1}^{RC}) + (\mu_{jk}^{CL} - \mu_{1k}^{CL}) \\
&= \mu_j^C + \mu_{ij}^{RC} + \mu_{jk}^{CL}.
\end{aligned}
\tag{7.23}
$$

In Eq. 7.23, μ_j^C corresponds to the intercept term, and μ_{ij}^{RC} and μ_{jk}^{CL} correspond to the β coefficients for R and L covariates in the multinomial logit model where C is regressed on R and L. Generalization of the preceding results to multiway tables is straightforward.

Numerical Example

Table 7.3 shows the cross-classification of race (A) ($1 =$ White/other, $2 =$ Black), father's education (B) ($1 =$ at least 12 years, $2 =$ more than 12 years), and 1985 employment status (C) ($1 =$ inactive, $2 =$ working, $3 =$ in-school), for a sample ($n = 978$) of 20–22 year old men from the NLSY. The data are in the form of a $2 \times 2 \times 3$ contingency table.[6]

We are interested in how a youth's self-reported major activity in the previous year (C) depends on race (A) and father's education (B). Fitting a loglinear model as an equivalent of a multinomial logit model requires that the AB interaction terms appear in the model along with all lower-order terms (A and B). To test the effects of A and B, we

---

[6]This is a grouping of the individual-level data used in the earlier example.

Table 7.3: Employment Status by Race and Father's Education

		Employment Status (C)		
Race (A)	Father's Education (B)	1	2	3
White/Other	≤12 yr	131	195	204
Black	≤12 yr	67	53	100
White/Other	>12 yr	28	90	78
Black	>12 yr	9	5	12

also fit the AC and BC interactions, along with a lower-order term (C). The results are reported in Table 7.4. Only the substantively meaningful coefficients involving C are presented. In this case, we have six parameters, which include two "constant" terms representing the baseline log-odds of membership in categories 2 vs. 1 and 3 vs. 1; two terms representing the main effects of Black pertaining to the log-odds above; and two terms for the effects of father's education.

Table 7.4: Multinomial Logit Estimates Derived from a Loglinear Model

		Employment Status			
	Model	2 vs. 1		3 vs. 1	
Variable	Terms	Estimate	(S.E.)	Estimate	(S.E.)
Constant	(μ_2^C, μ_3^C)	0.453	(0.110)	0.435	(0.111)
Black	(μ_2^{AC}, μ_3^{AC})	−0.071	(0.180)	−0.777	(0.203)
Father's Edu.	(μ_2^{BC}, μ_3^{BC})	−0.513	(0.216)	0.612	(0.219)
Model χ^2	32.05				
DF	4				

The results in Table 7.4 show that Blacks' odds of being in school vs. inactive are $\exp(-0.777) = 0.46$ times those of Whites and others. The odds of working vs. inactive for young men having fathers with more than 12 years of schooling are 1.67 times those for young men whose fathers have 12 years of schooling or less. Having educated fathers increases the odds of being in school vs. inactive by a factor of 1.84.

The loglinear model provides a flexible way of specifying multinomial logit models when the explanatory variables are categorical or can be treated as such. The same approach can be used to fit binomial logit models. It is particularly appropriate when the sample size is large (say, $n > 10,000$), and the data can be condensed in a tabular form. The approach is less appropriate when the sample size is small, and the cell counts are zero for some combinations of variables, since special treatment is required for dealing with zero frequencies for loglinear modeling (Clogg and Eliason 1988).

7.5   The Latent Variable Approach

The multinomial logit model can also be viewed as a natural extension of the latent variable model outlined in Chapter 3. In the case of exactly two choices, the model is the same as the binary choice model. A more general random-utility model framework can be used to deal with unordered choice models. Let u_{ij} denote the utility associated with the jth choice from J alternatives for the ith individual. Assume u_{ij} to be a linear function of explanatory variables plus a random component:

$$u_{ij} = \mathbf{x}_i' \beta_j + \varepsilon_{ij}. \tag{7.24}$$

That is, there are J potential utility functions for a given person, even though in practice we only observe one outcome for him/her. It is thus necessary to further assume the observation rule that

$$y_{ij} = j \text{ if } u_{ij} > u_{ij'} \qquad \text{for all } j \neq j'. \tag{7.25}$$

As with the binary logit model, the decision rule of Eq. 7.25 is necessary to identify the multinomial logit model with the latent variable approach. Economists often give it a behavioral interpretation and call it "revealed preference," meaning that the observed choice is one that maximizes a rational individual's utility function.

The error term (ε_{ij}) is further assumed to be independent over alternatives [i.e., $\mathrm{cov}(\varepsilon_{ij}, \varepsilon_{ij'}) = 0$] and follows a type-I extreme value distribution with cumulative distribution function[7]

$$F(\varepsilon_{ij}) = \exp\{-\exp(-\varepsilon)\}.$$

McFadden (1974) shows that under these conditions the probability $\mathrm{Pr}(y_i = j)$ follows the multinomial specification of Eq. 7.11.

7.6   The Conditional Logit Model

Although the standard model outlined in Section 7.3 is widely used by social scientists in general, a different form of the multinomial logit model is found in economic research. This model has come to be known as the discrete-choice model or *conditional* logit model, due to McFadden (1973, 1974). However, it is often also called a multinomial logit model, leading to a good deal of confusion. The conditional logit model differs from the standard model in considering the characteristics of the choices and their variations with the individual—in addition to those of the individual making a choice—as explanatory variables. Early applications of discrete-choice models involved research on consumer choices in which the "costs," "prices," or other characteristics of the choices were the major explanatory variables. A classical example considers alternative modes of transportation, such as car, bus, or train, which are assumed to differ with regard to transit time and cost (Hensher 1986). In the standard multinomial logit model, explanatory variables are invariant with outcome categories, but their parameters vary with outcome. In the conditional logit model, explanatory variables vary by outcome as well as by the individual, whereas their parameters are assumed constant over all the outcome categories.

In a random utility perspective, the utility associated with the jth alternative is

$$u_{ij} = \mathbf{z}'_{ij}\boldsymbol{\alpha} + \varepsilon_{ij},$$

---

[7]Note that this is the complement of the distribution function used for the complementary log-log model presented in Chapters 3 and 5.

where $\mathbf{z}_{ij} = (1, z_{ij1}, \ldots, z_{ijK})'$ denotes the vector of explanatory variables associated with the jth choice pertaining to the ith individual, and $\boldsymbol{\alpha}$ is a set of unknown parameters. The probability associated with the jth choice can be written as [8]

$$\Pr(y_i = j \mid \mathbf{z}_{ij}) = P_{ij} = \frac{\exp(\mathbf{z}_{ij}'\boldsymbol{\alpha})}{\sum_{h \in \mathcal{C}} \exp(\mathbf{z}_{ih}'\boldsymbol{\alpha})}. \qquad (7.26)$$

7.6.1 Interpretation

As in all the logit models discussed thus far, interpreting results from conditional logit models involves the use of log-odds and log-odds-ratios. The odds of choosing alternative j vs. j' can be expressed as

$$\frac{P_{ij}}{P_{ij'}} = \exp\left[(\mathbf{z}_{ij} - \mathbf{z}_{ij'})'\boldsymbol{\alpha}\right], \qquad (7.27)$$

which implies the following logit

$$\log\left(\frac{P_{ij}}{P_{ij'}}\right) = (\mathbf{z}_{ij} - \mathbf{z}_{ij'})'\boldsymbol{\alpha}. \qquad (7.28)$$

This expression states that the log-odds between alternatives j and j' is proportional to the weighted difference between the individual's values on the explanatory variables for the two alternatives, with the weights being the estimated parameters (α coefficients). Everything else being equal, the larger the value of an α coefficient, the more important is the explanatory variable associated with it. If the values of an explanatory variable are the same for two alternatives (j and j'), then the variable does not influence the respondent's choice between alternatives j and j'.

This interpretation is contrasted with the interpretation from the standard multinomial logit model, in which the differences in coefficients across response categories determine the direction of the change in the odds-ratio as the independent variable changes.

---

[8]This model allows the number of available choices to vary among individuals according to their particular choice set $\mathcal{C}$.

Numerical Example

The following example uses data on mode of transportation choice among 152 respondents.[9] The three choices, and the associated percentages making that choice, are 1 = train (41.5%), 2 = bus (19.7%), and 3 = car (38.8%). We assume that choice is a function of terminal waiting time (TTME), in-vehicle time (INVT), in-vehicle cost (INVC), and a generalized cost measure (GC) equal to INVC + INVT × VALUE, where VALUE is the subjective value of the respondent's time associated with each mode of transportation.

We maximize the same log-likelihood function as in the standard model.[10] Discrete-choice programs like LIMDEP and STATA, however, require a different arrangement of the data than that of the standard model. Because the values of the independent variables vary by choice, the data from one individual are recorded as J separate records.[11] The results provided in Table 7.5 are estimated using LIMDEP.

These estimates suggest that the attractiveness of a particular mode of transportation decreases as terminal waiting time, in-vehicle costs, and in-vehicle time increase, and increases as generalized costs (especially value of an individual's time) increase. In particular, the estimated log-odds of choosing train over car are

$$
\log\left(\frac{P_{i1}}{P_{i3}}\right) = -.002\ (\text{TTME}_1 - \text{TTME}_3) - .435\ (\text{INVC}_1 - \text{INVC}_3)
$$
$$
- .077\ (\text{INVT}_1 - \text{INVT}_3) + .431\ (\text{GC}_1 - \text{GC}_3). \tag{7.29}
$$

---

[9]We thank David Hensher for sharing these data, which were obtained from William Greene's LIMDEP programming examples. We have excluded the choice for "air travel."

[10]In the standard conditional logit model (i.e., without choice-specific constants), the DF for the model χ^2 is equal to the number of parameters.

[11]More generally, if the choice set varies among individuals, so that the ith individual faces a set of C choices, then the ith individual would contribute as many records as there are in his/her particular choice set. Alternatively, one could provide one record per individual but distinguish among the independent variables pertaining to each choice. The TDA program allows either approach to be used.

Table 7.5: Estimates from Conditional Logit Model

Variable	Estimate	Std. Error	t-Ratio
TTME	−0.002	0.007	−0.314
INVC	−0.435	0.133	−3.277
INVT	−0.077	0.019	−3.991
GC	0.431	0.133	3.237
Log L	−96.349		
Model χ^2	141.28		
DF	4		

The other log-odds-ratios can be computed in a similar manner.

7.6.2   The Mixed Model

The conditional logit model can be modified to include characteristics of the individual along with outcome characteristics. The *mixed* model combines the features of the standard model with those of the conditional logit model. This can be easily accomplished by incorporating individual-level covariates in the conditional logit model. In fact, we will show that the standard multinomial logit model can be written as a special case of the conditional logit model. The easiest way to implement this in practice is to create a set of dummy variables corresponding to each of the J alternatives and multiply each individual-level covariate by this set of dummies. The resulting model could contain outcome-specific constants (i.e., the dummy variables themselves) as well as individual-level traits. The corresponding utility function associated with the jth choice is now

$$u_{ij} = \mathbf{z}'_{ij}\boldsymbol{\alpha} + \mathbf{x}'_i\boldsymbol{\beta}_j + \varepsilon_{ij},$$

where $\mathbf{z}_{ij}$ and $\mathbf{x}_i$ respectively denote the outcome-varying and individual-varying covariates, and $\boldsymbol{\alpha}$ and $\boldsymbol{\beta}_j$ denote the associated effects. The general or *mixed* model can be written as

$$\Pr(y_i = j \mid \mathbf{x}_i, \mathbf{z}_{ij}) = P_{ij} = \frac{\exp(\mathbf{z}'_{ij}\boldsymbol{\alpha} + \mathbf{x}'_i\boldsymbol{\beta}_j)}{\sum_{h \in \mathcal{C}} \exp(\mathbf{z}'_{ih}\boldsymbol{\alpha} + \mathbf{x}'_i\boldsymbol{\beta}_h)}, \qquad (7.30)$$

which combines Eq. 7.11 and Eq. 7.26. To identify the model, we could normalize on any alternative and set the $\boldsymbol{\beta}$ for that alternative to zero. For example, we can set $\boldsymbol{\beta}_1 = \mathbf{0}$, which amounts to normalizing on the first alternative. Following this approach, the logit from the mixed multinomial model can be expressed as

$$\log\left(\frac{P_{ij}}{P_{ij'}}\right) = \mathbf{x}'_i(\boldsymbol{\beta}_j - \boldsymbol{\beta}_{j'}) + (\mathbf{z}_{ij} - \mathbf{z}_{ij'})'\boldsymbol{\alpha}. \qquad (7.31)$$

Excluding the outcome-varying covariates from this model results in the standard multinomial logit model.

Application

Using the preceding example, suppose that household income (HHINC) is included along with the choice-specific covariates. Because the value of this variable is constant across the choice set, it cannot be included in the model as $\mathbf{z}_{ij}$ with outcome-invariant coefficients. Thus, it is necessary to modify the data to identify the model. This can be accomplished by defining a dummy variable corresponding to each choice and using the product of the choice dummies and the individual-level covariate as regressors.

Omitting the lowest-coded category (train), we use dummy-choice variables (DB) for bus, and (DC) for car. HHINCB_DB = HHINC × DB stands for the income variable for bus, and HHINC_DC = HHINC× DC denotes the corresponding income variable for car. The estimates from the mixed model are provided in Table 7.6. We find, for example, that the attractiveness of bus and car vs. train increase with income but only the attractiveness of car vs. train shows a statistically significant increase with income. If we view the mixed model as a general case of the standard multinomial logit model, the model χ^2 test is based on 6 DF. This is because the null model contains $J - 1$ choice-specific intercepts. However, viewing the mixed model as a special case of the conditional logit model results in a model χ^2 with 8 DF. The null model in this case is one in which all parameters are fixed at zero.

Table 7.6: Results from the Mixed Model

Variable	Estimate	Std. Error	t-Ratio
TTME	−0.074	0.017	−4.360
INVC	−0.619	0.152	−4.067
INVT	−0.096	0.022	−4.361
GC	0.581	0.150	3.883
DB	−2.108	0.739	−2.577
HHINC_DB	0.031	0.021	1.404
DC	−6.147	1.029	−5.974
HHINC_DC	0.048	0.023	2.682
$\log L$	−59.66		
Model χ^2	214.66		
DF	8		

Conditional Logits Using Grouped Data

Conditional logit models can be estimated using the loglinear modeling techniques outlined earlier. In this case, we need to find covariates that map the interactions of the outcome and explanatory variables. Instead of specifying free interactions between the outcome and explanatory variables with observed categories, the researcher can use "interactive" covariates, established a priori, to explain the interactions. Let us consider the simple case of a two-way table of $R \times C$, with the variation in R indexed by $i = 1, \ldots, I$, and the variation in C indexed by $j = 1, \ldots, J$. C stands for the outcome variable. The loglinear specification with interactive covariates can be specified as follows:

$$\log F_{ij} = \mu + \mu_i^R + \mu_j^C + \sum_{k=1}^{K} \alpha_k z_{ijk}, \qquad (7.32)$$

where k denotes the kth covariate ($k = 1, \ldots, K$). Obviously, $K \leq (I-1)(J-1)$. It is easy to show that

$$\log\left(\frac{P_{ij}}{P_{ij'}}\right) = \log\left(\frac{F_{ij}}{F_{ij'}}\right) = (\mu_j^C - \mu_{j'}^C) + \sum_{k=1}^{K} \alpha_k(z_{ijk} - z_{ij'k}), \quad (7.33)$$

the same formulas as the conditional logit model of Eq. 7.28. For applications, see Breen (1994) and Xie and Shauman (1996).

7.7   Specification Issues

In this section we discuss limitations and extensions of the multinomial logit model. The most serious limitation concerns the assumption that the error terms are independent across choices. A violation of this assumption is likely when individuals view two alternatives as similar, or equivalent. We discuss some remedies, along with some useful extensions to the basic multinomial model.

7.7.1   Independence of Irrelevant Alternatives: The IIA Assumption

The various forms of the logit model presented before are simple representations of complicated social processes. As a result of the simplification, the aforementioned logit models possess the remarkable property that the relative odds between two alternative outcomes depend exclusively on characteristics pertaining to the two outcomes and are therefore independent of the number and the nature of all other outcomes that are simultaneously considered. This property is known as independence of irrelevant alternatives (IIA). To see what the IIA property means, the reader is referred to Eq. 7.18 for the basic multinomial logit model, Eq. 7.28 for the conditional logit model, and Eq. 7.31 for the mixed logit model. In these equations, it is shown that the odds between alternatives j and j' are only functions of the parameters for outcomes j and j' and thus unaffected by parameters pertaining to other outcomes.

The IIA assumption may oversimplify the real world and present difficulties for the researcher. This is especially true when two outcomes can be viewed as substitutes for one another. The classic example is discussed by McFadden (1974), in which a consumer's transportation choice set consists of the alternatives: (1) red bus, (2) blue bus, (3) car, and (4) train. This set of choices poses an analytical problem if, in fact, commuters have no preference over which type of bus they ride and view red bus and blue bus as equivalent, or equal substitutes. The problem is that a high (low) preference for red bus implies by IIA a low (high) preference for blue bus. For example, at a particular time, commuters may be equally likely to choose among red bus, blue bus, car, and train:

(j) Choice	(1) Red Bus	(2) Blue Bus	(3) Car	(4) Train
P_j	0.25	0.25	0.25	0.25

In this case, the odds between any pair of alternatives are 1. For simplicity, let us assume an extreme situation in which red bus and blue bus are perfect substitutes of each other so that commuters previously taking blue bus would all shift to red bus when the city closes the blue bus line. Thus, removing the blue bus line should result in the following distribution:

(j) Choice	(1) Red Bus	(2) Car	(3) Train
P_j	0.50	0.25	0.25

That is, our behavioral model leads us to expect the odds between red bus and car and between red bus and train to increase to 2 rather than to stay at 1 when we eliminate blue bus. The IIA property instead would predict the unrealistic distribution of

(j) Choice	(1) Red Bus	(2) Car	(3) Train
P_j	0.333	0.333	0.333

Testing the IIA Assumption

A general test, in the spirit of the Wald test, has been proposed by Hausman and McFadden (1984). This test also addresses issues of collapsibility by providing evidence for or against combining two or more categories into a single category.[12] To carry out the Hausman-McFadden test, the researcher first estimates a model with all choices and then estimates a model with a restricted choice set, keeping the same set of regressors in each model. Letting $\widehat{\beta}_u$ and $\widehat{\beta}_r$ denote the parameter estimates from the unrestricted and restricted model, the Hausman-McFadden test statistic (q) is calculated as

$$q = [\widehat{\beta}_u - \widehat{\beta}_r][\mathbf{V}_r - \mathbf{V}_u]^{-1}[\widehat{\beta}_u - \widehat{\beta}_r], \tag{7.34}$$

where $\mathbf{V}_r$ and $\mathbf{V}_u$ are the variance-covariance matrices of the estimates under the restricted and unrestricted models.

The Hausman-McFadden test statistic follows a χ^2 distribution with degrees of freedom equal to the difference in the number of parameters. The null hypothesis of this test states that the parameters from the restricted and unrestricted models are equal (or that their difference is zero) (i.e., $H_0 : \beta_u = \beta_r$). A large value of q leads to a rejection of the null hypothesis.[13] A less formal approach would be to exclude one choice, estimate the reduced model, and simply compare the estimates from the restricted and unrestricted models to see whether the interpretation of the results differs between the models. Combining categories on the basis of formal or informal methods usually results in a model that is easier to interpret and evaluate from a substantive standpoint. As will be shown later, it is often possible to gain some simplicity as well as insights by breaking down a multinomial problem into a series of binary choice problems. There are also special approaches (described later) that handle violations to the IIA assumption, although they are not widely used in applied work.

---

[12]For a review of this and other *choice-set partitioning* tests, see Fry and Harris (1998).

[13]Greene's LIMDEP program offers a convenient way to carry out this test.

The Multinomial Probit Model

When the IIA assumption is untenable, several alternative approaches have been suggested, most of which involve variations of the *multinomial probit* model. The multinomial probit model of Hausman and Wise (1978) relaxes the IIA assumption of independent errors across alternatives. This is best described in the latent variable approach. The utility function for a (mixed) multinomial probit is given by

$$u_{ij} = \mathbf{x}'_i \boldsymbol{\beta}_j + \mathbf{z}'_{ij} \boldsymbol{\alpha} + \varepsilon_{ij}, \tag{7.35}$$

where $\varepsilon_{ij}, \ldots, \varepsilon_{iJ}$ are normally distributed with mean 0 and covariance matrix $\boldsymbol{\Sigma}$. For a three-choice model, the probability that the third alternative is chosen is given by

$$\begin{aligned} \Pr(y_i = 3) &= \Pr(u_{i3} > u_{i2}, u_{i3} > u_{i1}) \\ &= \int_{-\infty}^{+\infty} \int_{-\infty}^{u_2} \int_{-\infty}^{u_3} f(u_1, u_2, u_3) du_1 du_2 du_3, \end{aligned} \tag{7.36}$$

where $f(\cdot, \cdot, \cdot)$ is the trivariate normal density function.[14] The attractiveness of this approach lies in the ability to estimate the covariances in errors across alternatives (σ_{12}, σ_{13}, and σ_{23} in this case), which provide information on the association among alternatives.[15] The main disadvantage of the multinomial probit is that, until very recently, technical issues associated with the computation of the multinormal integrals made these models impractical for most researchers, except in the case of up to four choices. Increased computing power, coupled with advances in the design of computer algorithms and the inclusion of these models in standard statistical packages, has now made these models feasible.[16] For a recent application of this model see Alvarez and Nagler (1995).

---

[14]In general, a multinomial probit model can be transformed so that with J choices, only $J - 1$ integrals need to be evaluated.

[15]Due to the arbitrary scaling of $\sigma = 1$ in probit models, covariances and correlations are equivalent.

[16]LIMDEP 7.0 can estimate multivariate and multinomial probit with up to 20 equations or alternatives.

Other Approaches

It is also possible to generalize the multinomial logit model to a non-independent logit model that relaxes the IIA assumption. McFadden (1978) suggests using a generalized extreme-value distribution. Although simpler to implement than the multinomial probit, this approach yields a single correlation estimate, not the full correlation structure. Gumble (1961) shows that the association parameter is linked to the Pearson correlation coefficient (ρ). However, the bivariate-logistic distribution constrains the values of ρ to lie in the interval $[-0.304, +0.304]$, which may be unrealistic for some applications.

Other approaches to the IIA problem involve simulating the underlying utilities ($u_{i1}, \ldots, u_{iJ}$) and using the observed relative frequencies to estimate the joint probabilities implied by Eq. 7.36 (Albright, Lerman, and Manski 1977).

7.7.2   Sequential Logit Models

Some multinomial response problems can be simplified by taking into account the temporal ordering of the responses. The approach takes advantage of the sequential nature of decision-making. The classical example involves school continuation decisions (see, e.g., Mare 1980). For example, suppose that a measure of educational attainment (y_i) takes the following values:

$y_i = 1$ if individual attains less than 12 years of schooling,
$y_i = 2$ if individual has attained at least 12 years of schooling,
$y_i = 3$ if individual has more than 12 years of schooling.

At first glance, it appears that this variable is ordinal and should be modeled by ordered response models discussed in Chapter 6. Recall, however, that ordered response models are restrictive in not allowing separate structural mechanisms across different categories. If the researcher suspects that different mechanisms are at work for different levels of school transitions, he/she may wish to break down the process into a sequence of transitions. In this case, we will work with *conditional* probabilities in modeling the probability that $y_i = j$ or higher for $j > 1$, given that $y_i = j - 1$, denoted as P_{ij}^+. That is

$$P_{ij}^+ = \Pr(y_i \geq j \mid y_i \geq j - 1) = \frac{\sum_{l=j}^{J} P_{il}}{\sum_{h=j-1}^{J} P_{ih}}, \qquad j > 1. \qquad (7.37)$$

This approach uses another form of the logit called the *continuation-ratio* logit, which is defined in terms of the conditional probabilities in Eq. 7.37. A continuation-ratio logit model can be written as

$$CRL_{ij} = \log \left(\frac{P_{ij}^+}{1 - P_{ij}^+} \right) = \mathbf{x}_i' \boldsymbol{\beta}_j, \qquad j = 2, \dots, J. \qquad (7.38)$$

The process of educational attainment can be viewed as a series of binary choices, which can be described diagrammatically:

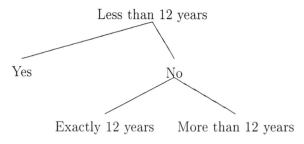

This implies that sequential models can be estimated by conditioning on the appropriate subsamples in the data. The entire sample is used to model the probability of 12 or more years of schooling (P_{i2}^+) using a continuation-ratio logit model. In the model for this first transition, the response variable is coded as 1 if the respondent has attained at least 12 years of schooling, 0 otherwise. Note $P_{i1} = 1 - P_{i2}^+$. The researcher then models the conditional probability for attaining more than 12 years of schooling (P_{i3}^+) with a continuation-ratio logit model using only the subset of respondents with at least 12 years of schooling. In the model for the second transition, the response variable is coded 1 if the respondent has more than 12 years of schooling and 0 otherwise. Note that $P_{i2} = P_{i2}^+(1 - P_{i3}^+)$ and $P_{i3} = P_{i2}^+ P_{i3}^+$. Hence, the results from a sequence of binary logit models completely describe the multinomial process.

Likelihood ratio tests can be carried out in the usual way. With the assumption of independence across transition levels, the *overall* log-likelihood for the model is the sum of the likelihoods from separate models. For grouped data, we can summarize the overall fit using the sum of the G^2 statistics from separate models.

Illustration

As an example, let us consider educational attainment by 1988 for a sample of 1,369 young men aged 18 or older in 1979 drawn from the NLSY. Completed schooling is assumed to be a function of race (BLK = 1, if respondent is Black, 0 otherwise; HSP = 1, if respondent is Hispanic, 0 otherwise), father's education (FEDU) and socioeconomic status (FSEI), number of siblings (NSIBS), and not living with both biological parents at age 14 (NONINT). The first panel of Table 7.7 models the logit of attaining 12 or more years of schooling (YRS). The second panel is a logit model for completing more than 12 years of schooling conditional on having completed at least 12 years.

Table 7.7: Educational Attainment

Variable	YRS ≥ 12 Estimate	YRS ≥ 12 t–Ratio	YRS > 12 | YRS ≥ 12 Estimate	YRS > 12 | YRS ≥ 12 t–Ratio
INTERCEPT	0.624	1.902	−1.550	−5.132
BLK	0.005	0.028	0.091	0.542
HSP	0.281	1.259	0.651	3.218
FEDU	0.117	5.300	0.011	0.481
FSEI	0.260	4.688	0.311	7.754
NSIBS	−0.173	−4.487	−0.012	0.350
NONINT	−0.875	−5.487	−0.235	−1.447
Log L	−589.06		−782.45	
n	1,369		1,097	
Model Log L		−1371.51		

We find, for example, that the odds of completing at least 12 years of schooling increase with father's education and socioeconomic status, and are decreasing functions of nonintact family structure and number of siblings. The odds of completing more than 12 years of schooling *conditional* on having completed at least 12 years are increasing with father's socioeconomic status; however, there is no evidence of an effect of father's education. The effects of family structure and number of siblings are also smaller for the later transitions. Consistent with previous research, we find some support for diminishing effects of social background (except for FSEI) with educational transitions (see, e.g., Mare 1980).

7.8   Summary

In this chapter we have presented an overview of methods for handling unordered multinomial responses ranging from familiar loglinear models to the multinomial, conditional, and mixed logit models derived from a random utility or behavioral choice framework. A concise review of these models is given by Hoffman and Duncan (1988). Ben-Akiva and Lerman (1985) provide a more detailed treatment of discrete-choice models. We examined how restrictive assumptions can be relaxed for more realistic models. We found that breaking the process into a sequence of choices can also lead to models that may be more appealing from a substantive standpoint and easier to interpret from a practical standpoint.

Appendix A

The Matrix Approach to Regression

A.1 Introduction

Matrix representation is used in multivariate statistics as a way of generalizing mathematical and statistical operations. Working with matrices has the advantage of eliminating the need for subscripts, thereby allowing the same notation to be used regardless of the number of independent variables. The disadvantage is that a different set of rules of arithmetic (matrix algebra) is required to carry out matrix operations.

A.2 Matrix Algebra

A matrix is a way of representing a set of variables as an arrangement of values arrayed by rows and columns. A single bold-faced letter is usually used to represent a matrix, while subscripted terms represent the distinct elements of a matrix. By convention, bold-faced, upper-case letters are used to denote matrices, whereas bold-faced, lowercase letters are used to denote vectors. The size or dimension of a matrix is determined by the number of rows (R) and number of columns (C). For example, a matrix $\mathbf{X}$, with 100 rows and 3 columns, would be described as a 100×3 matrix with elements x_{ij} ($i = 1, \ldots, 100;\ j = 1, \ldots, 3$). In this case, $\mathbf{X}$ stands for the set of variables, whereas each x_{ij} corresponds to the value in the ith row and jth column of $\mathbf{X}$. A vector may be defined as a matrix with a single row or column. For example, the vector $\mathbf{x}'_i$, which appears frequently in this book, denotes a single row of $\mathbf{X}$, corresponding to the set of covariate values for the ith observation.

A.2.1   The Matrix Approach to Regression

The regression equation can be written in matrix notation as

$$\mathbf{y} = \mathbf{X}\boldsymbol{\beta} + \boldsymbol{\varepsilon},$$

where $\mathbf{X}$ is the $n \times (K+1)$ matrix of independent variables, $\mathbf{y}$ is the $n \times 1$ vector of values for the dependent variable, $\boldsymbol{\varepsilon}$ is the $n \times 1$ vector of error terms, and $\boldsymbol{\beta}$ is the $(K+1) \times 1$ vector of regression coefficients. Letting x_{ik} denote the kth independent variable for the ith observation, the $\mathbf{X}$ matrix takes the form

$$\mathbf{X} = \begin{pmatrix} x_{10} & x_{11} & x_{12} & \cdots & x_{1K} \\ x_{20} & x_{21} & x_{22} & \cdots & x_{2K} \\ \vdots & \vdots & \vdots & \cdots & \vdots \\ x_{n0} & x_{n1} & x_{n2} & \cdots & x_{nK} \end{pmatrix}.$$

In most regression-type models, the first column is a vector of ones to allow for a constant term, so that $x_{i0} = 1$:

$$\mathbf{X} = \begin{pmatrix} 1 & x_{11} & \cdots & x_{1K} \\ 1 & x_{21} & \cdots & x_{2K} \\ \vdots & \vdots & \cdots & \vdots \\ 1 & x_{n1} & \cdots & x_{nK} \end{pmatrix}.$$

The $n \times 1$ vector of values of the dependent variable y takes the form

$$\mathbf{y} = \begin{pmatrix} y_1 \\ y_2 \\ \vdots \\ y_n \end{pmatrix}.$$

The $n \times 1$ vector of error terms is

$$\varepsilon = \begin{pmatrix} \varepsilon_1 \\ \varepsilon_2 \\ \vdots \\ \varepsilon_n \end{pmatrix}.$$

The $(K + 1) \times 1$ vector of regression coefficients is

$$\beta = \begin{pmatrix} \beta_0 \\ \beta_1 \\ \vdots \\ \beta_K \end{pmatrix}.$$

Putting these together, we have

$$\mathbf{y} = \mathbf{X}\beta + \varepsilon = \begin{pmatrix} y_1 \\ y_2 \\ \vdots \\ y_n \end{pmatrix} = \begin{pmatrix} 1 & x_{11} & \cdots & x_{1K} \\ 1 & x_{21} & \cdots & x_{2K} \\ \vdots & \vdots & \cdots & \vdots \\ 1 & x_{n1} & \cdots & x_{nK} \end{pmatrix} \begin{pmatrix} \beta_0 \\ \beta_1 \\ \vdots \\ \beta_K \end{pmatrix} + \begin{pmatrix} \varepsilon_1 \\ \varepsilon_2 \\ \vdots \\ \varepsilon_n \end{pmatrix}.$$

A.2.2   Basic Matrix Operations

Addition: Matrix addition requires that the two matrices being added are conformable, having the same number of rows and columns. That is, if $\mathbf{A}$ is $n \times K$ and $\mathbf{B}$ is $n \times K$, then $\mathbf{C} = \mathbf{A} + \mathbf{B}$. This is equivalent to adding the corresponding elements of each matrix $c_{ik} = a_{ik} + b_{ik}$.

$$\mathbf{A} + \mathbf{B} = \begin{pmatrix} a_{11} & a_{12} & \cdots & a_{1K} \\ \vdots & \vdots & \cdots & \vdots \\ a_{n1} & a_{n2} & \cdots & a_{nK} \end{pmatrix} + \begin{pmatrix} b_{11} & b_{12} & \cdots & b_{1K} \\ \vdots & \vdots & \cdots & \vdots \\ b_{n1} & b_{n2} & \cdots & b_{nK} \end{pmatrix}$$

$$= \begin{pmatrix} a_{11} + b_{11} & a_{12} + b_{12} & \cdots & a_{1K} + b_{1K} \\ \vdots & \vdots & \cdots & \vdots \\ a_{n1} + b_{n1} & a_{n2} + b_{n2} & \cdots & a_{nK} + b_{nK} \end{pmatrix}$$

$$= \begin{pmatrix} c_{11} & c_{12} & \cdots & c_{1K} \\ \vdots & \vdots & \cdots & \vdots \\ c_{n1} & c_{n2} & \cdots & c_{nK} \end{pmatrix} = \mathbf{C}.$$

Multiplication: Matrix multiplication requires that matrices to be multiplied are row-column conformable. For the multiplication of $\mathbf{A}$ and $\mathbf{B}$, this means that the number of columns in $\mathbf{A}$ must equal the number of rows in $\mathbf{B}$. For example, if $\mathbf{A}$ is $n \times K$ and $\mathbf{b}$ is $K \times 1$, then the product $\mathbf{C} = \mathbf{Ab}$ is the $n \times 1$ matrix with elements $c_i = \sum_k a_{ik} b_k$. In this case, $\mathbf{b}$ is premultiplied by $\mathbf{A}$ as follows:

$$\mathbf{C} = \begin{pmatrix} c_1 \\ \vdots \\ c_n \end{pmatrix} = \mathbf{Ab} = \begin{pmatrix} a_{11}b_1 + a_{12}b_2+ & \cdots & +a_{1K}b_K \\ a_{21}b_1 + a_{22}b_2+ & \cdots & +a_{2K}b_K \\ \vdots & \cdots & \vdots \\ a_{n1}b_1 + a_{n2}b_2+ & \cdots & +a_{nK}b_K \end{pmatrix}.$$

Matrix multiplication is accomplished by multiplying each row entry in $\mathbf{A}$ by the corresponding column entry in $\mathbf{b}$ and adding the results. Note that matrix multiplication is not communicative inasmuch as $\mathbf{Ab}$ does not necessarily equal $\mathbf{bA}$. In this case, it would not be possible to premultiply $\mathbf{A}$ by $\mathbf{b}$ because the number of columns of $\mathbf{b}$ (1) is not equal to the number of rows of $\mathbf{A}$ (n). It is often possible to rearrange the rows and columns of matrices to make them compatible for multiplication.

Matrix Transposition: Matrix transposition is an operation that alters the dimension of a matrix by interchanging rows and columns.

For example, if **b** is the $(K+1) \times 1$ matrix

$$\mathbf{b} = \begin{pmatrix} b_0 \\ b_1 \\ \vdots \\ b_K \end{pmatrix},$$

the transpose of **b** (**b**$'$) is the $1 \times (K+1)$ matrix

$$\mathbf{b}' = \begin{pmatrix} b_0 & b_1 & \cdots & b_K \end{pmatrix}.$$

The resulting matrix **b**$'$ can be premultiplied by any matrix having 1 column or postmultiplied by any matrix having $K+1$ rows.

Matrix Inverse: The division of matrices is accomplished by the inverse operator. Matrices must be square for matrix inversion. They must also be nonsingular. Suppose that **X** is the $n \times (K+1)$ data matrix and that a $(K+1) \times (K+1)$ square matrix, **M**, is constructed by premultiplying **X** by its transpose **X**$'$

$$\mathbf{M} = \mathbf{X}'\mathbf{X}.$$

If any columns of **X** can be expressed as linear functions of any other column or set of columns, then **M** is singular and cannot be inverted. If **M** is a nonsingular square matrix, it can be multiplied by its inverse $(\mathbf{M}^{-1})$, to yield a $(K+1) \times (K+1)$ identity matrix. The identity matrix is a square matrix with ones on the main diagonal and zeros elsewhere and is usually denoted by **I**:

$$\mathbf{I} = \mathbf{M}\mathbf{M}^{-1} = \mathbf{M}^{-1}\mathbf{M} = \begin{pmatrix} 1 & & & 0 \\ & 1 & & \\ & & \ddots & \\ 0 & & & 1 \end{pmatrix}.$$

Diagonal Matrices: The identity matrix is a special case of a diagonal matrix. Substituting values other than 1 will result in a general form of the diagonal matrix. This matrix arises in a number of situations. For example, in FGLS estimation, we minimize a weighted sum of squares

$$S(\beta) = \sum_{i=1}^{n} w_i (y_i - \mathbf{x}_i' \beta)^2,$$

where w_i is the value of the weight for the ith observation. The vector $\mathbf{w}$ would represent the $n \times 1$ vector of weights. If we define $\mathbf{W}$ to be the $n \times n$ matrix with w_i on the main diagonal, such that

$$\mathbf{W} = \begin{pmatrix} w_1 & & & \mathbf{0} \\ & w_2 & & \\ & & \ddots & \\ \mathbf{0} & & & w_n \end{pmatrix},$$

we can write the weighted sum of squares function in matrix notation as

$$S(\beta) = (\mathbf{y} - \mathbf{X}\beta)' \mathbf{W} (\mathbf{y} - \mathbf{X}\beta).$$

Matrix Operations for Regression: Given the regression model in matrix form

$$\mathbf{y} = \mathbf{X}\beta + \varepsilon,$$

the OLS estimator of β is found by minimizing the sum of squares

$$\begin{aligned} S(\beta) &= (\mathbf{y} - \mathbf{X}\beta)'(\mathbf{y} - \mathbf{X}\beta) \\ &= \mathbf{y}'\mathbf{y} - 2\mathbf{y}'\mathbf{X}\beta + \beta'\mathbf{X}'\mathbf{X}\beta. \end{aligned}$$

The vector of partial derivatives of the sum of squares with respect to β may be expressed as

$$\frac{\partial S(\beta)}{\partial \beta} = -2\mathbf{X}'\mathbf{y} + 2\mathbf{X}'\mathbf{X}\beta.$$

When we equate this expression to zero and solve, it yields the OLS estimator

$$\mathbf{b} = (\mathbf{X}'\mathbf{X})^{-1}\mathbf{X}'\mathbf{y},$$

where **b** is the $(K + 1) \times 1$ vector of OLS estimates.

The variance-covariance matrix of **b** is obtained by multiplying the mean square error, σ_ε^2, or its estimate, by the inverse of the sum of squares and cross-products matrix, $\mathbf{X'X}$, as follows:

$$\widehat{\mathrm{var}}(\mathbf{b}) = \hat{\sigma}_\varepsilon^2 (\mathbf{X'X})^{-1}.$$

This operation results in a square matrix with $\mathrm{var}(b_k)$ along the diagonal and $\mathrm{cov}(b_k, b_j)$ $(j \neq k)$ on the off-diagonal.

A.2.3 Numerical Example

Consider a simple regression model $y_i = \beta_0 + \beta_1 x_i + \varepsilon_i$, of y (exam score) on x (number of hours studied). This model is fit to a random sample of $n = 5$ students. The dependent variable is represented in matrix form as

$$\mathbf{y} = \begin{pmatrix} 80.0 \\ 90.0 \\ 92.0 \\ 70.0 \\ 67.0 \end{pmatrix} = \begin{pmatrix} y_1 \\ y_2 \\ y_3 \\ y_4 \\ y_5 \end{pmatrix}.$$

The matrix of independent variables includes x, along with a vector of ones to account for the constant term.

$$\mathbf{X} = \begin{pmatrix} 1.0 & 5.0 \\ 1.0 & 7.0 \\ 1.0 & 6.0 \\ 1.0 & 3.0 \\ 1.0 & 3.0 \end{pmatrix} = \begin{pmatrix} x_{10} & x_{11} \\ x_{20} & x_{21} \\ x_{30} & x_{31} \\ x_{40} & x_{41} \\ x_{50} & x_{51} \end{pmatrix} = \begin{pmatrix} 1 & x_{11} \\ 1 & x_{21} \\ 1 & x_{31} \\ 1 & x_{41} \\ 1 & x_{51} \end{pmatrix}.$$

The $\mathbf{X'X}$ matrix has a special form, with the sum of squares on the main diagonal and the sums of cross-products in the off-diagonal cells. However, since the first column of $\mathbf{X}$ is a vector of ones, this matrix simplifies to

$$\mathbf{X'X} = \begin{pmatrix} 5.0 & 24.0 \\ 24.0 & 128.0 \end{pmatrix} = \begin{pmatrix} n & \sum x_{i0} x_{i1} \\ \sum x_{i1} x_{i0} & \sum x_{i1} x_{i1} \end{pmatrix} = \begin{pmatrix} n & \sum x_{i1} \\ \sum x_{i1} & \sum x_{i1}^2 \end{pmatrix}.$$

The $\mathbf{X'y}$ matrix also simplifies, with $\sum y_i$ as the first element and $\sum y_i x_{i1}$ as the second element:

$$\mathbf{X'y} = \begin{pmatrix} 399.0 \\ 1993.0 \end{pmatrix} = \begin{pmatrix} \sum x_{i0} y_i \\ \sum x_{i1} y_i \end{pmatrix} = \begin{pmatrix} \sum y_i \\ \sum x_{i1} y_i \end{pmatrix}.$$

Inverting $\mathbf{X'X}$, we have,

$$(\mathbf{X'X})^{-1} = \begin{pmatrix} 2.0 & -0.375 \\ -0.375 & 0.078 \end{pmatrix}.$$

The least squares solution is

$$\mathbf{b} = \begin{pmatrix} 50.625 \\ 6.078 \end{pmatrix} = \begin{pmatrix} b_0 \\ b_1 \end{pmatrix},$$

where the first element of $\mathbf{b}$ is the estimated intercept (b_0) and the second is the estimated slope (b_1).

To obtain the standard errors of b_0 and b_1, it is necessary to estimate the error variance (σ_ε^2) using the mean squared error (s_e^2) from the model.

$$\begin{aligned} s_e^2 &= \frac{\sum_i (y_i - b_0 - b_1 x_i)^2}{n - K - 1} \\ &= \frac{(\mathbf{y} - \mathbf{Xb})'(\mathbf{y} - \mathbf{Xb})}{n - K - 1} \\ &= \frac{\mathbf{e'e}}{n - K - 1} \\ &= 13.307. \end{aligned}$$

The resulting variance-covariance matrix of $\mathbf{b}$ is

$$\widehat{\mathrm{var}}(\mathbf{b}) = s_e^2 (\mathbf{X'X})^{-1} = \begin{pmatrix} 26.614 & -4.990 \\ -4.990 & 1.040 \end{pmatrix}.$$

Taking the square roots of the diagonal elements gives the standard errors of $\mathbf{b}$. Thus, the OLS estimates (standard errors in parentheses) are $b_0 = 50.625$ (5.159) and $b_1 = 6.078$ (1.020).

Appendix B

Maximum Likelihood Estimation

B.1   Introduction

Maximum likelihood estimation is one of several methods used to obtain parameter estimates. Other methods include least squares, method of moments, and expectation maximization (EM). In many cases, alternative methods yield maximum likelihood estimates.

B.2   Basic Principles

If one observes a random sample, $x_1, x_2, \ldots, x_n$, of values drawn independently from a distribution, say $f(x_1, x_2, \ldots, x_n \mid \theta)$ governed by an unknown parameter θ, we may express the probability of obtaining the data given a value of θ. This expression is called the likelihood of the sample (or likelihood on the data). We may think of this as the chance of obtaining the sample data we actually obtained given θ. Because θ is unknown, it must be estimated from the data. As an estimate of θ, we select the value $\widehat{\theta}$ such that, when evaluated at $\widehat{\theta}$, the expression for the likelihood of the sample reaches a maximum. This process of finding estimated values of unknown parameters is called maximum likelihood estimation. Estimates obtained in this manner are known as maximum likelihood estimates or MLEs.

B.2.1   Example 1: Binomial Proportion

Suppose we observe the outcome of an experiment of tosses of a fair coin, recording the number of heads, x, in n tosses. In this case, the sample contains n realizations. The expected value of the random variable X in the population is $E(X) = np$, where p denotes the probability of success on a single toss. We are interested in estimating p (of course, in this case p is known since the coin is assumed to be fair). The likelihood of the sample is the probability function for a binomial random variable:

$$L(p) = L = \binom{n}{x} p^x (1 - p)^{n-x}. \tag{B.1}$$

If we plot L as a function of p only, (i.e., n and x are fixed), we get something similar to that shown in Fig. B.1. In this case, $0 \leq p \leq 1$ and $0 \leq L \leq 1$ because each is a probability (p is the probability of success in a single trial, and L is the probability of exactly x successes in n trials). The quantity $\widehat{p}$ is the value of p that maximizes L.

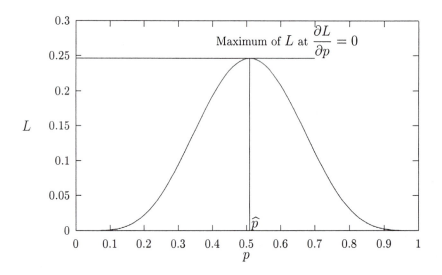

Figure B.1: Maximum of Likelihood Function

How do we find $\widehat{p}$? First, we need to observe that the maximum value of L occurs at a point where its rate of change with respect to p is zero. Geometrically, the tangent to the curve L at the MLE has a slope of zero. We can find an analytic or numerical expression for the rate of change of a function relative to a variable on which the function depends. This expression is the first derivative of the function; it is the expression for the rate of change or slope of the function.

To summarize, in order to find the value at which L reaches its maximum, we find the expression for the first derivative of L with respect to p. Then we find the estimated value of p that makes this expression equal to zero. Strictly speaking, one must make sure that the estimated value corresponds to a maximum rather than a minimum of L because when L reaches a minimum, the tangent at that point will also have a slope of zero. How can we distinguish between these situations?

To ensure that—when setting the first derivative equal to zero and solving for p—we are getting a maximum, we must also make sure that the second derivative of L is negative. That is, the first derivative of the first derivative of L is negative. This means that the slope of L is decreasing in the neighborhood of $\widehat{p}$. Returning to the example, we have

$$L(p) = L = \binom{n}{x} p^x (1-p)^{n-x} = c p^x (1-p)^{n-x}, \qquad (\text{B.2})$$

where c does not involve p. If we take the logarithm of L, we obtain

$$\log L(p) = \log c + x \log p + (n-x) \log(1-p). \qquad (\text{B.3})$$

Working with $\log L$ rather than L does not change things since a logarithm is a monotonic transformation. Usually, working with $\log L$ simplifies the computations. Note, however, that $0 \leq L \leq 1$; hence, $-\infty \leq \log L \leq 0$. If we take the first derivative of $\log L$ (defined previously), we get

$$\frac{\partial \log L(p)}{\partial p} = \frac{x}{p} - \frac{n-x}{1-p}. \qquad (\text{B.4})$$

Setting the left-hand side equal to zero and solving for p leads to the MLE (i.e., $\widehat{p} = x/n$). In other words, the MLE of p is the observed proportion of heads.

B.2.2   Example 2: Normal Mean and Variance

Suppose we observe n normally distributed random variables drawn from a population with mean μ and variance σ^2. The likelihood of a single observation is given by

$$L(\mu, \sigma^2) = \frac{1}{\sqrt{2\pi}\sigma} \exp\left(-\frac{x_i - \mu}{2\sigma}\right)^2. \tag{B.5}$$

Since the observations are independent, it follows that the likelihood of the sample is the product

$$L(\mu, \sigma^2) = \prod_{i=1}^{n} L(\mu, \sigma^2) = \frac{c}{\sigma^n} \exp\left\{-\sum_{i=1}^{n}\left[(x_i - \mu)/2\sigma\right]^2\right\}, \tag{B.6}$$

where c is the component that does not involve μ or σ.

Unlike Example 1, this example involves two unknown parameters, but the principles are the same. To obtain $\widehat{\mu}$, the MLE of μ, find an expression for the rate of change of $\log L$ relative to μ while the other parameter, σ^2, is held constant. This is the first partial derivative with respect to μ. Setting this expression equal to zero and solving for μ leads to $\widehat{\mu} = \sum_{i=1}^{n} x_i/n$. The MLE of μ is the sample mean. To obtain the MLE of σ^2, find an expression for the rate of change of $\log L$ relative to σ^2 while holding μ constant. This expression is the first partial derivative of $\log L$ with respect to σ^2. You will find that, after substituting the MLE of μ, $\widehat{\sigma}^2 = \sum_{i=1}^{n}(x_i - \widehat{\mu})^2/n$, the sample variance.[1]

General Principles of ML Estimation

1. If $\log L_i$ is the log-likelihood of one observation out of n independent observations drawn from the same distribution, then the log-likelihood of the sample is $\log L = \sum_{i=1}^{n} \log L_i$.

2. Let $\boldsymbol{\theta} = (\theta_1, \theta_2, \ldots, \theta_K)'$ denote a $K \times 1$ vector of parameters that describe some aspect of the distribution of the data (i.e., mean,

---

[1]Note that this formula is different from the usual formula for the sample variance, which has $(n - 1)$ in the denominator.

variance, regression slopes, model effects. The MLE of $\boldsymbol{\theta}$ is obtained by the following steps:

(a) Find the vector of partial derivatives of $\log L$ relative to $\boldsymbol{\theta}$,

$$\mathbf{U}(\boldsymbol{\theta}) = \frac{\partial \log L(\boldsymbol{\theta})}{\partial \boldsymbol{\theta}}. \tag{B.7}$$

Specifically, let u_k denote the partial derivative of $\log L$ with respect to θ_k, then

$$u_k = \frac{\partial \log L(\boldsymbol{\theta})}{\partial \theta_k}, \qquad k = 1, \dots, K. \tag{B.8}$$

Set each of these equations equal to zero and solve for θ_k. This will yield K equations with K unknowns. $\mathbf{U}(\boldsymbol{\theta})$ is the $K \times 1$ vector of first derivatives with respect to $\log L$, called the *score* function (or score vector). The u_k $(k = 1, \dots, K)$ are the individual elements of the score vector.

(b) Second, to make sure that the first-order conditions identify a maximum, it should be checked that the second derivative of $\log L$ with respect to $\boldsymbol{\theta}$ is a negative definite matrix, that is,

$$\mathbf{H}(\boldsymbol{\theta}) = \frac{\partial^2 \log L(\boldsymbol{\theta})}{\partial \boldsymbol{\theta} \partial \boldsymbol{\theta}'} \tag{B.9}$$

should be negative definite. Let h_{kl} denote the second derivative of $\log L$ with respect to θ_k and θ_l, then

$$h_{kl} = \frac{\partial^2 \log L(\boldsymbol{\theta})}{\partial \theta_k \partial \theta_l}, \qquad k, l = 1, \dots, K.$$

The *negative* of the resulting $K \times K$ matrix formed from the elements h_{kl} is called the information matrix, which we will denote by $\mathbf{I}(\boldsymbol{\theta})$. In certain cases, it is possible to obtain this matrix directly. In other situations, the expectation, or a reasonable approximation of $-\mathbf{H}(\boldsymbol{\theta})$ can be obtained. One such approximation is available as the outer product of the gradient vector (or individual score functions). For example, if we let $\log L_i$ denote the contribution of the ith individual to the sample log-likelihood, the $n \times K$ matrix of first derivatives (or individual score functions) is called the gradient vector $\mathbf{g}(\boldsymbol{\theta})$. The estimated information matrix can be obtained as the following cross-product:

$$\widehat{\mathbf{I}(\boldsymbol{\theta})} = \mathbf{g}(\boldsymbol{\theta})'\mathbf{g}(\boldsymbol{\theta}). \tag{B.10}$$

(c) The square roots of the diagonal entries of the inverse of the information matrix (or negative second-derivative matrix) provide the standard errors of the MLEs. That is, when evaluated at $\widehat{\boldsymbol{\theta}}$, $\mathbf{I}(\boldsymbol{\theta})^{-1}$ gives the asymptotic variance-covariance matrix of $\widehat{\boldsymbol{\theta}}$. The diagonal elements of $\mathbf{I}(\boldsymbol{\theta})^{-1}$ are $\text{var}(\widehat{\boldsymbol{\theta}})$. Because maximum likelihood estimates are asymptotically normally distributed, this information can be used to construct confidence intervals around $\boldsymbol{\theta}$.

B.2.3   Example 3: Binary Logit Model

As outlined in Chapter 3, the likelihood function for a grouped or individual-level binomial response model can be written as

$$\log L(\boldsymbol{\beta}) = \sum_i \left\{ \log \binom{n_i}{y_i} + y_i \log F(\mathbf{x}_i'\boldsymbol{\beta}) + (n_i - y_i) \log[1 - F(\mathbf{x}_i'\boldsymbol{\beta})] \right\}.$$

$$\tag{B.11}$$

The constant multiplier $\binom{n_i}{y_i}$ appearing in the likelihood function does not involve unknown parameters, so it can be ignored during estimation. Moreover, in the case of individual-level data, this term is always equal to 1 so the log-likelihood function for the binary logit model simplifies to

$$\log L(\boldsymbol{\beta}) = \sum_i \left\{ y_i \log \Lambda_i + (1 - y_i) \log[1 - \Lambda_i] \right\},$$

where $\Lambda_i = \exp(\mathbf{x}_i'\boldsymbol{\beta})/\{1 + \exp(\mathbf{x}_i'\boldsymbol{\beta})\}$.

Solving the first-order conditions for the logit model, we obtain the following expression for the score function

$$u_k = \sum_i (y_i - \Lambda_i)x_{ik}, \qquad k = 0, \dots, K.$$

In matrix notation, this expression is written as

$$\mathbf{U} = \mathbf{X}'(\mathbf{y} - \mathbf{\Lambda}).$$

The klth element of the second derivative matrix for the logit model is given by the expression

$$h_{kl} = -\sum_i x_{ik}x_{il}\Lambda_i(1 - \Lambda_i),$$

or in matrix notation,

$$\mathbf{H} = -\mathbf{X}'\mathbf{W}\mathbf{X},$$

where $\mathbf{W}$ is a diagonal matrix with $w_i = \Lambda_i(1 - \Lambda_i)$ on the main diagonal.

Iterative methods must be used to obtain the MLEs because Λ_i is nonlinear in the unknown parameters, meaning that no *closed form* solution for the MLE exists. We substitute parameter estimates in the expression for the likelihood equations, so Λ_i is replaced by $\widehat{\Lambda}_i = \exp(\sum_k b_k x_{ik})/\{1+\exp(\sum_k b_k x_{ik})\}$. Two competing iterative methods, the Newton-Raphson method and the Fisher scoring method, yield identical results in this case because the expected and actual Hessians are identical.[2] The resulting matrix is negative definite, and because the functions to be maximized are globally concave, the resulting estimates provide a global maximum.

---

[2] As stated earlier, one may also estimate the Hessian as the cross-product of the first derivatives, resulting in the estimator of Berndt et al. (1974) (or BHHH estimator). This estimator may be preferred when formulas for the expected or actual Hessians are difficult to express or do not exist. Other estimation methods, such as the Davidon-Fletcher-Powell (or DFP method) rely on updating procedures to obtain an estimate of the second derivative matrix (or its inverse). For the models described here, such methods are not needed.

The Newton-Raphson and scoring methods usually begin with initial estimates, or *starting values* from OLS regressions on either the binary variable y, or in the case of grouped data, the empirical logits.

At the $(t+1)$th iteration, estimates are updated based on quantities from the previous iteration as

$$\widehat{\boldsymbol{\beta}}^{(t+1)} = \widehat{\boldsymbol{\beta}}^{(t)} - [\mathbf{H}^{(t)}]^{-1}\mathbf{U}^{(t)}, \tag{B.12}$$

where $\widehat{\boldsymbol{\beta}}$ is the $(K+1) \times 1$ vector of parameter estimates, and $\mathbf{H}$ and $\mathbf{U}$ are the second and first partial derivatives of $\log L$ with respect to $\boldsymbol{\beta}$.

The iterative procedure is said to converge when the difference $\Delta\widehat{\boldsymbol{\beta}} = \widehat{\boldsymbol{\beta}}^{(t)} - \widehat{\boldsymbol{\beta}}^{(t-1)}$ is negligible, when the proportionate change in the value of the log-likelihood is less than some small number δ, or when the score vector is sufficiently close to zero. Most computer programs check each of these criteria to determine convergence. The asymptotic variance-covariance matrix of the estimates is obtained from the final iteration as the inverse of the information matrix (negative Hessian), $\mathbf{I}(\widehat{\boldsymbol{\beta}})^{-1}$. The maximum likelihood estimates are asymptotically normally distributed, with estimated variances equal to the diagonal elements of the inverse information matrix, Diag $\mathbf{I}(\widehat{\boldsymbol{\beta}})^{-1}$. The quantity $\widehat{\boldsymbol{\beta}}/\text{Diag}\sqrt{\mathbf{I}(\widehat{\boldsymbol{\beta}})^{-1}}$ follows an asymptotic standard normal distribution (z-distribution). This can be used to conduct significance tests on the individual parameters.

Grouped Data

Estimating parameters of logistic models using grouped data requires some slight modifications to the foregoing formulas. The kernel of the log-likelihood function for the grouped binomial logit model can be written as

$$\log L(\boldsymbol{\beta}) = \sum_i \left\{ y_i \log \Lambda_i + (n_i - y_i) \log(1 - \Lambda_i) \right\}, \tag{B.13}$$

where y_i now represents the number of successes in n_i trials (i.e., the observed cell frequencies). Differentiating $\log L$ with respect to β, we have

$$u_k = \frac{\partial \log L(\boldsymbol{\beta})}{\partial \beta_k} = \sum_i y_i x_{ik} - \sum_i n_i x_{ik} \Lambda_i, \qquad k = 0, \dots, K,$$

or in matrix notation,

$$\mathbf{U} = \mathbf{X}'(\mathbf{y} - \mathbf{m}),$$

where $\mathbf{y}$ is the column vector of "success" counts, $\mathbf{X}$ is the matrix of independent variables, and $\mathbf{m}$ is the column vector with elements $m_i = n_i \Lambda_i$.

The klth element of the second derivative matrix is

$$h_{kl} = \frac{\partial^2 \log L(\boldsymbol{\beta})}{\partial \beta_k \beta_l} = -\sum_i x_{ik} x_{il} n_i \Lambda_i (1 - \Lambda_i), \quad k, l = 0, \dots, K,$$

or in matrix notation,

$$\mathbf{H} = -\mathbf{X}'\mathbf{W}\mathbf{X},$$

where $\mathbf{W}$ is the diagonal matrix with $w_i = n_i \Lambda_i (1 - \Lambda_i)$ on the main diagonal.

Numerical Example

We will illustrate the mechanics of the Newton-Raphson method for obtaining maximum likelihood estimation using individual-level data on a subsample of $n = 647$ nonwhite males from the NLSY. The program and dataset are available from the book's website. The binary dependent variable is whether a school-aged youth (aged 14–17 in 1979) graduated from high school ($y = 1$) by the 1985 survey. We fit the following binary logit model to the data using information on family structure, $x_1 = $ NONINT, and $x_2 = $ INCOME in tens of thousands of dollars:

$$y_i^* = \beta_0 + \beta_1 x_{i1} + \beta_2 x_{i2} + \varepsilon_i.$$

A value of $-2\times$ log-likelihood of 677.82 is obtained from the model. The estimates, standard errors, and t-ratios are given in Table B.1.

Table B.1: Binomial Logit Model of High School Graduation

Variable	Estimate	Std. Error	t-Ratio
Constant (x_0)	0.667	0.210	3.171
NONINT (x_1)	−0.149	0.195	−0.766
INCOME(x_2)	1.237	0.326	3.795

The iterative procedure begins with a set of starting values $(\widehat{\beta}^{(0)})$. The easiest way to obtain these is from the OLS regression on the binary dependent variable, y,

$$\widehat{\beta}^{(0)} = \begin{pmatrix} 0.695 \\ -0.031 \\ 0.163 \end{pmatrix}.$$

The score vector at the first iteration is

$$\mathbf{U}^{(1)} = \begin{pmatrix} 55.93 \\ 15.90 \\ 43.58 \end{pmatrix}.$$

The negative Hessian matrix at the first iteration is

$$-\mathbf{H}^{(0)} = \begin{pmatrix} 139.88 & 59.36 & 73.94 \\ 59.36 & 59.36 & 25.23 \\ 73.94 & 25.23 & 59.31 \end{pmatrix}.$$

The resulting inverse information matrix at the first iteration is

$$[\mathbf{I}^{(0)}]^{-1} = \begin{pmatrix} 0.0315 & -0.0181 & -0.0316 \\ -0.0181 & 0.0309 & 0.0094 \\ -0.0316 & 0.0094 & 0.0523 \end{pmatrix}.$$

Multiplying the inverse information matrix by the score vector, we obtain the direction vector $\Delta\widehat{\beta}^{(0)}$, which denotes the change or increment in the parameter vector:

$$[\mathbf{I}^{(0)}]^{-1}\mathbf{U}^{(0)} = \Delta\widehat{\beta}^{(0)} = \begin{pmatrix} 0.0984 \\ -0.1108 \\ 0.6593 \end{pmatrix}.$$

The first iteration is completed when the parameter vector is updated by adding this increment to the initial (OLS) parameter vector:

$$\widehat{\boldsymbol{\beta}}^{(0)} + \Delta\widehat{\boldsymbol{\beta}}^{(0)} = \begin{pmatrix} 0.695 \\ -0.031 \\ 0.163 \end{pmatrix} + \begin{pmatrix} 0.0984 \\ -0.1108 \\ 0.6593 \end{pmatrix} =$$

$$\widehat{\boldsymbol{\beta}}^{(1)} = \begin{pmatrix} 0.793 \\ -0.141 \\ 0.822 \end{pmatrix}$$

A $-2\times$ log-likelihood value of 716.37 is obtained by evaluating the expression for the log-likelihood at the end of the first iteration using the current estimates, $\widehat{\boldsymbol{\beta}}^{(1)}$.

The entire process is repeated until the differences, $\Delta\widehat{\boldsymbol{\beta}}$, are less than 0.00001. At the end of the fourth iteration, the parameter vector is

$$\widehat{\boldsymbol{\beta}}^{(4)} = \begin{pmatrix} 0.667 \\ -0.149 \\ 1.237 \end{pmatrix},$$

and we find that the score vector at the current parameter vector is approaching 0, meaning that the slope of the log-likelihood function is nearly zero at these estimates:

$$\mathbf{U}^{(4)} = \begin{pmatrix} 2.01\mathrm{E}{-06} \\ 6.10\mathrm{E}{-07} \\ 2.28\mathrm{E}{-06} \end{pmatrix}.$$

Similarly, the direction vector, $\Delta\widehat{\boldsymbol{\beta}}$, indicates that the parameter vector is changing little near the MLE:

$$\Delta\widehat{\boldsymbol{\beta}}^{(4)} = \begin{pmatrix} -4.86\mathrm{E}{-08} \\ 6.87\mathrm{E}{-09} \\ 1.42\mathrm{E}{-07} \end{pmatrix}.$$

Updating the parameter vector results in the MLEs of

$$\widehat{\boldsymbol{\beta}}^{(5)} = \begin{pmatrix} 0.6667 \\ -0.1492 \\ 1.2374 \end{pmatrix}.$$

The inverse information matrix evaluated at the final estimates is

$$
\mathbf{I}^{-1}(\widehat{\beta}) = \begin{pmatrix} 0.0442 & -0.0238 & -0.0540 \\ -0.0238 & 0.0379 & 0.0139 \\ -0.0540 & 0.0139 & 0.1063 \end{pmatrix}.
$$

Taking the square root of the diagonal elements of $\mathbf{I}^{-1}(\widehat{\beta})$, we obtain the following standard errors of the MLEs:

$$
\widehat{\mathrm{SE}}(\widehat{\beta}) = \begin{pmatrix} 0.2102 \\ 0.1947 \\ 0.3260 \end{pmatrix}.
$$

These results, along with the t-ratios are reported in Table B.1.

B.2.4   Example 4: Loglinear Model

This example draws on the data on education and attitude toward premarital sex presented in Table 4.1. We will begin by rearranging the data in a column format suitable for an analysis by most standard computer programs as shown in Table B.2.

Table B.2: Column-Formatted Data from Table 4.1

x_0	x_1	x_2	y
1	0	0	873
1	1	0	533
1	0	1	1190
1	1	1	1208

Each cell in Table 4.1 will be denoted by a row in the data set, and the variables (education and attitude) will each be represented by a dummy variable, resulting in Table B.2. The first column in Table B.2 is a vector of ones for the intercept. The second and third columns are vectors of dummy variables corresponding respectively to education and attitude toward premarital sex. Let x_{0i}, x_{1i}, x_{2i} denote the row vector of independent variables corresponding to the ith cell.

This set of variables corresponds to the independence model [i.e., it fits only the mean frequency (via x_0) and the marginal distributions of x_1 and x_2]. The fourth column contains the observed cell frequencies denoted by y, which is the dependent variable in this analysis. The independence model can be written as a multiplicative (or loglinear) model for counts as

$$m_i = \exp(\beta_0 + \beta_1 x_{1i} + \beta_2 x_{2i}), \tag{B.14}$$

where m_i is the expected frequency in the ith cell under the independence model, and the β's are parameters to be estimated.

The *kernel* of the log-likelihood under Poisson sampling is

$$\log L(\boldsymbol{\beta}) = \sum_{i=1}^{n} (y_i \log m_i - m_i).$$

Again, an iterative strategy is needed because of the nonlinearity of the model. As was the case with the logit model, estimation involves repeatedly updating the estimates of the β's using the first and second derivatives of $\log L(\boldsymbol{\beta})$ with respect to $\boldsymbol{\beta}$.

We begin by obtaining starting values from the OLS regression of $\log y_i$ as

$$\log y_i = \beta_0 + \beta_1 x_{1i} + \beta_2 x_{2i}. \tag{B.15}$$

We calculate the expected counts, $m_i = \exp(\sum_k \beta_k x_{ik})$ at each iteration, substituting the current parameter estimates in this expression. Next, the observed and expected counts, along with the design matrix, are used to obtain the score vector,

$$u_k = \frac{\partial \log L(\beta_k)}{\partial \beta_k} = \sum_{i=1}^{n} x_{ik}(y_i - m_i), \qquad k = 0, \ldots, K, \tag{B.16}$$

or, in matrix notation,

$$\mathbf{U} = \mathbf{X}'(\mathbf{y} - \mathbf{m}), \tag{B.17}$$

where $\mathbf{y}$ and $\mathbf{m}$ are respectively the vector of observed and predicted cell counts, and $\mathbf{X}$ is the design matrix of independent variables.

The same quantities are used to form the matrix of second derivatives. The klth element of the second derivative matrix, $\mathbf{H}$, is

$$h_{kl} = -\frac{\partial^2 \log L(\boldsymbol{\beta})}{\partial \beta_k \partial \beta_l} = -\sum_{i=1}^{n} x_{ik} x_{il} m_i, \qquad k, l = 0, \dots, K. \quad \text{(B.18)}$$

In matrix notation, this can be expressed as

$$\mathbf{H} = -\mathbf{X}'\mathbf{W}\mathbf{X}, \qquad \text{(B.19)}$$

where $\mathbf{W}$ is the diagonal matrix with elements of m_i (evaluated at the
current estimates) on the main diagonal.

Finally, the parameter vector at the $(t+1)$th iteration is updated
according to the usual Newton-Raphson formula given by Eq. B.12.

Numerical Example

Again, we will use the GAUSS programming language to illustrate
the process of obtaining MLEs using the Newton-Raphson algorithm.
Example programs are provided on this book's website.

The first step (at iteration 0) is to obtain starting values via OLS.
In our example, these are

$$\widehat{\boldsymbol{\beta}}^{(0)} = \begin{pmatrix} 6.645 \\ -0.239 \\ 0.564 \end{pmatrix}.$$

We now enter the iteration loop and compute the updated parameter vector as

$$\widehat{\boldsymbol{\beta}}^{(1)} = \widehat{\boldsymbol{\beta}}^{(0)} - [\mathbf{H}^{(0)}]^{-1}\mathbf{U}^{(0)}.$$

Thus, at the end of the first iteration, the estimated parameters are

$$\widehat{\boldsymbol{\beta}}^{(1)} = \begin{pmatrix} 6.6372 \\ -0.1691 \\ 0.5336 \end{pmatrix} = \begin{pmatrix} 6.645 \\ -0.239 \\ 0.564 \end{pmatrix} +$$

$$\begin{pmatrix} 0.000935 & -0.00047 & -0.00073 \\ -0.000471 & 0.00107 & 1.10\text{E}{-}20 \\ -0.000728 & 1.10\text{E}{-}20 & 0.00114 \end{pmatrix} \begin{pmatrix} 14.856 \\ 71.945 \\ -17.103 \end{pmatrix}.$$

By the end of the fourth iteration, the score vector is nearly zero, and the estimated parameters do not depart much from the OLS starting values or those from the earlier iterations:

$$\widehat{\beta}^{(4)} = \begin{pmatrix} 6.6366 \\ -0.1697 \\ 0.5339 \end{pmatrix}.$$

The inverse information matrix at the last iteration is

$$\mathbf{I}^{-1}(\widehat{\beta}) = \begin{pmatrix} 0.00093 & -0.00048 & -0.00071 \\ -0.00048 & 0.00106 & -6.80E-20 \\ -0.00071 & -6.80E-20 & 0.00112 \end{pmatrix}.$$

The standard errors of the estimates are obtained from the square roots of the diagonal elements of this matrix:

$$\widehat{SE}(\widehat{\beta}) = \begin{pmatrix} 0.0305 \\ 0.0325 \\ 0.0336 \end{pmatrix}.$$

B.2.5   Iteratively Reweighted Least Squares

Statistical packages rely on different methods to estimate logit, probit, and loglinear models. The iteratively reweighted least squares technique can be used to estimate these models as generalized linear models. Several computer packages utilize this approach, which—in the case of the logit, probit, loglinear, and many other models—is equivalent to maximum likelihood estimation.

To show this equivalence, let us note that the procedure for updating the estimates given by Eq. B.12 used in the preceding examples can be generalized to

$$\widehat{\beta}^{(t+1)} = \widehat{\beta}^{(t)} + [\mathbf{X}'\mathbf{W}^{(t)}\mathbf{X}]^{-1}\mathbf{X}'(\mathbf{y} - \mathbf{m}^{(t)}), \qquad (B.20)$$

where the various models have different forms of $\mathbf{W}^{(t)}$ and $\mathbf{m}^{(t)}$. For example, in the case of logit models, $\mathbf{W}^{(t)}$ is a diagonal matrix with elements $w_i = n_i \Lambda_i (1 - \Lambda_i)$ on the main diagonal, and $n_i = 1$ for individual-level data. For the probit model, $\mathbf{W}^{(t)}$ has diagonal entries $w_i = n_i \phi_i^2 / \{\Phi_i(1 - \Phi_i)\}$, where ϕ_i and Φ_i are the standard normal density and cumulative distribution functions evaluated at the estimates. For loglinear models, $\mathbf{W}^{(t)}$ is a diagonal matrix with $\mu_i^{(t)} = \exp(\sum_k \beta_k^{(t)} x_{ik})$ on the main diagonal.

The vector of conditional mean responses $(\mathbf{m}^{(t)})$ under the logit and probit models are the predicted number of successes. For the logit model, the individual elements of $\mathbf{m}^{(t)}$ are

$$\mu_i^{(t)} = n_i \Lambda_i^{(t)}.$$

For the probit model, these are

$$\mu_i^{(t)} = n_i \Phi_i^{(t)}.$$

For the loglinear model, the expected counts are

$$\mu_i^{(t)} = \exp(\sum_k \beta_k^{(t)} x_{ik}).$$

We could also write the updating formula in Eq. B.20 as

$$\widehat{\boldsymbol{\beta}}^{(t+1)} = [\mathbf{X}'\mathbf{W}^{(t)}\mathbf{X}]^{-1}\mathbf{X}'\mathbf{W}^{(t)}\mathbf{z}^{(t)}, \qquad (B.21)$$

where $\mathbf{z}^{(t)}$ is an "adjusted" or "linearized" dependent variable, with elements

$$z_i^{(t)} = \sum_k \beta_k^{(t)} x_{ik} + (y_i - \mu_i^{(t)})/w_i^{(t)}. \qquad (B.22)$$

The last term on the right in Eq. B.22 can be expressed as

$$\frac{y_i - \mu_i}{w_i} = (y_i - \mu_i)\frac{\partial g(\mu_i)}{\partial \mu_i}. \qquad (B.23)$$

The term $g(\mu_i)$ is referred to as the "link" function that transforms the mean response function to make the model linear in the parameters.

Equation B.22 is a heteroscedastic linear model that can be estimated using weighted least squares. The *iterated* weighted least squares estimates are obtained from repeated applications of Eq. B.21, by updating $\mathbf{W}$ and $\mathbf{z}$ until the difference in successive estimates $(\Delta\widehat{\boldsymbol{\beta}})$ becomes negligible. The process usually converges to the ML estimates in a few iterations. The next section presents a more formal development of generalized linear models.

B.2.6   Generalized Linear Models

Generalized linear models are a class of statistical models generalized from the classical linear regression, which provide a systematic way to handle categorical dependent variables. Methods for estimating GLMs involve straightforward applications of the generalized least squares techniques described earlier. Here we present a brief outline of generalized linear models. McCullagh and Nelder (1989) offer a more detailed treatment of this subject.

As in the classical regression model, the GLM begins with a dependent variable (y), a conditional expectation (or mean value function) μ_i, and variance function v_i. Let $\mathbf{x}'_i = x_{i0}, x_{i1}, \dots, x_{iK}$ denote the explanatory variables, with $x_{i0} = 1$ to allow for the intercept. As in the classical regression model, the structural component is a *linear* function of $\mathbf{x}$:

$$\eta_i = \mathbf{x}'_i \boldsymbol{\beta}, \tag{B.24}$$

where η_i represents some function of the dependent variable y. In classical linear models, the objective is to estimate the conditional mean of y. In this case, we have an identity link between μ_i and η_i:

$$\mu_i = \eta_i.$$

More generally, however, the link function may be written as

$$g(\mu_i) = \eta_i. \tag{B.25}$$

The link function, $g(\mu_i)$, relates μ_i to the linear predictor η_i. Therefore, specifying a GLM is equivalent to transforming the dependent variable to make the model linear in the structural parameters. In this way, a nonlinear model may be transformed to a model that is linear in the parameters.

Equations B.24 and B.25 constitute the basic structure of a GLM. Estimation of the model is based on the *linearization* of the link function through

$$g(y_i) \approx g(\mu_i) + (y_i - \mu_i) g'(\mu_i), \tag{B.26}$$

where $g'(\mu_i) = \partial \eta_i / \partial \mu_i$ is the derivative of the link function with respect to the mean value function.

Except in the case of very simple models, all these terms must be evaluated at the current estimates and updated iteratively. This specifies a process that is carried out until the values of the estimates of the structural parameters (β) stabilize. One may think of transforming the dependent variable y into a new variable $g(y)$. Let $\hat{z}$ be this "adjusted" dependent variable. At each step, the estimated values of $\hat{\eta}$ and $\hat{\mu}$—evaluated at the current estimates—give rise to new estimated values of the adjusted dependent variable

$$\hat{z}_i = \hat{\eta}_i + (y_i - \hat{\mu}_i)(\partial \hat{\eta}_i / \partial \hat{\mu}_i),$$

where the expression $\partial \hat{\eta}_i / \partial \hat{\mu}_i$ is the current iteration's value of the derivative of linear predictor function with respect to the mean function of y. The regression weights for the model are

$$\hat{w}_i = \frac{(\partial \hat{\eta}_i / \partial \hat{\mu}_i)^2}{\hat{v}_i},$$

where $\hat{v}_i$ is the variance function of y evaluated at the current estimates.

The solution for β is a GLS formula modified to allow for successive updating. At the tth iteration cycle, the estimates of β are given by Eq. B.20.

In practice, any model could be fit in this manner. When densities of exponential families are involved, this procedure yields maximum likelihood estimates. With nonexponential densities, the estimates are not ML but possess many of the desirable properties of ML estimates. This procedure is identical to the iterative reweighted least squares estimator presented earlier.

Example 1: OLS Regression

The simplest application of a generalized linear model would be where y is drawn from a normal distribution with constant variance, in which case the linear predictor and the mean value of y coincide such that

$$\eta_i = \mu_i = \mathbf{x}_i' \boldsymbol{\beta}.$$

Due to the identity between the link and mean function, it follows that $\partial \eta_i / \partial \mu_i = 1$, $\widehat{z} = y$, and the estimating equations can be solved in a single iteration as

$$\mathbf{b} = (\mathbf{X}'\widehat{\mathbf{W}}\mathbf{X})^{-1}(\mathbf{X}'\widehat{\mathbf{W}}\widehat{z}) = (\mathbf{X}'\mathbf{I}\mathbf{X})^{-1}(\mathbf{X}'\mathbf{I}y) = (\mathbf{X}'\mathbf{X})^{-1}(\mathbf{X}'y),$$

where $\mathbf{I}$ is the $n \times n$ identity matrix.

Example 2: Logit Model

Let y_i represent the number of successes in n_i trials of a binomial experiment, where the probability of success on the ith trial, p_i, is assumed to depend on a set of unknown parameters. The conditional mean function of y is $\mu_i = n_i p_i$, with variance function $v_i = n_i p_i (1-p_i)$. A complication in this case is that the mean and variance functions depend on p_i, which itself involves unknown parameters that must be estimated from data. Moreover, p_i must lie in the range $[0, 1]$. One way to guarantee this is to assume that y is drawn from a standard logistic distribution such that

$$p_i = \frac{\mu_i}{n_i} = \frac{\exp(\eta_i)}{1 + \exp(\eta_i)} = \frac{1}{1 + \exp(-\eta_i)}.$$

Therefore, p_i is a nonlinear function of η_i, but the linear predictor function given by the "logit" transformation (or link) makes the model linear in the logit scale

$$\eta_i = \log\left(\frac{p_i}{1 - p_i}\right) = \mathbf{x}_i'\boldsymbol{\beta}.$$

The adjusted dependent variable is

$$\widehat{z}_i = \widehat{\eta}_i + (y_i - n_i\widehat{p}_i)/\widehat{v}_i,$$

where $\widehat{v}_i = n_i\widehat{p}_i(1 - \widehat{p}_i)$, and the iterative weights are given by

$$\widehat{w}_i = n_i\widehat{p}_i(1 - \widehat{p}_i).$$

Combining these expressions with the iterative estimation strategy given by Eq. B.21 yields maximum likelihood estimates.

Example 3: Probit Model

Estimation of the probit model follows the same principles. Now, however, the expected probabilities are

$$p_i = \Phi(\eta_i).$$

The model is linear in the probit link function,

$$\eta_i = \Phi^{-1}(p_i).$$

The adjusted dependent variable is

$$\widehat{z}_i = \widehat{\eta}_i + (y_i - n_i\widehat{p}_i)/\widehat{v}_i,$$

where $\widehat{v}_i = n_i\phi(\widehat{\eta}_i)$, and the iterative weights are

$$\widehat{w}_i = n_i\phi(\widehat{\eta}_i)/\widehat{p}_i(1 - \widehat{p}_i).$$

Example 4: Complementary Log-Log Model

Like logit and probit models, in complementary log-log models, the mean response function for the number of successes (y_i) in n_i trials is $\mu_i = n_ip_i$, where p_i is given by

$$p_i = 1 - \exp\{-\exp(\eta_i)\}.$$

The model is linear in the complementary log-log link function,

$$\eta_i = \log\{-\log(1 - p_i)\}.$$

The adjusted dependent variable in the GLM takes the form

$$\widehat{z}_i = \widehat{\eta}_i + (y_i - n_i\widehat{p}_i)(\partial\widehat{\eta}_i/\partial\widehat{\mu}_i),$$

where

$$\partial\widehat{\eta}_i/\partial\widehat{\mu}_i = \{-\log(1 - \widehat{p}_i)n_i(1 - \widehat{p}_i)\}^{-1}.$$

The iterative weights are

$$\widehat{w}_i = \{(\partial\widehat{\eta}_i/\partial\widehat{\mu}_i)^2 n_i\widehat{p}_i(1 - \widehat{p}_i)\}^{-1}.$$

Example 5: Loglinear Model

The mean response function for a loglinear model with counts, y_i, is given by

$$\mu_i = \exp(\eta_i).$$

The model is linear in the log of the mean response function (i.e., a log link function)

$$\eta_i = \log(\mu_i).$$

The adjusted dependent variable is

$$\widehat{z}_i = \widehat{\eta}_i + (y_i - \widehat{\mu}_i)/\widehat{\mu}_i.$$

The mean and variance functions are the same for Poisson variables, so the iterative weights are simply

$$\widehat{w}_i = \widehat{\mu}_i.$$

B.2.7   Minimum χ^2 Estimation

When the data are grouped, we can obtain estimates that are close to those of ML by using a simple weighted least squares regression on the empirical logits or probits.[3]

As shown earlier, with grouped or replicated data, the number of "successes" (y_i) and the number of trials (n_i) can be used to obtain the empirical probabilities, $\widetilde{p}_i = y_i/n_i$. We now describe an alternative to the ML estimation method that uses sample proportions (empirical probabilities) to form empirical logits and probits. This approach will yield consistent estimates. This method is intuitively appealing because of its similarity to standard regression.

We begin with a heteroscedastic linear model, much like the linear probability model. However, the dependent variable is now the empirical logit or probit, obtained as a transformation of the empirical

---

[3]In some cases, the adjustment of adding a small constant to each cell is needed to ensure that the log transformation in the logit model will work.

probability. The reciprocal (or inverse) of the error variance is used to construct the weights in a FGLS regression.

The minimum χ^2 method begins with a linear model for a transformation of the "theoretical" population response probability, p_i,

$$g(p_i) = \mathbf{x}_i'\boldsymbol{\beta} = \eta_i,$$

where $g(p_i)$ denotes the "theoretical" logit or probit. As before, the expression $g(\cdot)$ is known as the "link" function that makes the model linear in $\boldsymbol{\beta}$.

We can express this as a heteroscedastic linear regression model

$$g(\widetilde{p}_i) = \mathbf{x}_i'\boldsymbol{\beta} + \varepsilon_i,$$

where $\widetilde{p}_i = y_i/n_i$ and $\varepsilon_i = \widetilde{p}_i - p_i$. The empirical logit is $g(\widetilde{p}_i) = \log\{\widetilde{p}_i/(1 - \widetilde{p}_i)\}$, whereas the empirical probit is $g(\widetilde{p}_i) = \Phi^{-1}(\widetilde{p}_i)$.

A Taylor series expansion of $\widetilde{p}_i$ around p_i—omitting higher-order terms—gives

$$
\begin{aligned}
g(p_i) &= \mathbf{x}_i'\boldsymbol{\beta} + \frac{\partial g(p_i)}{\partial p_i}(\widetilde{p}_i - p_i) \\
&= \eta_i + \frac{\partial \eta_i}{\partial p_i}(\widetilde{p}_i - p_i),
\end{aligned}
\tag{B.27}
$$

where $\partial\eta_i/\partial p_i$ is the derivative of the link function with respect to the mean response function. For the logit and probit models, the mean response functions (p_i) are $\Lambda(\mathbf{x}_i'\boldsymbol{\beta})$ and $\Phi(\mathbf{x}_i'\boldsymbol{\beta})$, respectively.

The weighted least squares problem is to minimize

$$\sum_i \frac{(\widetilde{p}_i - p_i)^2}{w_i}$$

with respect to $\boldsymbol{\beta}$, where w_i are the weights given by the inverse of the variance. The FGLS solution is

$$\mathbf{b}_{GLS} = \left[\mathbf{X}'\mathbf{W}\mathbf{X}\right]^{-1}\mathbf{X}'\mathbf{W}g(\widetilde{\mathbf{p}}).$$

Minimum Logit χ^2 Method: The minimum logit χ^2 estimator uses the empirical logit as the dependent variable. A linear model can be written as

$$\text{logit}(\widetilde{p}_i) = \log\left(\frac{\widetilde{p}_i}{1 - \widetilde{p}_i}\right) = \mathbf{x}_i'\boldsymbol{\beta} + \varepsilon_i, \qquad (B.28)$$

where $\text{E}(\varepsilon) = 0$ and $\text{var}(\varepsilon) = 1/[n_i p_i (1 - p_i)]$, which is estimated using the empirical probabilities, $1/[n_i \widetilde{p}_i (1 - \widetilde{p}_i)]$. In this case, we minimize the *weighted* sum of squares

$$\sum_i w_i \left[\text{logit}(\widetilde{p}_i) - \mathbf{x}_i'\boldsymbol{\beta}\right]^2$$

with respect to $\boldsymbol{\beta}$ using FGLS with weights equal to $w_i = n_i \widetilde{p}_i (1 - \widetilde{p}_i)$.

Minimum Probit χ^2 Method: The minimum probit (or normit) χ^2 estimator requires that we evaluate the inverse of the cumulative normal distribution function (or z-score) corresponding to the empirical probability, $\Phi^{-1}(\widetilde{p})$. This inverse function is provided in many statistical packages, along with the cumulative normal distribution function. A linear model can be written using the empirical probits as follows:

$$\text{probit}(\widetilde{p}_i) = \Phi^{-1}(\widetilde{p}_i) = \mathbf{x}_i'\boldsymbol{\beta} + \varepsilon_i, \qquad (B.29)$$

where $\text{E}(\varepsilon) = 0$. The error variance is estimated as

$$\widehat{\text{var}}(\varepsilon) = \frac{\widetilde{p}_i(1 - \widetilde{p}_i)}{n_i \phi(\widehat{z}_i)^2},$$

where $\widehat{z}_i = \Phi^{-1}(\widetilde{p}_i)$.

As with the logit model, estimation involves minimizing a weighted sum of squares using the inverse of the error variances as weights. Thus, a weighted least squares regression using the empirical probits with weights equal to $w_i = n_i \phi(\widehat{z}_i)^2/\widetilde{p}_i(1 - \widetilde{p}_i)$ is used to estimate the β's.

Minimum χ^2 Estimator for Loglinear Models: The minimum χ^2 estimator for the loglinear model is particularly simple. Let y_i denote the value of a count variable (or cell frequency) for the ith individual (or the ith cell in a contingency table). The mean response function is $\mu_i = \exp(\sum_k \beta_k x_{ik})$, which implies a linear model in the log of the mean response,

$$\log(y_i) = \mathbf{x}_i'\boldsymbol{\beta} + \varepsilon_i,$$

where $\varepsilon_i = y_i - \mu_i$. Assuming a Poisson distribution for the observed counts, we can use a weighted least squares regression on $\log y$ with weights equal to $w_i = y_i$. This model requires that the counts be greater than 0, so a small constant may need to be added to some y-values to ensure this. The FGLS solution is

$$\mathbf{b}_{GLS} = \left[\mathbf{X}'\mathbf{W}\mathbf{X}\right]^{-1}\mathbf{X}'\mathbf{W}\log\mathbf{y}.$$

   Minimum χ^2 (FGLS) estimates will usually differ from the ML estimates. They are asymptotically as efficient as ML estimates and easy to obtain using almost any regression package (MINITAB for example). These methods provide a linkage between generalized linear models and ordinary linear regression. Because these models involve transformations of the dependent variable, they offer a particularly instructive view of the transformational approach for certain nonlinear models.

Bibliography

Agresti, A. (1990), *Categorical Data Analysis*, New York: Wiley.

Albright, R. L., S. R. Lerman, and C. F. Manski (1977), "Report on the Development of an Estimation Program for the Multinomial Probit Model." Washington, D.C.: Federal Highway Administration.

Allison, P. D. (1982), "Discrete-Time Methods for the Analysis of Event Histories," pp. 61-98. In S. Leinhardt (Ed.), *Sociological Methodology*, San Francisco: Jossey-Bass.

Allison, P. D. (1984), *Event History Analysis*, Beverly Hills: Sage Publications.

Alvarez, R. M., and J. Nagler (1995), "Issues, Economics, and the Perot Candidacy: Voter Choice in the 1992 Presidential Election," *American Journal of Political Science*, 39:714-744.

Amemiya, T. (1991), "Qualitative Response Models: A Survey," *Journal of Economic Literature*, 19(4):483-536.

Andersen, E. B. (1970), "Asymptotic Properties of Conditional Maximum Likelihood Estimators," *Journal of the Royal Statistical Society, Ser. B*, 32:283-301.

Andersen, J. A. (1984), "Regression and Ordered Categorical Variables," *Journal of the Royal Statistical Society, Ser. B*, 46:1-30.

Aptech Systems (1997), *GAUSS Version 3.2.34*, Maple Valley: Aptech Systems, Inc.

Avery, R. B., and V. J. Hotz (1985), *HotzTran User's Manual.* Unpublished Manuscript, Economics Research Center/NORC, Chicago.

Aranda-Ordaz, F. J. (1983), "An Extension of the Proportional Hazards Model for Grouped Data," *Biometrics*, 39:109-117.

Barlow, R. E., and F. Proschan (1975), *Statistical Theory of Reliability and Life Testing*, New York: Holt, Rinehart and Winston.

Becker, M. P., and C. C. Clogg. (1989), "Analysis of Sets of Two-Way Contingency Tables Using Association Models," *Journal of the American Statistical Association*, 84:142-151.

Ben-Akiva, M., and S. R. Lerman (1985), *Discrete-Choice Analysis*, Cambridge: MIT Press.

Berndt, E., B. Hall, R. Hall, and J. Hausman (1974), "Estimation and Inference in Nonlinear Structural Models," *Annals of Economic and Social Measurement*, 3/4:653-666.

Bickel, P. J., E. A. Hammel, and J. W. O'Connell (1975), "Sex Bias in Graduate Admissions: Data from Berkeley," *Science*, 187:398-404.

Blossfeld, H. P., A. K. Hamerle, and K. U. Mayer (1989), *Event History Analysis: Statistical Theory and Applications in the Social Sciences*, Hillsdale: Lawrence Earlbaum and Associates.

Breen, R. (1994), "Individual Level Models for Mobility Tables and Other Cross-Classifications," *Sociological Methods and Research*, 23:147-173.

Butler, J. S., and R. Moffitt (1982), "A Computationally Efficient Quadrature Procedure for the One-Factor Multinomial Probit Model," *Econometrica*, 50:761-764.

Buse, A. (1973), "Goodness of Fit in Generalized Least Squares Estimation," *American Statistician*, 27:106-108.

Camic, C., and Y. Xie (1994), "The Advent of Statistical Methodology in American Social Science—Columbia University, 1880–1915: A Study in the Sociology of Statistics," *American Sociological Review*, 59:773-805.

Candy, S. G. (1984), "Fitting a Parametric Log-Linear Hazard Function to Grouped Survival Data," *GLIM Newsletter*, No. 13:28-31.

Center for Human Resource Research (1979), *The National Longitudinal Survey of Youth Handbook*, Columbus: The Ohio State University.

Chamberlain, G. (1980), "Analysis of Covariance with Qualitative Data," *Review of Economic Studies*, 47:225-238.

Chamberlain, G. (1984), "Panel Data," pp. 1247-1317. In Z. Griliches, and M. D. Intriligator (Eds.), *Handbook of Econometrics*, Vol II, Cambridge: MIT Press.

Clogg, C. C. (1978), "Adjustment of Rates Using Multiplicative Models," *Demography*, 15:523-539.

Clogg, C. C. (1982), "Using Association Models in Sociological Research: Some Examples," *American Journal of Sociology*, 88:114-134. Also reprinted in Goodman (1984).

Clogg, C. C. (1992), "The Impact of Sociological Methodology on Statistical Methodology," *Statistical Science*, 7:183-207.

Clogg, C. C., and S. R. Eliason (1988), "A Flexible Procedure for Adjusting Rates and Proportions, Including Statistical Methods for Group Comparisons," *American Sociological Review*, 53:267-283.

Clogg, C. C., and E. S. Shihadeh (1994), *Statistical Models for Ordinal Variables*, Thousand Oaks: Sage Publications.

Cox, D. R. (1970), *The Analysis of Binary Data*, London: Chapman and Hall.

Cox, D. R. (1972), "Regression Models and Life Tables," *Journal of the Royal Statistical Society, Ser. B*, 34:187-220.

Cox, D. R. (1975), "Partial Likelihood," *Biometrica*, 62:269-276.

Davies, R. B. (1987), "Mass-Point Methods for Dealing with Nuisance Parameters in Longitudinal Studies," pp. 88-107. In R. Crouchley (Ed.), *Longitudinal Data Analyis*, Aldershort: Avebur.

DiPrete, T. A. (1990), "Adding Covariates to Loglinear Models for the Study of Social Mobility," *American Sociological Review*, 55:757-773.

Duncan, O. D. (1961), "A Socioeconomic Index for All Occupations," pp. 109-138, In A. Reiss, Jr. (Ed.), *Occupations and Social Status*, New York: Free Press.

Duncan, O. D. (1979), "How Destination Depends on Origin in the Occupational Mobility Table," *American Journal of Sociology*, 84:793-803.

Duncan, O. D. (1984), *Notes on Social Measurement: Historical and Critical*, New York: Russell Sage Foundation.

Dunnett, C. W. (1989), "Multivariate Normal Probability Integrals with Product Correlation Structure" (Algorithm AS 251), *Applied Statistics*, 38:564-579.

Erikson, R., J. H. Goldthorpe, and L. Portocarero (1979), "Intergenerational Class Mobility in Three Western European Societies: England, France, and Sweden," *British Journal of Sociology*, 30:415-441.

Featherman, D. L., F. L. Jones, and R. M. Hauser (1975), "Assumptions of Social Mobility Research in the US: The Case of Occupational Status," *Social Science Research*, 4:329-360.

Fineberg, S. E., (1980), *The Analysis of Cross-Classified Categorical Data*, 2nd ed., Cambridge: MIT Press.

Finney, D. J. (1971), *Probit Analysis*, 3rd ed., Cambridge: Cambridge University Press.

Freedman, D., R. Pisani, and R. Purves (1978), *Statistics*, 1st ed., New York: Norton.

Fry, T. R. L., and M. N. Harris (1998), "Testing for the Independence of Irrelevant Alternatives: Some Empirical Results,"

Sociological Methods and Research, 26:401-423.

Goodman, L. A. (1972), "Some Multiplicative Models for the Analysis of Cross-Classified Data," pp. 649-696. In *Proceedings of the Sixth Berkeley Symposium on Mathematical Statistics and Probability,* Berkeley: University of California Press.

Goodman, L. A. (1979), "Simple Models for the Analysis of Association in Cross-Classifications Having Ordered Categories," *Journal of the American Statistical Association,* 74:537-552.

Goodman, L. A. (1981a), "Three Elementary Views of Log-Linear Models for the Analysis of Cross-Classifications Having Ordered Categories," pp. 193-239. In S. Leinhardt (Ed.), *Sociological Methodology.* San Francisco: Jossey-Bass.

Goodman, L. A. (1981b), "Association Models and Canonical Correlation in the Analysis of Cross-Classifications Having Ordered Categories," *Journal of the American Statistical Association,* 76:320-334.

Goodman, L. A. (1984), *The Analysis of Cross-Classified Data Having Ordered Categories,* Cambridge: Harvard University Press.

Goodman, L. A. (1986), "Some Useful Extensions of the Usual Correspondence Analysis Approach and the Usual Log-Linear Models Approach in the Analysis of Contingency Tables," *International Statistical Review,* 54:243-309.

Goodman, L. A., and M. Hout (1998), "Understanding the Goodman-Hout Approach to the Analysis of Differences in Association and Some Related Comments," pp. 249-261. In A. Raftery (Ed.), *Sociological Methodology 1998,* Washington, DC: American Sociological Association.

Gumble, E. J. (1961), "Bivariate Logistic Distributions," *Journal of the American Statistical Association,* 56:335-349.

Guo, G., and G. Rodríguez (1992), "Estimating a Multivariate Proportional Hazards Model for Clustered Data Using the EM Algorithm, with an Application to Child Survival in Guatemala," *Journal of the American Statistical Association*, 420:969-976.

Greene, W. H. (1991), *Econometric Analysis*, New York: Macmillan.

Greene, W. H. (1995), *LIMDEP Version 7.0*, Bellport: Econometric Software Inc.

Grusky, D. B., and R. M. Hauser (1984), "Comparative Social Mobility Revisited: Models of Convergence and Divergence in 16 Countries," *American Sociological Review*, 49:19-38.

Hauser, R. M. (1978) "A Structural Model of the Mobility Table," *Social Forces*, 56:919-953.

Hauser, R. M. (1979), "Some Exploratory Methods for Modeling Mobility Tables and Other Cross-Classified Data," pp. 413-458. In K. F. Schuessler (Ed.), *Sociological Methodology 1980*, San Francisco: Jossey-Bass.

Hauser, R. M. (1984), "Vertical Class Mobility in England, France and Sweden," *Acta Sociologica*, 27:87-110.

Hauser, R. M., and J. R. Warren (1997), "Socioeconomic Indexes for Occupations: A Review, Update, and Critique," pp. 177-298. In A. E. Raftery (Ed.), *Sociological Methodology 1997*, Washington, DC: American Sociological Association.

Hausman, J. A., and D. McFadden (1984), "Specification Tests for the Multinomial Logit Model," *Econometrica*, 52:1219-1240.

Hausman, J. A., and D. A. Wise (1978), "A Conditional Probit Model for Qualitative Choice: Discrete Decsisions Recognizing Interdependence and Heterogeneous Preferences," *Econometrica*, 46:403-426.

Heckman, J. J., and R. J. Willis (1976), "Estimation of a Stochastic Model of Reproduction: An Econometric Approach," In N. Terleckyj (Ed.), *Household Production and Consumption*, New York: Bureau of Economic Research.

Heckman, J. J. (1979), "Sample Selection Bias as a Specification Error," *Econometrica*, 47:153-161.

Heckman, J. J., and B. Singer (1984), "A Method for Minimizing the Impact of Distributional Assumptions in Econometric Models for Duration Data," *Econometrica*, 52:271-320.

Hensher, D. (1986), "Simultaneous Estimation of Hierarchical Logit Mode Choice Models," Macquarie University, School of Economic and Financial Studies, Working Paper Number 34, 1986.

Hoem, J. M. (1990), "Limitations of a Heterogeneity Technique: Selectivity Issues in Conjugal Union Disruption at Parity Zero in Contemporary Sweden," pp. 133-153. In J. Adams *et al.* (Eds.), *Convergent Issues in Genetics and Demography,* New York: Oxford University Press.

Hoffman, S. D., and G. J. Duncan (1988), "Multinomial and Conditional Logit Discrete-Choice Models in Demography," *Demography*, 25:415-427.

Holford, T. R. (1980), "The Analysis of Rates and of Survivorship Using Log-Linear Models," *Biometrics*, 36:299-305.

Hout, M. (1984), "Status, Autonomy, and Training in Occupational Mobility," *American Journal of Sociology*, 89:1379-1409.

Hsiao, C. (1986), *Analysis of Panel Data*, Cambridge: Cambridge University Press.

Laird, N., and D. Oliver (1981), "Covariance Analysis of Censored Survival Data Using Log-Linear Analysis Techniques," *Journal of the American Statistical Association*, 76:231-240.

Lancaster, T. (1990), *The Analysis of Transition Data*, Cambridge: Cambridge University Press.

Lin, G., and Y. Xie (1998), "Some Additional Considerations of Loglinear Modeling of Interstate Migration: A Comment on Herting, Grusky, and Rompaey," *American Sociological Review*, 63:900-907.

Li, R. M., Y. Xie, and H. S. Lin (1993), "Division of Family Property in Taiwan," *Journal of Cross-Cultural Gerontology,* 8:49-69.

Lithell, U-B. (1981), "Breast-Feeding Habits and Their Relation to Infant Mortality and Marital Fertility," *Journal of Family History,* 6-7:182-193.

Long, J. S. (1997), *Regression Models for Categorical and Limited Dependent Variables,* Thousand Oaks: Sage Publications.

Louis, T. A. (1982), "Finding the Observed Information Matrix When Using the EM Algorithm," *Journal of the Royal Statistical Society, Ser. B,* 44:226-233.

McCullagh, P. (1980), "Regression Models for Ordinal Data (with Disscussion)," *Journal of the Royal Statistical Society Ser. B,* 42:109-142.

McCullagh, P., and J. A. Nelder (1989), *Generalized Linear Models,* 2nd ed., New York: Chapman and Hall.

McFadden, D. (1973), "Conditional Logit Analysis of Qualitative Choice Behavior," pp. 105-135. In P. Zarembka (Ed.), *Structural Analysis of Discrete Data With Economometric Applications,* Cambridge: MIT Press.

McFadden, D. (1974), "The Measurement of Urban Travel Demand," *Journal of Public Economics,* 3:303-328.

McFadden, D. (1978) "Modeling the Choice of Residential Location," pp. 75-96. In A. Karlqvist *et al.* (Eds.), *Spatial Interaction Theory and Planning Models,* Amsterdam: North-Holland.

McKelvey, R., and W. Zavoina (1975), "A Statistical Model for the Analysis of Ordinal Level Dependent Variables," *Journal of Mathematical Sociology,* 4:103-120.

Maddala, G. S. (1983), *Limited-Dependent and Qualitative Variables in Econometrics,* Cambridge: Cambridge University Press.

Maddala, G. S. (1987), "Limited Dependent Variable Models Using Panel Data," *The Journal of Human Resources*, 22:307-338.

Manski, C. F., and D. A. Wise (1983), *College Choice in America*, Cambridge: Harvard University Press.

Mare, R. D. (1980), "Social Background and School Continuation Decisions," *Journal of the American Statistical Association*, 75:295-303.

Mare, R. D. (1991), "Five Decades of Educational Assortative Mating," *American Sociological Review*, 56:15-32.

Numerical Algorithms Group (1986), *The GLIM System*, Release 3.77, Oxford: Numerical Algorithms Group Ltd.

Petersen, T. (1985), "A Comment on Presenting Results from Logit and Probit Models," *American Sociological Review*, 50:130-131.

Raftery, A. E. (1986), "Choosing Models for Cross-Classifications (Comment on Grusky and Hauser)," *American Sociological Review*, 51:145-46.

Raftery, A. E. (1995), "Bayesian Model Selection in Social Research," pp. 111-163. In P. Marsden (Ed.), *Sociological Methodology*, Washington, DC: The American Sociological Association.

Rohwer, G. (1995), *TDA: Transition Data Analysis*, Cambridge: Free Software Foundation.

SAS Institute (1990), *SAS/STAT User's Guide, Version 6.0*, 3rd ed., Cary: SAS Institute, Inc.

Shryock, H. S., and J. S. Siegel (1976), *The Methods and Materials of Demography*, Orlando: Academic Press.

Simonoff, J. S. (1998), "Logistic Regression, Categorical Predictors, and Goodness-of-Fit: It Depends on Who You Ask," *The American Statistician*, 52:10-14.

Sobel, M. E., M. Hout, and O. D. Duncan (1985), "Exchange, Structure, and Symmetry in Occupational Mobility," *American Journal of Sociology*, 91:359-372.

Stata Corporation (1995), *Stata Reference Manual: Release 4.0*, College Station: Stata Corporation.

Thurstone, L. L. (1927), "A Law of Comparative Judgment," *Psychological Review*, 34:273-286.

Trussel, J., and T. Richards (1985), "Correcting for Unobserved Heterogeneity in Hazard Models Using the Heckman-Singer Procedure," pp. 242-276. In N. B. Tuma (Ed.), *Sociological Methodology*, San Fransisco: Jossey-Bass.

Trussel, J., and G. Rodríguez (1990), "Heterogeneity in Demographic Research," pp. 111-134. In J. Adams *et al.* (Eds.), *Convergent Issues in Genetics and Demography*, New York: Oxford University Press.

Tuma, N. B., and M. T. Hannan (1984), *Social Dynamics: Models and Methods*, New York: Academic Press.

Vaupel, J. W., and A. I. Yashin (1985), "Heterogeneity's Ruses: Some Surprising Effects of Selection on Population Dynamics," *The American Statistician*, 39:176-185.

Winship, C., and R. D. Mare (1984), "Regression Models with Ordinal Variables," *American Sociological Review*, 49:512-525.

Xie, Y. (1989), "An Alternative Purging Method: Controlling the Composition-Dependent Interaction in an Analysis of Rates," *Demography*, 26:711-716.

Xie, Y. (1992), "The Log-Multiplicative Layer Effect Model for Comparing Mobility Tables," *American Sociological Review*, 57:380-395.

Xie, Y., and C. F. Manski (1989), "The Logit Model and Response-Based Samples," *Sociological Methods and Research*, 17:283-302.

Xie, Y., and K. A. Shauman (1996), "Modeling the Sex-Typing of Occupational Choice: Influences of Occupational Structure," *Sociological Methods and Research,* 26:233-261.

Yamaguchi, K. (1991), *Event History Analysis,* Newbury Park: Sage Publications.

SUBJECT INDEX